H ANGED AT
PENTONVILLE

STEVE FIELDING

The History Press

First published in 2008
Reprinted 2013

The History Press
The Mill, Brimscombe Port,
Stroud, Gloucestershire, GL5 2QG
www.thehistorypress.co.uk

British Library Cataloguing in Publication Data
A catalogue record for this book is available from the British Library.

ISBN 978 0 7509 4950 7

Typesetting and origination by
The History Press.
Printed and bound in England.

CONTENTS

ACKNOWLEDGEMENTS

I would like to thank the following people for help with this book. Firstly to Lisa Moore for her help in every stage in the production, but mainly with the photographs and proofreading. I offer my sincere thanks to both Matthew Spicer and Tim Leech, who have been willing to share information along with rare documents, photographs and illustrations from their own collections. I would also like to acknowledge the help given by Janet Buckingham who helped to input the original data and to Gillian Papaioannou who proofread and edited the final drafts.

RESEARCH MATERIAL & SOURCES

As with my other books on capital punishment and executions, many people have supplied information and photographs over the years, some of whom have since passed away. I remain indebted to the help with rare photographs and material given to me by the late Syd Dernley, (assistant executioner), and former prison officer, the late Frank McKue.

The bulk of the research for this book was done many years ago, and extra information has been added to my database as and when it has become available. In most instances, contemporary local and national newspapers have supplied the basic information, which has been supplemented by material found in PCOM, HO and ASSI files held at the National Record Office at Kew. I have been fortunate to have access to the Home Office Capital Case File 1901–1948, along with personal information in the author's collection from those directly involved in some of the cases.

Space doesn't permit a full bibliography of books and websites accessed while researching this project. I have tried to locate the copyright owners of all images used in this book, but a number of them were untraceable. In particular, I have been unable to locate the copyright holders of a number of images, mainly those sourced from the National Archives. I apologise if I have inadvertently infringed upon any existing copyright.

The author, Steve Fielding.

Steve Fielding, 2008
www.stevefielding.com

INTRODUCTION

HM Prison Pentonville is one of the most famous prisons in the country. Situated in north London, it has housed a host of famous prisoners including Oscar Wilde and spy Dr Klaus Fuchs. It was opened in 1842 to replace the Millbank Penitentiary, the first modern prison, which, although only 25 years old, had proved unsatisfactory and outdated. Designed by Lt-Col Jebb, RE, it had taken two years to build the new Pentonville Prison, and cost over £84,000.

Standing in 8 acres, surrounded by an 18ft perimeter wall, its radial wing design was influenced by the 'separate system' developed at Eastern State Penitentiary in Philadelphia. This meant that a single prison officer standing in the centre could, by turning his head, view all four wings in turn.

The new prison had separate cells for 520 prisoners, and its design proved so satisfactory to the government that a programme of prison building began. This was two fold; the increase in population brought with it an increase in the crime rate, and with the use of transportation to the colonies for convicted criminals coming to an end, new prisons were now needed.

The cells at Pentonville, which under the separate system meant each convict had his own cell which measured 13ft long, 7ft wide and 10ft high, with a small window 4½ins square, high on the wall, which could be opened for ventilation. Conditions in the new prison were a vast improvement on the archaic Newgate Gaol and other older establishments. Prisoners were encouraged to undertake work, such as coir picking (un-threading old tarred rope) and basket weaving.

In the twentieth century, the cells were updated and modernised, with the installation of electric light and improved sanitation. In 1941, the gaol suffered a direct hit from an enemy bomb on C Hall and as a result, the hall was split into two. The gable ends were bricked up, and the isolated building, sometimes known as the 'stump', or H Hall, was partially separated from the rest of the prison and linked only by a corridor.

At the turn of the twentieth century, the execution chamber was situated in the prison grounds at the end of B Hall, which also housed the original condemned cells. This necessitated the condemned men having to walk from the cell to the gallows, which often proved to be an ordeal for a terrified prisoner. In 1928, in line with the modernisation of many other prisons, a new execution suite was built at Pentonville. It was now located in A Hall, close to the prison entrance, and consisted of a gallows room situated between two condemned cells built into the prison wing. The execution suite was constructed over three floors. The ground floor cell ceiling housed the trapdoors through which the prisoner dropped. The middle floor was the gallows room into

Front gate of Pentonville Prison in the 1940s. (T.J. Leech Archive)

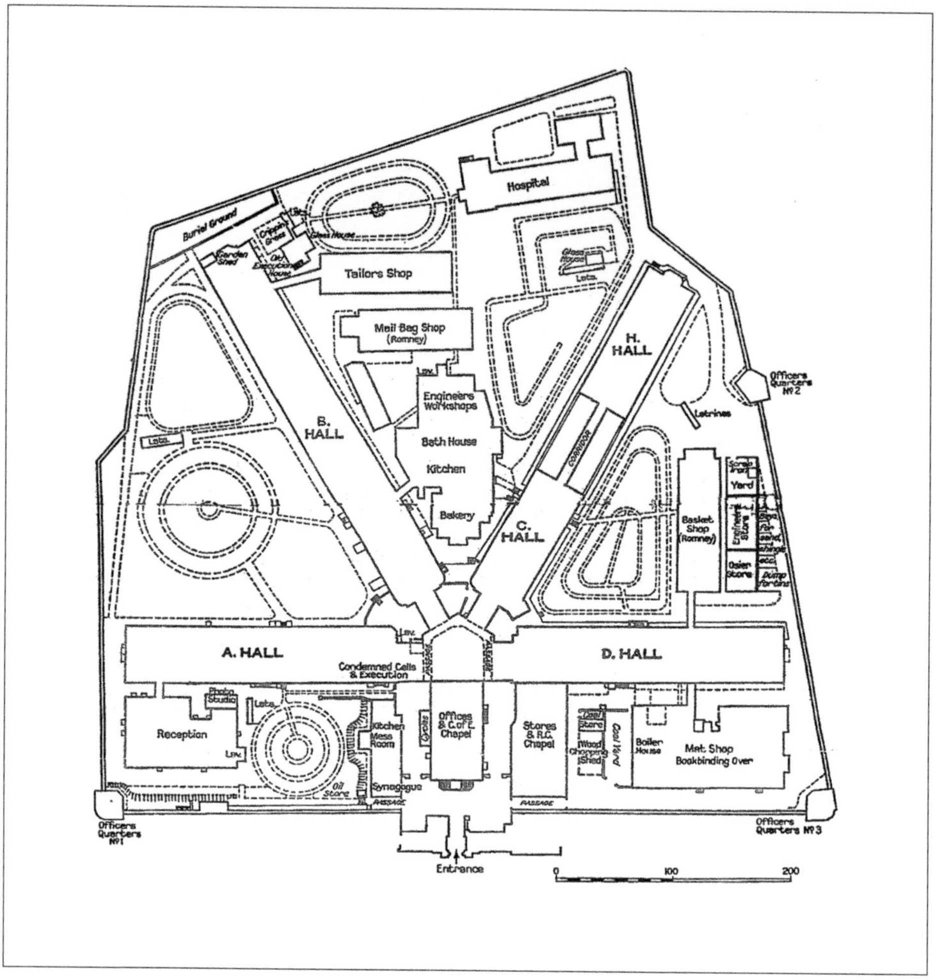

Plan of Pentonville Prison in the 1950s. (Author's collection)

Pentonville Prison at the turn of the twentieth century. (Author's collection)

The Old Bailey in the early part of the twentieth century. Most men hanged at Pentonville had been sentenced to death here. (Author's collection)

which the condemned would walk directly from the condemned cell, a distance of just a few feet. Painted pale green, it contained the lever and trapdoors of two heavy oak leaves, each measuring 8ft 6ins long by 2ft 6ins wide. The cell above housed the beams and chain mechanisms to which the noose was attached.

It wasn't until the closure of Newgate in 1902 that prisoners under sentence of death were housed at Pentonville, and following the closure of the former, the gallows, supports and beams, along with the trapdoors and mechanisms were transported across the city and installed.

Following an upheaval in the whole procedure of recruiting and training executioners in the late 1890s, anyone wishing to become an executioner would have to attend a course of instruction before being placed on the official list. The first courses took place at Newgate in 1900, but following its closure, the executioners' training school was transferred to Pentonville. Among the first hangmen to graduate were Tom Pierrepoint and William Willis, who both went on to have long careers on the gallows. All would-be hangmen graduated at Pentonville until 1960 when training was transferred to Wandsworth Prison, South London.

People who applied to be added to the Home Office list of executioners had to first of all face an interview at a prison close to their home. This was designed to weed out unsuitable applicants whose motives to apply may have been fuelled by a gruesome or perverted interest. Those who were successful were invited to attend the one-week course at Pentonville, with expenses and travel paid for by the Home Office, where they were taught how to pinion the prisoner, calculate and rig the drop, and to carry out a mock execution using a dummy. The applicants were constantly monitored, and speed, efficiency, nerve and discretion were all requisites of a hangman.

LP.C4 sheet used by prison officials for recording information on executions. (Author's collection)

Equipment needed to rig the gallows, including the ropes and straps, along with the block and chains used for removing the prisoner from the gallows, were housed in special execution boxes and stored at Pentonville. They would be despatched by rail to prisons around the country where needed.

❖   ❖   ❖

Apart from its fellow London prison at Wandsworth, Pentonville was the busiest prison in the country for executions, with 120 people ending their lives on the gallows there. There are a number of reasons for the higher than normal count: several spies and German PoWs convicted by court-martial were hanged at Pentonville, and the prison also received prisoners sentenced to death from further afield than north London, when many provincial prisons were down-graded around the time of the First World War. Therefore, prisoners, who may once have been hanged at rural prisons such as Chelmsford and Hertford, were now transferred to Pentonville for execution.

The first hangmen to officiate at Pentonville were William and John Billington, the last members of that family, whose dynasty stretched back to the 1880s. Both members were assisted by Henry Pierrepoint, the first of a new family of executioners, and a name that stayed at the head of the short official list of hangmen until the late 1950s.

Rochdale barber John Ellis' first engagement as chief executioner at Pentonville was to hang Dr Crippen, and in the next thirteen years, he made over twenty visits to the prison in the capacity of executioner. In 1925, Hertford hangman Robert Orridge Baxter took over the mantle of chief executioner at the prison, and for the next decade carried out every execution at the gaol, until his failing eyesight meant that he was no longer fit for duty.

EXECUTIONS.—TABLE OF DROPS (October, 1913).

The length of the drop may usually be calculated by dividing 1,000 foot-pounds by the weight of the culprit and his clothing in pounds, which will give the length of the drop in feet, but no drop should exceed 8 feet 6 inches. Thus a person weighing 150 pounds in his clothing will require a drop of 1,000 divided by 150 = 6⅔ feet, i.e., 6 feet 8 inches. The following table is calculated on this basis up to the weight of 200 pounds :—

TABLE OF DROPS.

Weight of the Prisoner in his Clothes.	Length of the Drop.		Weight of the Prisoner in his Clothes.	Length of the Drop.		Weight of the Prisoner in his Clothes.	Length of the Drop.	
lbs.	ft.	ins.	lbs.	ft.	ins.	lbs.	ft.	ins.
118 and under	8	6	138 and under	7	3	167 and under	6	0
119 ,,	8	5	140 ,,	7	2	169 ,,	5	11
120 ,,	8	4	141 ,,	7	1	171 ,,	5	10
121 ,,	8	3	143 ,,	7	0	174 ,,	5	9
122 ,,	8	2	145 ,,	6	11	176 ,,	5	8
124 ,,	8	1	146 ,,	6	10	179 ,,	5	7
125 ,,	8	0	148 ,,	6	9	182 ,,	5	6
126 ,,	7	11	150 ,,	6	8	185 ,,	5	5
128 ,,	7	10	152 ,,	6	7	188 ,,	5	4
129 ,,	7	9	154 ,,	6	6	190 ,,	5	3
130 ,,	7	8	156 ,,	6	5	194 ,,	5	2
132 ,,	7	7	158 ,,	6	4	197 ,,	5	1
133 ,,	7	6	160 ,,	6	3	200 ,,	5	0
135 ,,	7	5	162 ,,	6	2			
136 ,,	7	4	164 ,,	6	1			

When for any special reason, such as a diseased condition of the neck of the culprit, the Governor and Medical Officer think that there should be a departure from this table, they may inform the executioner, and advise him as to the length of the drop which should be given in that particular case.

Hangman's Table of Drops: devised at the end of the nineteenth century to help the hangman work out the correct drop. This version dates from 1913. (Author's collection)

William Billington, the first hangman to officiate at Pentonville. (Author's collection)

'Crippen's Grass' at
the end of B Hall.
(Author's collection)

Tom Pierrepoint, William Willis and Alfred Allen also pulled the lever at executions there, and it was at a Pentonville execution that Willis' conduct was brought into question and led to his dismissal (see Chapter 44). Another hangman whose career ended at Pentonville was Stanley Cross of Fulham. Cross had graduated from Pentonville in the autumn of 1932 and was promoted to chief executioner at the start of the Second World War. He executed Udham Singh in July 1940 and three spies that December, and on each occasion Dr James Liddell, Chief Medical Officer at the gaol, noted on the official post execution forms that he didn't think Cross was competent in calculating the drops needed to dispense instant death, despite his having access to a Table of Drops.

Albert Pierrepoint made his debut as chief executioner at Pentonville on 31 October 1941, and vied with his uncle, Tom, for work at the prison during the war. From 1946, with his uncle now pensioned off, Albert carried out every execution until the temporary suspension of capital punishment in 1956, when the death penalty was being debated in parliament and which led to the passing of the Homicide Act in 1957. This new Act categorised types of murder and led to a drastic reduction in executions being carried out.

By the time hangings were re-introduced, Pierrepoint had tendered his resignation, and the chief executioner was now Harry Allen, a publican living in the Manchester area. Allen officiated at three of the four post-Homicide Act executions at Pentonville, with Robert Leslie 'Jock' Stewart carrying out the other, that of Norman Harris. Both Stewart and Allen had assisted Albert Pierrepoint at the gaol on many occasions.

Like many Victorian prisons, Pentonville is believed to be haunted. One of the ghostly apparitions said to walk the grounds at the prison is Dr Crippen, hanged in November 1910 for the murder of his wife. A piece of grass adjacent to the original execution shed, is known to this day as 'Crippen's Grass', and it is here that it is claimed that his ghost, complete with a crooked neck, can be seen to wander.

HMP Pentonville remains in use as a major London prison to this day, holding around 1,100 prisoners remanded both by Magistrates and Crown Court, along with those serving short sentences or beginning longer sentences.

This book looks in detail at the stories behind why 120 murderers, spies and traitors were all *Hanged at Pentonville*.

1

THAT DOLLAR I LOST

❖ *John MacDonald, 30 September 1902* ❖

On a hot July evening in 1902, a small sum of money was stolen from John MacDonald, a 24-year-old costermonger, as he slept in a run down Salvation Army shelter on Middlesex Street in London's Aldgate district. Discovering the theft, he looked at the other lodgers, and instantly suspected 30-year-old Irish ex-soldier Henry Groves. Confronted with the accusation, Groves, known as 'Mickey the Irishman' denied the theft, but MacDonald was not satisfied and Groves' disappearance from the lodging house on the following day seemed to confirm his suspicions.

Scotsman MacDonald was not going to let the matter drop, and a few days later he was seen at the shelter sharpening his knife, muttering that he was going to 'kill Groves over that dollar I lost.'

On Thursday, 28 August, seeing Groves enter a shop in Old Castle Street, MacDonald followed him inside, and when a row broke out between the two, they were asked to leave. Groves left first and began walking towards Wentworth Street. MacDonald followed a few moments behind, and as they approached a school at the top end of the street, where Groves worked as the caretaker, MacDonald approached, grabbed him by the shoulder and began to punch him. Groves hit back, knocking MacDonald to the ground. As the fight escalated, Sam Dodds, a friend of Groves, tried several times to pull them apart, as another man ran to find a policeman. Groves gave as good as he got, but as his strength began to sap, he attempted

SLAIN IN A CROWD.

MAN STABBED TO DEATH IN THE EAST END

A startling tragedy occurred on Thursday night in the East End. In Wentworth-street, off Commercial-road, hundreds of people, mostly Jews, were shopping, a little before eight o'clock. Flaring oil lamps illuminated coster stalls, and itinerant organ-grinders were playing to dancing crowds when a piercing shriek was heard. In the heart of the throng a tall man, ill-clad, under the full glare of shop-window lights, fell to the ground with a knife through his throat. A moment later a costermonger had upset on to the road the contents of his barrow, lifted the injured man into it, and set off at a rapid trot for the London Hospital. Four other coster-mongers seized a small man alleged to have been the assailant whose name proved to be John McDonald, and held him until two police officers arrived. In ten minutes the coster brought his barrow to a stand oppo-site the hospital. But its occupant was dead, his head almost severed from his body. Policemen were soon amid the horror-stricken crowds at Wentworth-street investigating the tragedy. They were im-mediately confronted with a difficulty of identification. While dozens of men and women were familiar with the dead man as "Micky the Irishman," and the alleged murderer as "Scottie," no one knew their real names. Beyond that a casual history of both men was soon obtained. "Scottie," who was taken to the Commercial-street

PRISONER.

Newspaper report and sketch of John MacDonald. (T.J. Leech Archive)

to make his escape. As Groves turned on his heels, Dodds saw MacDonald draw a knife from his pocket, and although he tried one last time to help, he watched helplessly as MacDonald caught Groves by the arm, twisted him around and plunge the knife into his neck, severing an artery and cutting his windpipe. Groves staggered along the street, with blood oozing from the terrible wound, as Dodds managed to wrestle MacDonald to the ground and detain him until the police arrived. Groves collapsed and died from his injuries before medical assistance could be given.

At his Old Bailey trial before Mr Justice Walton on Thursday, 11 September, MacDonald's defence was that he was so drunk when the murder took place, he had no recollection of committing any crime. Evidence of his threats to kill Groves over the money he had stolen was given in court, as was evidence of a friend of MacDonald's who testified that less than an hour before the murder, he had made a similar threat. Evidence was also heard of a statement MacDonald made at Spitalfield's police station. When pointing to the knife he claimed; 'That's the knife I did it with… I did it intentionally.'

Hanged just thirty-three days after committing the brutal murder, John MacDonald holds the dubious honour of being the first man to be executed at Pentonville, the gallows' beams and posts having been recently installed, following removal from the recently closed and soon to be demolished Newgate Gaol.

2

'MAY GOD BLESS HER DEAR LITTLE HEART'

❖ *Henry Williams, 11 November 1902* ❖

Having fought bravely on the front line in the Boer War, 31-year-old Henry Williams left the 4th East Surrey Militia and returned to his lodgings at Fulham in July 1902, expecting to resume his relationship with widow Ellen Andrews, the mother of his beloved 5-year-old daughter, Margaret 'Maggie' Anne Andrews. Although they had not married, Williams and Ellen had been together for almost a decade, and they had kept in regular contact by letter while he was in South Africa.

Returning home that summer, Williams began to suspect that Ellen had been unfaithful to him, and had been carrying on an affair with a sailor while he was away fighting for his country. Although she admitted knowing the sailor, Ellen denied that anything untoward had taken place, but Williams was not convinced.

In early September, Ellen took Maggie to stay in Worthing, Sussex, and on 10 September, Williams travelled down to see them, in order to collect Maggie and take her back to London with him. Still convinced Ellen had been unfaithful, the visit ended in a fierce quarrel, and as he was leaving to return to London, Williams made a chilling parting statement: 'I will not hurt you Ellen' he said coldly, 'but I will do something which will break your heart and brand you so that you will never hold your head up in this world again.' Quite what she imagined he would do is not known, but it probably never crossed her mind the lengths to which her suspected infidelity had driven him.

Later that evening and back in London, Williams was having a drink in the Lord Palmerston public house on the Kings Road, Fulham. Williams was sitting with friends when he began to speak about his feelings for his daughter. He pulled out a photograph and tears welled up in his eyes as he spoke: 'Do you think I can let my little Maggie call another man daddy? It would

Henry Williams as sketched in court. (T.J. Leech Archive)

Hangman Henry Pierrepoint assisted William Billington at the execution of Henry Williams. He later described Williams as the bravest man he ever hanged. (Author's collection)

drive me stark raving mad.' He then began to ramble, but the gist of it seemed to suggest that he had killed his daughter. One of his friends became so concerned at what he was hearing that he went in search of a policeman. When he returned in the company of Detective Inspector Walter Dew (later to find fame as the man who caught Dr Crippen), Williams finished his drink and climbed to his feet. 'I know what you have come for – for killing my little girl. God bless her. I will swing for it like a man.'

With Williams held in the local police station, officers went to his lodgings and discovered the body of his beloved daughter lying on a bed, covered over with the Union Jack flag. Beside the body was a note which read, 'May God bless her dear little heart, and may her good soul go to heaven, and may I, her heartbroken father, be forgiven.'

Tried at the Old Bailey before Mr Justice Jelf on 23 October, Williams' defence was based on insanity through jealousy at the time of the murder. Ellen Andrews, whose infidelity Williams strongly suspected but had never confirmed, was the subject of verbal abuse from a large section of the crowd when she made her way into court. She sat in tears in the dock as the court heard Williams say he had killed Maggie 'so that she wouldn't grow up to be like her mother'.

Williams said that after putting his daughter to bed, he told her they were going to play a game. He covered her eyes with a handkerchief and then cut her throat, placing a doll next to her body.

The jury returned a guilty verdict with a recommendation for mercy, and when asked if he had anything to say before sentence was passed, Williams stood erect and in a firm voice said, 'Nothing whatsoever; I am only too pleased to receive it and get out.'

Williams kept his composure throughout his time in the condemned cell, chatting and playing cards with the warders. On the night before his execution he said he had killed his daughter because he feared that if she was brought up by her mother, she would grow up to be unfaithful and would break men's hearts.

Henry Pierrepoint, who assisted hangman William Billington, later recorded that Williams was the gamest and bravest man he had ever executed and that he had shown no fear as he was led to the gallows.

3

BEFORE 12 O'CLOCK TOMORROW

❖ *Thomas Fairclough Barrow, 9 December 1902* ❖

It was a most unusual relationship. Thirty-two-year-old Emily Coates was the illegitimate stepdaughter of Thomas Fairclough Barrow, a 49-year-old dock labourer. When Barrow was widowed fifteen years before, Emily stayed with her stepfather and the relationship soon developed into a semi-incestuous one, and during that time she bore him several children, although only one, a boy, survived.

By the autumn of 1902, they were living together to all intents and purposes as man and wife in a two-room apartment on Red Lion Street, in a run down part of Wapping. Strange as the relationship was, it was also an unhappy one. Emily frequently complained to friends that Tommy beat her, and following one particularly fierce assault, she fled and took refuge in a friend's house at nearby Shadwell.

On Friday night, 10 October, Emily turned up in tears on the doorstep of her friend and neighbour, Jane Corker's house, complaining of being beaten and kicked by Barrow, and asked if she could stay the night. Her neighbour agreed. Six days later, Emily served Barrow with a writ for assault which needed to be responded to within forty-eight hours. On the following night, warrant in hand, Barrow went to where Emily was staying and demanded to see her. Told she was out, he began issuing a number of threats that he would resolve his grievances with her imminently. Shouting through the letterbox, Barrow proclaimed coldly that they weren't idle threats as, 'you shall know before 12 o'clock tomorrow.'

On the following morning, as Emily walked to work down nearby Glamis Road, Barrow ran up behind her and stabbed her five times – once in the heart – killing her instantly. Barrow was arrested within minutes and seemed resigned to his fate. 'This will end it all. Now all I want is a rope around my neck.'

During his trial at the Old Bailey on 19 November, Dr James Scott, medical officer at Brixton Prison, who had examined Barrow while he was on remand, told the court that the prisoner had complained of headaches and claimed to have suffered from sunstroke while serving in the Navy.

His counsel pleaded vainly that when Barrow had killed Emily, he was temporarily not responsible for his actions and was therefore not guilty of wilful murder. The jury rejected those claims; not even leaving the dock before indicating to Mr Justice Bigham that they believed Barrow was indeed guilty as charged.

UNWANTED ADVANCES

To 20-year-old barmaid Martha Jane Hardwick, he was becoming a pest. She was used to the flirting and suggestive chat from the regulars at the Lord Nelson public house at Whitechapel, but whereas most customers knew where to draw the line, 28-year-old Charlie Slowe was beginning to make her feel uncomfortable.

Martha lived at the pub, which was owned and run by her sister, Jane Starkey, and throughout the summer of 1903, she had grown to dread the pint sized, stockily built, dock labourer entering the bar. Without fail, Slowe would make a point of asking Martha to go out with him, usually when he was drunk. When it became clear that he was taking no heed of her refusals, she took to avoiding him when he came to the pub, and would busy herself with other customers or find some other chore to take her away from the bar if business was quiet.

Slowe gradually began to feel that she was making a fool of him by discussing his failed advances with other barmaids, and early in September a lodger at the Lord Nelson heard Slowe threaten to stab Martha if she continued to shun him.

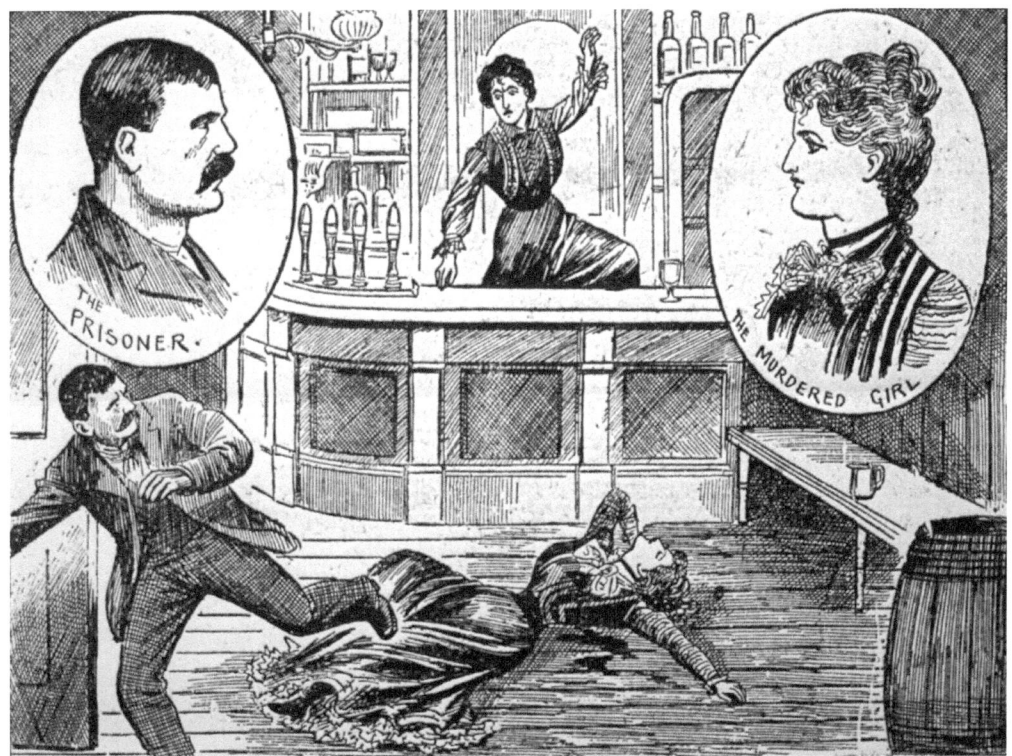

How the Illustrated Police News *depicted the murder of Martha Hardwick.* (T.J. Leech Archive)

BARMAID MURDERED IN WHITECHAPEL.

ANOTHER murder of a barmaid has taken place—this time in a Whitechapel public-house.

The story of the crime was given in evidence before the Worship Street magistrate, when Charles Jeremiah Slowe, twenty-eight years of age, described as a dock labourer, was placed in the dock on a charge of murdering Mary Jane Hardwick in the bar of the Lord Nelson, 299, Whitechapel Road.

With a sprightly step Slowe went into the dock—he has served in the Militia—and listened to the evidence given with his head resting on his left hand. His face bore a serious expression, however.

Newspaper cutting relating to the murder of Martha Hardwick. (T.J. Leech Archive)

In the early evening of Wednesday, 23 September, Slowe visited the pub, and seeing him enter the bar, Martha immediately went to serve in another room. When she went back into the main bar a short time later, she saw that he had gone and breathed a sigh of relief as she carried on serving. There were no licensing laws of note in the early part of the twentieth century and unfortunately for Martha, Slowe returned to the Lord Nelson shortly after midnight. Seeing her standing close to the bar, Slowe approached and struck out, hitting her on both shoulders. Although witnesses thought he had used his fists, he had in fact been holding a sharp knife.

'I've got you now,' he shouted as Martha slumped to the floor, fatally wounded. Slowe fled from the bar, with landlady Jane Starkey in pursuit, shouting for help and asking people to stop him. A burly docker detained Slowe who was brought back to the public house. In his pocket was a bloodstained knife.

Tried before Mr Justice Bigham at the Old Bailey on 21 October, Slowe's defence stated that a mixture of provocation and drink had led him to commit murder. The prosecution refuted this by saying the police surgeon who had examined him shortly after his arrest confirmed that he was only mildly drunk, certainly not enough to have been unaware of his actions. They also dismissed the issue of provocation, saying that rather than being provoked, he had simply killed Martha because she had rejected his unwanted advances.

5

MURDER ON THE HIGH SEAS

❖ *John Sullivan, 12 July 1904* ❖

'I consider that the judge summed up the case as if he had a personal spite against me, and he also went to sleep while my lawyer was pleading for my life.' (Statement by John Sullivan, following the passing of the sentence of death.)

After two months on the high seas, the relationship between 40-year-old seaman, John Sullivan and 17-year-old cabin boy, Derek Lowthian had started to turn sour. Both had joined the SS *Waiwera* at London prior to it departing on 6 January 1904, bound for New Zealand, via South Africa and Uruguay.

Sullivan, a native of County Durham, soon formed an attachment to the young boy, which quickly developed into an intimate relationship. The older man had a very jealous nature and would often berate Lowthian if he saw him chatting to other deckhands, and by the time the ship reached the Cape of Good Hope, Lowthian had made it clear to Sullivan that he did not want the relationship to continue.

Sullivan, however, was smitten and had no intention of letting things go. They had a fierce quarrel that resulted in a coming to blows, and only ended when Sullivan pulled out a knife on Lowthian and threatened to 'cut his head off!' He was put in irons, brought before the Captain, fined and imprisoned for seven days.

When Sullivan had served his sentence and was freed to resume his duties, the two men would quarrel whenever they saw each other. On one occasion Sullivan was seen by one of his shipmates holding an axe and claiming, 'This would be a good thing to use to do away with someone.'

On the evening of 18 May, as the ship steamed towards Tenerife, Sullivan warned Lowthian to 'beware' and when asked what he meant by that, he replied, 'wait and see', adding, 'I will break your neck. I can't stand this much longer and there will be a murder done before morning!'

Later that night, as Lowthian was talking to the quartermaster on deck, Sullivan appeared, carrying an axe. Before Lowthian could speak, Sullivan rained down blows on his head. The quartermaster hurried to fetch a doctor, but as medical assistance was vainly given to the stricken boy, Sullivan stood by and shouted, 'You don't need no doctor. He's dead enough, I've knocked his brains out!'

MURDER ON THE HIGH SEAS.
John Sullivan, 40, able seaman, was indicted at the Old Bailey, before Mr. Justice Grantham, for the murder of Dennis Lowthian, 17, a native of New Shildon, Durham, on the high seas, on May 18.—Prisoner

SULLIVAN.

Murderer John Sullivan sketched in the dock.
(T.J. Leech Archive)

Lowthian died within minutes and Sullivan was again put in irons. He asked to see the Captain and said there was a letter in his pocket, which would explain everything. The letter ended with the sentence, 'I shall cut off his head and take it overboard with me'. On Thursday, 2 June, as the ship docked in the Thames, Inspector Reed boarded the vessel and arrested Sullivan. 'I am sorry I did it, I am sorry for his parents,' he said as he was led away.

Sullivan stood trial at the Old Bailey before Mr Justice Grantham on Thursday, 23 June. His defence claimed insanity, stating that since joining the Navy, Sullivan had suffered from heart disease, melancholia and bad teeth! The jury debated whether there were grounds for reducing the charge to manslaughter through provocation; they quickly returned a verdict of guilty as charged, but requested mercy on the grounds of provocation.

6

'NO MURDER WAS INTENDED'

❖ *Joseph Potter & Charles Wade, 13 December 1904* ❖

The hangmen were asleep in their quarters, and in the gallows chamber two ropes hung taut, stretched with sandbags that would allow the executioners on the morrow to fix a drop accurate to the half inch. Inside two condemned cells at Pentonville, prisoners 12298 and 12299 were spending their last nights on earth oblivious to an extraordinary turn of events taking place outside.

Matilda Farmer – murdered by Potter and Wade in her shop at Stepney. (T.J. Leech Archive)

At a few minutes to midnight on 12 December 1904, a man had walked into Whitechapel police station and asked to speak to a detective. He then made a full confession to a murder that had assistant commissioner Sir Melvin MacNaughten roused from his bed and hurrying to the station to deal with the situation. Detectives who had been investigating the brutal murder were all present, as discussions took place whether to advise the Home Secretary to cancel the executions pending further enquiries.

The confessor was grilled on several points, and after an intensive interrogation, the officers came to the conclusion his story was false. Gradually his confession was unravelled as a pack of lies, and as he was removed down to the cells, he was asked why he had volunteered a false confession. 'I just wanted to do them a good turn' he said, admitting that he knew neither of the two condemned men whose last hours were quickly ticking by.

It was early in the morning of Wednesday, 12 October 1904, when a paper-boy arriving for work at a newsagent and tobacconist's shop at 478 Commercial Road, Stepney, started a major murder enquiry. Surprised to find the shop unlocked and with no sign of the proprietor, the fearsome Miss Matilda Farmer, he waited around, unsure of what to do. A short time later, another boy turned up at the shop and when told of Miss Farmer's absence, he reported this to his employer.

The police were called, and when an officer entered the shop he found a set of false teeth and a boot lying near the counter, and a pair of glasses on the stairs. Miss Farmer was discovered lying face down on her bed, hands tied behind her back and a towel forced into her mouth. Although there was a faint pulse when the policeman checked, by the time the doctor arrived, she was dead.

The bedroom had been ransacked, and there was no sign of any money or jewellery. Evidently the killer, or killers, had found what they had come for, and with the back door locked and the windows barred, had presumably left via the front door.

A witness told detectives he had seen two men, one of whom he recognised as Charles Wade, loitering by the newsagents the night before, and then again early in the morning of the murder, shortly after Miss Farmer had opened the shop when the newspapers had been delivered. Kept under surveillance for several days, as police followed different lines of enquiry, 22-year-old Charles Wade and his 35-year-old half brother Joseph Potter (also known as Conrad Donovan), were eventually arrested, and when picked out in an identity parade at Brixton Prison, charged with wilful murder. Both had long criminal records for robbery and violence.

Appearing before Mr Justice Grantham at the Old Bailey in November, both vociferously proclaimed their innocence. None of the stolen jewels were found in either man's house, and one of the police witnesses admitted that he had seen pictures of Wade and Potter prior to the identity parade, during which two other witnesses had failed to recognise them. Despite this, the jury took less than ten minutes to find both guilty of wilful murder.

Eight days before the men were to be hanged, workmen at the shop lifted a floorboard and discovered the hoard of cash and missing jewellery. The killers' haul had been nothing like the police had surmised.

Although there had been some public disquiet regarding the outcome of the trial, moments before Potter was led to the gallows he turned to the prison chaplain and made a brief statement that showed that the verdict was indeed the correct one: 'No murder was intended.'

'WHEN THE TIME COMES'

❖ *Albert Bridgeman, 26 April 1905* ❖

An ear piercing scream rang out. It was in the early hours of Sunday, 5 March 1905, when Alice Shadbolt opened her door at her lodgings on Compton Street, St Pancras, and saw a man fleeing down the stairs. She ran out of her room and followed him onto the street, but he soon vanished in the warren of side streets. Returning to her home she entered the room of fellow tenant, 44-year-old Catherine Ballard, and found her lying on the floor. She had been battered on the head with a poker found beside the body, but death was due to a hideous throat wound. Her hysterical daughter told police that the killer was her former boyfriend, 22-year-old Albert Bridgeman, and a few hours later he was picked up on nearby Hunter Street. In his pocket was a bloodstained razor.

One month later at the Old Bailey, before Mr Justice Jelf, the background into the brutal murder was told before a packed courtroom. Shortly before Christmas 1904, former soldier Bridgeman and his girlfriend Catherine Ballard had called off their engagement. Although not to his choosing, the break-up was amiable enough, and they had remained on good terms. The same could not be said for relations between Bridgeman and the girl's mother, also called Catherine Ballard.

Blaming her for the break-up, Bridgeman had re-enlisted in the army before Christmas, but keen to try to repair the broken relationship, on Wednesday, 28 February 1905, he bought his discharge. He went round to see Catherine and discovered that while he had been away, her mother had been spreading gossip about him.

On Friday, 2 March, Bridgeman had called at the lodging house on Compton Street and lost his temper with Mrs Ballard. Words were exchanged and threats made, but seeing that Bridgeman was clearly the worse for drink, they weren't taken seriously.

On the following day, Bridgeman and Catherine spent the day in a local pub before staggering back to Compton Street. It was then during a quarrel with Catherine's mother that he had lost his temper and cut her throat.

Bridgeman's counsel pleaded insanity on account of head injuries he had sustained while serving in South Africa, but it was to be in vain. Upon his arrest, Bridgeman had told officers he was ready to swing for his crime 'when the time comes.' Three weeks later, the time came.

SHOCKING MURDER OF A SWEETHEART'S MOTHER.

" I am ready to swing for it, is the statement attributed to Albert Bridgeman, 21, a labourer, formerly in the Militia, who stands accused of having murdered Catherine Ballard, 43, at Compton-street, St. Pancras, on March 4. Bridgeman is a short, sturdy young man and he looked exceedingly anxious as he stepped into the dock at Clerkenwell, where the preliminary magisterial investigation was held. Inspector Dew told the story of the crime. He said

BRIDGEMAN

Albert Bridgeman sketched in court as sentence of death is passed on him. (Author's collection)

THE BODIES IN THE TRUNK

❖ *Arthur Devereux, 15 August 1905* ❖

In February 1905, removal men from Messrs Bannisters were detailed to move the contents from a house on Milton Road, Harlesden, across North London to a new address on Harrow Road, Wembley. Four boxes were delivered, as directed by the occupier, but the fifth, a large metal trunk, containing chemicals, was to be put into storage and taken to the company's warehouse in Buller Road, Kensal Rise.

A short time later, Mrs Ellen Gregory called at the house on Milton Road, intending to go shopping with her daughter. She was shocked to find the house empty, and enquiries among neighbours revealed that the family had moved from the area. She was given the name of the removal company who had loaded a van a week earlier, and calling at the Kensal Rise offices, she was told of the mysterious heavy trunk in the warehouse. Suspicious at the sudden disappearance of her daughter along with her son-in-law and their young family, she contacted the police.

On 13 April, detectives examined the trunk and found it padlocked, strapped and sealed with wax. Lifting the lid, they discovered a layer of wooden planks, tightly butted together and screwed securely into place. The planks had then been sealed with a layer of glue and boric acid, making the trunk totally airtight. Once inside, detectives removed the layer of wood and found a bed quilt and a tablecloth. Finally the trunk yielded its sinister contents: the bodies of 31-year-old Beatrice Devereux and her 2-year-old twin sons, Laurence and Evelyn.

With the identities of the victims already known, a search for the prime suspect, missing husband 36-year-old Arthur Devereux, took the police to Coventry where he had recently taken a new position as a chemist's assistant. Placed under arrest and brought back to London, Devereux confessed that he had concealed the bodies, but denied having anything to do with their deaths.

Arthur Devereux in court. (T.J. Leech Archive)

He stood trial before Mr Justice Ridley at the end of July, where it was shown that Devereux had previously earned a good wage as a pharmacist until the new additions to the family stretched the budget to almost breaking point. In 1904, he took over as the manager of a chemist shop in Kilburn, but just when things began to look up, on 2 January 1905, he was given his notice when the shop closed down.

Now unemployed and with a young family to maintain, Devereux looked for ways to save money. His first step was to downsize and move into a new and smaller home on Milton Avenue, Harlesden. It was here, Devereux said, that on 28 January, having returned home after spending the day looking for work, he found the house smelling strongly of chloroform. Upstairs, his wife and twin sons lay dead in their beds. Devereux kept chloroform, along with morphine locked in his desk, for which his wife had a spare key. Both bottles were now empty. Convinced that his wife had killed the children before taking her own life, he said that he had put their eldest son, Stanley, to bed, then set about concealing the three bodies in the trunk. Devereux then worked out his plan to hide the bodies. On 30 January, he told the milkman that his wife and the twins had gone away for a while. At the beginning of February, he took temporary lodgings in Harrow Road and contacted the removal company to move his belongings.

Prosecution counsel showed several flaws in Devereux's testimony. The most damning was a letter he had written to the company in Coventry penned on 13 January, over a fortnight before the death of his wife and sons, in which Devereux claimed he was a widower with one child. This, they claimed, showed clearly that it was a premeditated killing. Devereux countered this by claiming he had been refused other jobs on account of his young family, and had passed himself as a widower as he was desperate to find a job.

His intention, he maintained, had always been to firstly secure the job, move with Stanley to Coventry, and have his wife and the twins stay with her mother until he could find them a place where they could all be together.

With the case against the accused looking strong, the defence introduced evidence to suggest traces of insanity, claiming that Devereux came from an unstable family, that his thought process were not as lucid as the average man's, and that he had merely panicked upon finding the bodies and had chosen to hide them, rather that contact the police.

Summing up, the judge said that he could see no reason why Beatrice Devereux would murder her sons and then commit suicide. The jury took just ten minutes to agree.

9

'NO IDLE THREATS'

❖ *George William Butler, 7 November 1905* ❖

You must not be surprised if I am charged with murder,' the father told his son, as they shared a pint of beer in a north London public house on Sunday, 24 September 1905. Believing it was just the beer talking, the son ignored the boast, but within a few hours those fatal words came back to haunt him.

Forty-seven-year-old Mary Allen had been married twice before when she took up with George William Butler, a 50-year-old shoe and book maker. For the past three years, the two had been living together on Union Road, Marylebone. Mary had a grown up son from a previous marriage called George Melhuish, and in the summer of 1905, Melhuish went to stay with his mother and Butler. From the beginning, the men failed to hit it off, and by the end of July, the tension between the two finally erupted into violence. The short fight ended when Melhuish punched Butler in the face, knocking him to the ground. The blow was so severe it had broken his jaw and he needed medical attention at the local hospital. Released on the following day, Butler was still in great pain.

On the morning of 17 September, Butler argued with Mary Allen, and in front of neighbours later that afternoon, he insulted Mary and blamed her for encouraging her son to assault him. He told the neighbours that he would 'do for the two of them'. On 24 September, his own son visited Butler and they headed for a public house where a large amount of beer was drunk. With his jaw still causing pain and being unable to fully open it, Butler suffered the ignominy of having to drink his ale through a straw. He explained to his son that Mary's son had assaulted him, and said that when his jaw had healed he would buy a revolver and blow out their brains. He ended by making the sinister threat about being charged with murder.

On the following Monday morning, Mary Allen was heard crying for help. Her son ran to her room and found that Butler had stabbed her four times. The police were summoned and as Butler was led away, he shouted that it was Melhuish's fault for breaking his jaw. Mary Allen died two days later, and in due course Butler stood trial before Mr Justice Jelf at the Old Bailey. His defence put forward a plea that due to the large amount he had drunk, he was unaware of his actions at the time of the attack, but the prosecution countered by claiming that threats he had made to neighbours and to his own son, were 'no idle threats,' and showed that the murder was premeditated.

10

DEATH ON SHAFTESBURY AVENUE

❖ *John Esmond Murphy, 6 January 1909* ❖

It was Saturday morning, 7 November 1908, on London's busy Shaftesbury Avenue. The streets bustled with shoppers, while outside the offices of bankers and foreign moneychangers Messrs Cartnell and Schlitte, a cab driver waited to pick up a fare. At shortly after 11.30 a.m., a large metal paperweight crashed through the bank window. Seemingly having been thrown from the inside, passers-by peered inside and saw two men in the midst of a scuffle. The smaller of the two men appeared to have the upper hand and was seen to be thrusting at the other with what looked like a dagger.

The fight carried on into the doorway before the assailant made his escape. 'For God's sake someone help me!' the stricken banker cried as the man took flight. Cabbie George Carter, who had just deposited a fare outside the bank, saw the man escape and tried to detain him. Seeing his path blocked, the fleeing man responded by lashing out with the knife, badly wounding Carter on the hand. PC Albert Howe, alerted by the fracas, also made an attempt to apprehend the knifeman, and he too received a stab wound to the shoulder and slumped to the pavement.

This latest struggle resulted in the knife being wrestled from the attacker's hand, and as an angry mob converged on him, he was detained until PC Howe got to his feet and was able to drag him into custody.

Giving his name as James McDonald, a 21-year-old engineer of no fixed abode, he was charged with the attempted murder of Freidrich George Wilhelm Schlitte, a German banker with a home in Kingston-upon-Thames. The victim was able to make a deathbed identification of his attacker before he succumbed to his injuries forty-eight hours later.

When he stood trial before Mr Justice Pickford on 14 December, the accused gave his correct name as John Esmond Murphy, and said he was born in India. Murphy was charged with the wilful murder of Schlitte and with wounding Carter and Howe. The motive for the attack had been a botched robbery which had yielded nothing. Schlitte's deathbed statement was retold in court. He claimed that on the morning of the attack he had looked up to see Murphy standing before him in the banking hall, with a gun levelled at his chest. Without a word, Murphy had simply fired the gun once, the heavy calibre bullet burying itself in Schlitte's flesh.

Schlitte had then thrown himself at the attacker, knocking the gun from his hand. They fell to the floor, at which point Murphy had drawn a knife and stabbed the banker repeatedly. Schlitte had finally managed to throw something through the window in the hope of attracting attention.

Murphy claimed to have no memory of the attack other than hearing the gun going off. Witnesses told the court that previously Murphy was of excellent character, but they had noticed a change coming over him of late, and in the months before the murder he had been practising shooting at a range in Haymarket.

Suggestions were made that he was suffering from *petit mal*, a form of epilepsy, that he had also suffered badly from sunstroke as a child, and had undergone some sort of seizure when he went into the offices on that fateful morning. His counsel launched an appeal on the grounds of insanity but it was met with little success, and was quickly dismissed a few days before Christmas.

11

THE BROTHERS

❖ *Morris & Marks Reubens, 20 May 1909* ❖

As the steamer *Dorset* made its way up the Thames at the end of a long voyage from Australia, the crew were more than ready to set foot back on dry land and spend some of their hard earned wages in the dockside bars and clubs. It was Monday, 15 March 1909, and later that night, with the boat safely moored up in Victoria docks, second mate Charles McEachran and second engineer William Sproull, each with around £5 in their respective pockets, went off in search of fun.

After catching a train to Fenchurch Street, the first stop was the Three Nuns Hotel. After a meal and a few drinks elsewhere, they returned and a short time later, at around 11 p.m., they were approached by two women, Emily Allen and Ellen Stevens. Their intentions were soon clear, and, after some small talk and another drink, the men accompanied the women back to a room at 3 Rupert Street, off Leman Street, near Aldgate.

With business concluded, the sailors prepared to leave, when two men suddenly appeared from behind a curtain and began to attack them. McEachran was struck over the head with a heavy cosh and slumped to the ground unconscious. Thirty-four-year-old Sproull fought for his life, and as they spilled out into the street, the fight was brought to an abrupt end when one of the attackers pulled out a knife and dealt a fatal wound.

A short time later, a police officer found McEachran slumped against a wall in Whitechapel Road, and the body of Sproull was later discovered in nearby Rupert Street. A trail of blood led the police straight to the door of no. 3, where Marks Reubens, described by the arresting officer as a 22-year-old 'scallywag', was questioned and arrested.

Inside the house, officers also found Ellen Stevens in bed, too drunk to make any sense, and 23-year-old Morris Reubens, who was trying to dress when the police entered the house. Morris soon admitted that he had robbed Sproull, but claimed that the sailors had started the fight, and that he and his brother had only intervened to protect the women. Clearly disbelieving his account, both Reubens brothers, along with the two women, were taken into custody and later charged with murder.

When the case came to the Old Bailey in the spring of 1909, it was shown that Emily Allen had lived with Morris Reubens for two-and-a-half-years, and between them they had devised a simple arrangement. Ellen Stevens would look out for men, usually ones likely to be carrying a few shillings, or preferably pounds. These were often sailors on shore leave with money burning holes in their pockets.

She would use her charms to persuade the men to buy both her and Emily a few drinks, and once the bait was hooked, they would head back to Rupert Street where the Reubens brothers would be waiting to relieve their victims of cash and any other items about the person they took a shine to.

With no evidence being offered against either woman, Emily Allen was persuaded to give evidence for the prosecution. She claimed that Morris had first struck the men with a heavy sjambok, before Marks had dealt the fatal knife wound. With her confession and testimony, it took the jury less than ten minutes to return guilty verdicts on the brothers. Both struggled with their guards in the dock as sentence of death was passed, and as they were led below dock, Morris screamed out 'Why is there no recommendation to mercy?'

At their appeal, attempts were made to spare Morris from the gallows on the basis that it was not his hand that had struck the fatal blow. His counsel argued that for this reason the murder verdict, in his case, should be reduced to manslaughter. In dismissing the appeal, the panel explained that as the Reubens brothers had a common design in committing robbery that night, they were therefore equally guilty of wilful murder and the appeals were rejected.

The execution was unique in the history of capital punishment. The Reubens brothers were led to their deaths by executioner Harry Pierrepoint and his brother Thomas. On the morning of their executions, the brothers ignored each other as they were led onto the drop, but as a rabbi read out prayers as they reached the scaffold, the younger brother spoke one last time before the drop fell. 'Goodbye, Morris. I am sorry!'

12

A HUMBLE REVENGE

❖ *Madar Lal Dhingra, 17 August 1909* ❖

It had clearly been a longed planned crime. Slightly built Indian engineering student Madar Lal Dhingra had been in London since 1905, studying engineering at University College, and living in lodgings in Bayswater. On 20 January 1909, the 25 year old went to Hatton Garden post office and obtained a licence to carry a revolver. On the following day, he purchased a Colt automatic and later obtained a Belgian six-shot pistol, and throughout that winter and spring he was a regular visitor to a shoot gallery called 'Fun Land' off the Tottenham Court Road, where he became quite proficient in shooting the hand guns. Now he was ready to carry out his 'mission.'

On the evening of Thursday, 1 July, the Imperial Institute hosted a concert, witnessed by many dignitaries and other distinguished guests. As guests began to disperse at the end of the evening, small groups formed, discussing the performance and other issues. Sir William Curzon Wyllie, the 61-year-old Aide-de-Camp to the Secretary of State for India, was engaged in a discussion with Dhingra when the student suddenly pulled out a pistol and fired five shots. The first skimmed past, but the next four struck him in the head. He was killed instantly.

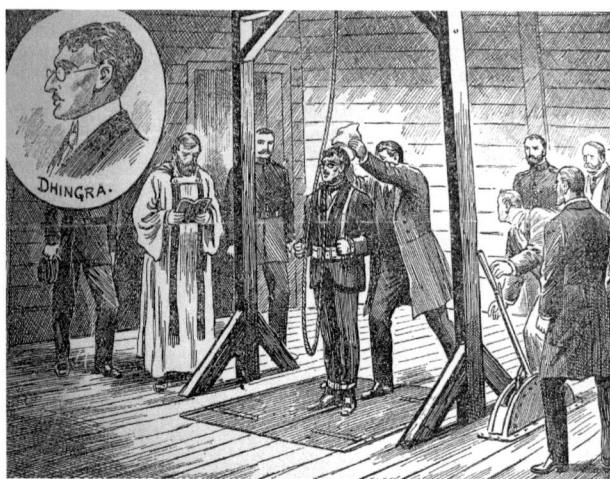

EXECUTION OF DHINGRA.

SIR CURZON WYLLIE'S ASSASSIN PAYS THE PENALTY.

[Subject of Illustration.]

Madar Lal Dhingra, the young Indian student who murdered Sir Curzon Wyllie and Dr. Lalcaca at the Imperial Institute on July 1, was executed last week at Pentonville Prison, Pierpoint being the executioner. About a hundred persons gathered outside to await the official announcement, but there were no natives of India among them.

Dhingra rose at six o'clock after a restless night, and dressed in his own clothes. He hardly touched the tea and bread and butter which were brought to him for breakfast, but he displayed perfect calmness and self-possession. He walked firmly to the scaffold, and died without making any statement respecting his crime.

How the Illustrated Police News *depicted the execution of Dhingra.* (T.J. Leech Archive)

Newspaper headline announcing the execution of Dhingra. (T.J. Leech Archive)

Shocked by what they had seen, several guests stood motionless for several seconds. Bombay-born 48-year-old Dr Cowas Lalcaca was the closest to the gunman and, as he moved forward, Dhingra aimed the gun and fired two shots at him. Lalcaca slumped to the ground fatally wounded, as Dhingra waved the gun at the crowd who had now closed in. Realising escape was hopeless, the Indian pointed the gun at his head and pulled the trigger. There was an empty click and within seconds he was overpowered and bundled to the ground.

Taken into custody, Dhingra made a detailed statement confessing to the crime and stating his motives. He said he believed passionately in the cause of freeing India from British rule to the extent he was prepared to assassinate those he blamed responsible for the troubles and to die for his country.

Before Lord Chief Justice Alverstone at the Old Bailey on 23 July, Dhingra refused legal representation and claimed not to recognise the court. In his eyes, he had committed no crime, as Sir William Curzon Wyllie had been assassinated because he was an enemy of his people. With regards to the second charge, the murder of Dr Lalcaca, this had been unfortunate and accidental, and that he had shot him in self-defence to evade arrest.

He asked for a statement to be read out, in which he blamed the British government for the deaths of millions of his countrymen, and for taking millions of pounds from the subcontinent every year. He said it was a humble revenge for years of occupation and brutality. In his eyes, he had as much right to resist the English occupying forces as the English would have if the Germans occupied England. Asked if he had anything to say before the sentence was passed, Dhingra simply reiterated that he did not recognise the court.

13

THE EALING MURDER

❖ *George Henry Perry, 1 March 1910* ❖

George Henry Perry acknowledged his guilt and saw no reason to deny that he had committed a brutal murder. But to Mr Justice Coleridge, that wasn't the way it was done, and he told the prisoner he would not accept the plea, telling him to arrange for a counsel to defend him. Two days later, with Henry, later Sir Henry, Curtis Bennett representing him, Perry was returned to the Old Bailey for what was to all intents, a formality of a trial.

Twenty-seven-year-old Perry had served for seven years in the Royal Garrison Artillery before leaving the army in 1908. With little money and unable to find a steady job, the parents of his girlfriend, Annie Covell, allowed him to live with them at Ealing until he was able to find a place of his own. Although willing to help their daughter's boyfriend, they soon felt that Perry was taking advantage of their hospitality and making no real effort to find work or support himself. He had set up as a window cleaner with the little money he had saved from the army, but in the following year and a half, he worked barely fifty days.

Eventually Annie Covell had had enough, and on Sunday, 9 January 1910, she told Perry he was to find somewhere else

George Perry – the Ealing Murderer.
(T.J. Leech Archive)

to live. On the following morning, Perry packed his few belongings and left as instructed, but later that afternoon he returned and asked to see Annie. Her mother invited him in, and the couple had been in Annie's room for a matter of minutes when a fearful scream rang out. Mrs Covell hurried to the room and found Alice lying on the floor, with Perry kneeling on top of her holding a bloodstained bread knife. She rushed into the street to find a policeman, and, left alone with Annie, Perry completed the job by cutting her throat. He made no attempt to flee, and surrendered himself to the police who arrived moments later.

Curtis Bennett put forward a plea of insanity, claiming that Perry's offering to plead guilty was as good as putting his head in the noose, and this was surely the work of someone suffering from a mental illness. The prosecution simply said that Perry was angered at losing both his girlfriend and his home and had committed the murder in revenge and anger.

14

BEYOND ENDURANCE

❖ *Hawley Harvey Crippen, 23 November 1910* ❖

It was to be friends' suspicions that eventually lead to a transatlantic murder hunt, and the name of a killer going down in the annals of crime as one of the most notorious on record. But the truth of the matter was somewhat different, and, far from being the brute that history has painted him, Hawley Harvey Crippen was a mild mannered man who, in all probability, was pushed beyond endurance and had accidentally killed his wife, and it was only sheer panic that made him dismember and conceal her remains before attempting to flee for his life back to his homeland.

Born in Coldwater, Michigan, in 1862, Crippen was a widower when, in 1893, he met his second wife, known to friends as Cora, in New York. Although using the stage name Belle Elmore, she had in fact been christened Kunigunde Mackamotzki, the daughter of a Russian-Polish father and a German mother. They married shortly afterwards in Jersey City and spent the rest of the century in various parts of America while Crippen worked as a medical practitioner, although he mainly dealt in quack medicines.

In April 1900, Crippen came to London, alone at first, and after acquiring a house in St John's Wood he took a position with a firm that produced homoeopathic remedies, also helping to run a dental practice in New Oxford Street.

His wife joined him in August. With her ambitions to be an opera singer, Crippen paid for Cora to have extra tuition, but lacking the talent to make the big time, she turned to music hall. Although limited in ability, she was able to find work, and in due course made many friends, eventually becoming treasurer of the Music Hall Ladies Guild.

In September 1905, they took tenancy of 39 Hilldrop Crescent, Holloway. Belle became close to American music hall artist Bruce Miller, and now began to find fault in her meek husband. Crippen was not unduly worried: he himself had fallen for his pretty young typist, Ethel Le Neve. If husband and wife had chosen to separate at this point, that would probably have been enough to save both from an untimely death, but with Cora threatening to leave him penniless if they spilt up, he chose to endure the situation, satisfied at least in the comfort of his young mistress.

On New Year's Eve 1910, Paul and Clara Martinetti, friends of the Crippens, dined at Hilldrop Crescent. They left at about 1 a.m. on the following morning, and were the last people to see Belle alive. Crippen told friends that, following a quarrel, Belle had left him and gone back to America. When he later told them that she had subsequently fallen ill and died, they were incredulous with disbelief. Their suspicions were heightened when Ethel Le Neve moved into Hilldrop Crescent shortly afterwards, and, within days, began wearing Belle's jewellery.

Dr Crippen – arrested in Canada after a
transatlantic chase. (Author's collection)

Hangman John Ellis. His first senior engagement at
Pentonville was to hang Dr Crippen.
(Author's collection)

Following a visit by Belle's concerned friends to Scotland Yard on 8 July, Chief Inspector Walter Dew went to Hilldrop Crescent. Crippen showed Dew around the house, and told the Inspector a slightly different tale to the one he had told Belle's friends. He admitted that stories of her death were lies, and that he had made them up to cover his shame at her having left him and run off with her lover, who he suspected was Bruce Miller.

Chief Inspector Dew was not completely satisfied and told Crippen that it was in his interests to locate his wife and to clear up the mystery. Crippen promised he would and the Inspector left. The visit had clearly shaken the doctor, and on the following morning, with Ethel disguised as a boy, the couple headed for Antwerp via Brussels, where they purchased tickets for Canada, and boarded a steamer, *Montrose*.

Dew returned to Hilldrop Crescent to ask Crippen a couple of follow-up questions and, finding the house deserted, he ordered a thorough search. Discovering some loose bricks on the cellar floor, he had them lifted and found the headless, limbless remains of a human body.

Suspecting Crippen had fled the country, Dew asked all ships' officers to be on the lookout for the missing couple. Although disguised as father and son, the actions of Crippen and his mistress alerted Captain Kendall on the *Montrose* and, as the ship passed the south coast of England he telegraphed a message to Scotland Yard. Satisfied they were the missing fugitives, Dew boarded a faster ship, the *Laurentic*, at Liverpool. The race was now on.

With the eyes of the world watching the chase through the pages of national newspapers, on Sunday, 31 July, Dew boarded the *Montrose* as it sailed up the St Lawrence River. Chief Inspector Dew arrested Crippen and Le Neve and they were taken into custody.

The trial of Hawley Harvey Crippen began on 18 October at the Old Bailey, before the Lord Chief Justice Alverstone. The prosecution claimed that the body was that of Crippen's wife and that cause of death was hyoscine poisoning. Identification was confirmed by a particular piece of flesh showing a scar, one that Belle was known to have had on her lower abdomen. They could also show that Crippen had bought five grains of hyoscine poison in January 1910, three weeks before Belle had disappeared, and poison found in the remains was consistent with the victim having ingested half a grain, almost twice the fatal dose. Crippen's defence was based around the surmise that the body in the cellar was not that of his wife, and that he was therefore innocent of her murder.

The most damning evidence was to be a pyjama jacket in which the remains had been concealed. Crippen maintained that the jacket was not his and must have been put there by previous owners before the Crippens took residency in 1905. This statement was effectively destroyed when it was shown that the jacket had a label inside giving the manufacturer as Jones Brothers Ltd, Holloway. Jones Brothers had only become a limited company in 1909, and therefore the jacket could not have been concealed after this date, proving that only Crippen could have put the body there.

Faced with this, the jury took less than half an hour to return their guilty verdict. Three days later, Ethel Le Neve stood trial but was quickly found not guilty. She continued to visit Crippen in the condemned cell, and after her last visit, he went to the bathroom where he snapped off a piece of his spectacle frame with the intention of puncturing an artery and bleeding to death. He was prevented from doing so and spent his last hours on earth under the careful watch of prison guards to make sure he did not cheat the hangman.

15

GOD'S WILL BE DONE

❖ *Noah Woolf, 21 December 1910* ❖

Noah Woolf was not a popular resident at the Home for Aged Hebrew Christians at St John's Villas, Upper Holloway. The 58-year-old German bookbinder had been a resident at the

Noah Woolf. (T.J. Leech Archive)

Home until the summer of 1910, when he was asked to leave. At the end of June, Revd Michael Machim, superintendent of the London mission linked to the Home, arranged a meeting, and one of the first to speak to him was Andrew Simon, a 65-year-old retired hawker. Simon said that he had come to the Home to live and die in peace as a Christian, and strongly objected to Woolf's atheistic utterances. He had consulted with other residents, and it was decided that Woolf would have to go. On 4 July, Woolf was given notice to leave, but the kindly reverend granted him an allowance of 10s, and a smaller sum of money to be paid every week for the next three months.

On 27 October, with the monies having now run out, Woolf returned to the Home and was seen talking to Simon, whom he clearly blamed for his eviction. They had words, and Woolf went away, only to return on the following day shortly before lunchtime, when he was seen heading towards Simon's room. Later that afternoon, Woolf walked into the police station at Upper Holloway Road, pulled out a bloodstained knife, and said that he wished to confess to the murder of Andrew Simon. Police went to the Home, and found the body as Woolf had described. He said that he had asked Simon to withdraw the accusations he had made, believing that if he did so, Woolf would be allowed to return to the Home.

Woolf said that Simon told him he was unwilling to withdraw anything, and even if he did, it was too late for him to return to the house. In a rage, Woolf then stabbed him in the neck and chest, and as he fell to the floor, he finished him off with several more knife wounds to his back and chest.

At his brief trial before Mr Justice Darling three weeks later, there was never any doubt about the verdict, although the jury did recommend Woolf to mercy. Moments before his execution, Woolf dispelled the atheist beliefs that had led to his situation. He wrote a message on a slate addressed to the chaplain and prison doctor. It read: 'Thank one and all for their great kindness to me, while in your charge. I pray God's will be done. Lord receive my spirit – Noah Woolf.'

16
'NOTHING BUT DEATH SHALL PART US'
❖ *Michael Collins, 24 May 1911* ❖

Taxi driver Michael Collins had been dating recently-widowed Elizabeth Kempster since Christmas 1910, and within weeks, she had decided to move in with the 30-year-old army reservist who had a house in Stepney. He seemed to dote on her 6-year-old son, and their future together looked happy.

Then, for some unknown reason, things suddenly changed. On Sunday, 19 March 1911, after spending the evening out drinking, Collins asked Elizabeth what seemed to be troubling her, as she was obviously unhappy. She merely told him that she wished he would leave her alone. On the following day, relations deteriorated to the extent that she would not even speak to him. This continued for a further day, with Collins becoming increasingly upset and concerned. He pleaded for her to confide in him, but all she would say was that she wanted him to leave, and she would face the trouble she was in by herself.

On Saturday, 25 March, Collins spent some time with his friend and neighbour, George Crease. Clearly depressed, Collins told Crease that he had had yet another quarrel with Elizabeth, and that he thought it best if he did away with both her and himself. On the way home, he purchased a new razor from a shop in Whitechapel. At 6 p.m., Collins approached Crease as he was talking to another neighbour. Collins's hands were covered in blood, and he told them quietly he had just killed Elizabeth.

At his Old Bailey trial in April, Collins said he had spent a week fretting over whether Elizabeth would be ending their relationship. Finally, he pleaded with her to make a decision. 'Are we to live together or part?' he asked. Elizabeth thought for a moment before replying, 'Part.'

At that, he picked up a hammer and cried, 'Nothing but death shall part us,' and struck her on the temple.

Cut-throat killer Michael Collins.
(T.J. Leech Archive)

'Oh Mike, don't!' Elizabeth cried out as she fell to the ground. He pulled out the razor he had bought on the way home and cut her throat. 'Goodbye, we shall meet above!' he cried, kissing her as she lay dead on the floor.

Collins' counsel put forward a defence of insanity, but as Mr Justice Grantham explained in his summing up, the facts in the case were straightforward, and that Elizabeth's wishing to end their relationship was a clear motive for the vicious and murderous assault.

17

THE LAST VOYAGE

❖ *Francisco Carlos Godhino, 17 October 1911* ❖

If I say my fault, will they pardon me? Is King George here? If I say my fault and ask pardon perhaps he relieve me. It was his Coronation ten days ago. If he no relieve me will they put me in gaol or hang me up? It was both our faults. We fighting. (Statement made by Godhino at Bow Street Magistrates Court, 3 July 1911)

The P&O liner *China* was slowly making its way from Sydney to London. On 8 June 1911, she departed from Colombo, Ceylon, and set course for Aden. Three days into this leg of the voyage, just before dawn, Goa-born bath attendant Francisco Godhino woke stewardess Annie Crutchley and asked which was the cabin of head stewardess, 40-year-old Alice Brewster.

It was Godhino's turn to wake the staff for morning duties and, told that she was in the cabin opposite, he went to wake Miss Brewster, while Annie Crutchley began to run her bath. Moments later, Godhino returned looking shocked and shouted for her to come quickly. Returning to Alice Brewster's cabin, they found her lying on the floor of the cabin covered by a mattress. She had been battered to death, and it seemed that someone had tried and failed to push her through the open porthole.

The ship's captain launched an immediate investigation, and it soon became clear that Godhino was the main suspect. The victim had been his immediate superior, and it was made known to the captain that she had often found fault with his work. Asked to account for his movements on the night of the murder, he explained that as it had been a hot night, he had opted not to sleep in his cabin, choosing instead to sleep on deck.

Waking around midnight, he had gone to get a drink of water, and on the way, had passed the security officer on duty. He had then returned to the fore hatch and slept until around 5 a.m. when he went to wake Miss Crutchley. The security man confirmed seeing Godhino on deck, but said that it was closer to 3 a.m. than midnight. Godhino could not produce his porthole key, a heavy item capable of sustaining the wounds found on the body, and he had also changed his pair of trousers shortly after the murder was discovered. They were found soaking in a tub, still clearly showing bloodstains. The heavy key was also found in the sink of a steward's bathroom.

Godhino was placed under arrest, and when the *China* docked in England in early July, he was taken into police custody. Before his first court appearance at Bow Street Magistrate's Court, he made a statement asking if the king would pardon him. Before Mr Justice Avory at the Old Bailey, in September, Godhino's counsel fought to have the statement made at Bow Street inadmissible as evidence, but after lengthy debate, it was decided that it could to be heard. But the prosecution's main evidence from the ship's captain was enough to convince the jury of Godhino's guilt.

Alice Brewster had intended this to be her last voyage: she probably would never have imagined it would end in her brutal, cold-blooded murder.

THE FIRE-STARTER

❖ *Edward Hill, 17 October 1911* ❖

For a man who had once earned his living as a marine fireman, Edward Hill kept a sinister secret. Just months before his wedding, he had been paroled, having served a ten-year prison sentence for arson. On his release, the 41 year old preferred to avoid any type of work, and had, in fact, lived a persistently dishonest and violent life since his first convictions in 1891. It seems though that his wife-to-be was unaware of his history when she agreed to be his wife.

On 16 July, Mary Jane Hill, ten years older than her new husband, walked out of the church as his wife. They took unfurnished rooms on the top floor of a house at 22 Caledonia Street, Kings Cross, but within days, their landlady noticed that her new tenants had been drinking. She told them that she expected certain standards from her tenants and would not tolerate people with intemperate habits. Hill apologised, explaining that the couple had recently wed and were still celebrating. A few hours after Hill had received the warning from his landlady, his new wife borrowed 22s from a relative in order that she could then lend it to a friend. Mary later found that this money was missing, and the only person who could have taken it was her new husband.

Hill denied it but Mary was not convinced. On the following day, they had a fierce quarrel about the missing money. Hill became so enraged, he picked up a knife and slashed at the bedding and pillows, scattering feathers around the room. Later that night, he went out drinking, and in the early hours of 25 July, the landlady heard Hill knocking on the front door and saw Mary letting her husband in.

Around 10 a.m. that morning, Mary Hill borrowed a further sum from her relative and asked the landlady to look after it until she could pass it on to her friend. Mary returned to her room, and a short time later the landlady heard footsteps on the stairs. Looking out of the window, she saw Hill leaving the house and walking briskly up the street.

Within the hour, smoke was seen coming from under the door to Hill's room, and when fellow tenants forced entry into the room, they saw a fire raging on the bed. It was soon extinguished, and to their horror, they found the body of Mary Hill. She lay on the floor, a bandage knotted tightly around her neck, and her face covered with two pillows. A paraffin lamp had been thrown onto the bed, which had also been doused in paraffin. It seemed clear that the intention of the killer was to cause a severe fire to cover up the strangulation.

Edward Hill was soon located, as he drank in a public house close to his mother's house in St George's Road, Southwark. He initially tried to tell police officers that he was in fact his own twin

Habitual criminal Edward Hill, who collapsed on the scaffold. (T.J. Leech Archive)

brother, but his diminutive size, standing a little over 5ft tall, made him easy to identify. He denied any knowledge of the fire, and claimed he was at his mother's house at the time the fire had been started.

Placed under arrest, Hill became violent at the police station and had to be forcibly restrained. He made a vain attempt to escape when removed to Kings Cross police station in a taxi cab, fighting violently with the officers until they could subdue him.

On 12 September, he stood before Mr Justice Avory, where it became a case of believing Hill's account that he was at his mother's at the time of the murder, or the testimony of his landlady who had seen him leave the house shortly before the fire broke out. The jury chose to believe the latter, and Hill was duly convicted.

On the morning of his execution, Hill scribbled a last message on a slate, thanking the governor, doctors and officers of Pentonville Prison for their kindness during his stay in the condemned cell. As he took his place on the gallows – alongside convicted murderer Franscisco Godhino – Hill's courage and bravado deserted him, and he slumped in a faint as the hangman's rope was placed around his neck.

19

THE GAMBLING DEN MURDERS

❖ *Myer Abramovitch, 6 March 1912* ❖

Hanbury Street, Spitalfields, was no stranger to murder. In September 1888, in a yard at the rear of No. 29, the second victim of Jack the Ripper, Annie Chapman, met her grisly end. Almost a quarter of a century later, the grim reaper returned to the East End streets.

In the early hours of Wednesday, 27 December 1911, firemen, following up an alarm, called at a café at 62 Hanbury Street, where they found the side door open and smoke bellowing from a locked back room. They forced the door to the back room and discovered a small blaze which they easily contained, but they also made a gruesome discovery. On the bed, in a pool of blood, lay the bodies of a 35-year-old Pole, Solomon Milstein, and his 37-year-old wife, Annie. Police arrived and found that the couple had been battered to death with a pair of heavy tongues and a poker which lay beside the bed. They also saw that paraffin had been poured over the bed before hot fire irons were placed on top.

Detective Inspector Wensley was placed in charge of the investigation, and began to piece together events that led up to the brutal double murder. Solomon and Annie Milstein had successfully run the Jewish café and teashop in Hanbury Street until November 1911, when, following a strike at the nearby warehouses, trade began to drop off to such extent that Milstein came up with the idea of converting the basement into a gambling den.

With gambling being against the law, his wife was unhappy at the move, but chose to keep quiet and not make a fuss. To keep troublemakers out, Milstein went into partnership with former professional boxer Joe Goldstein and another local tough, and from the start the cellar proved a popular meeting place. Any number of card games would take place, many for fun, but the most popular was the gambling game, Faro. They would charge three pence per game and divide the profits three ways, after paying Milstein 5s rent for the cellar.

As business boomed, the threesome hit upon another lucrative sideline. Once a customer had lost his stake, they would be willing to provide extra funds in the form of a loan, secured against personal property, such as watches and gold chains.

After a while, Mrs Milstein began to fear for the safety of both her husband and of the premises. A number of disgruntled gamblers had been heard to make threats, having suffering

An artist's impression of the horrific murder at Spitalfields. (T.J. Leech Archive)

heavy losses, and while she didn't object to the cellar being used as a meeting place for cards and other board games, the illegal gambling was a different matter. She reasoned that it would only be a matter of time before the police got involved and they would face prosecution.

On 26 December, Milstein told his partners that he was winding up operations, and later that night Goldstein decided to leave early. They counted up the money, divided it out, and when the last of the gamblers had left the cellar, Milstein locked the doors and retired to bed. Within the next four hours, he and his wife were brutally murdered.

Wensley set about tracing anyone who had been present at the cellar on the previous night. All were found and eliminated with one exception; Myer Abramovitch, a 28-year-old Polish Jew who worked as a fruit seller at the local market. He was a regular visitor to the cellar on Hanbury Street, but was not thought to be a heavy gambler, though one or two witnesses suggested that he might have lost heavily at Faro on the previous evening. Abramovitch had been wearing a silk neck scarf on the night of the murder. A similar scarf had been found close to the bodies.

Twenty-four hours later, Henry Seychur, one of those in the cellar on the night of the murder, was at the corner of Leman Street when he saw Abramovitch at a coffee stall. Aware that detectives were looking to interview Abramovitch, he asked him why he had not been to the police. Abramovitch just shook his head but agreed to Seychur's offer to accompany him to Leman Street police station.

Shown the silk neckerchief found beside the body, Abramovitch immediately confessed to detectives: 'I done it. That is mine; I done it because I lost all my money in gambling.'

Following the confession, the trial at the Old Bailey in February 1912 was a formality. Mr Justice Ridley heard Abramovitch's counsel put forward a defence of insanity, claiming he was known locally as 'Myer the Insane'. Following the inevitable passing of the death sentence, Abramovitch broke down and wept, and spent his time in the death cell highly agitated and distressed. On the morning of his execution, he stumbled slowly along the short walk to the drop.

20

A STUDY IN GREED

❖ *Frederick Henry Seddon, 18 April 1912* ❖

Eliza Mary Barrow passed away suddenly on 14 September 1911. Two days later, she was buried in a pauper's grave, and only when her cousin Frank Vonderahe called at her home at 63 Tollington Park, Islington, to see his cousin, did he learn that the 50-year-old spinster was dead and buried. Vonderahe was immediately concerned. Why had relatives not been informed of her death, and why had she been buried in Islington when the family had their own plot in Kensal Green cemetery?

Vonderahe wanted answers and demanded to see the owner of the house, 40-year-old insurance agent, Frederick Henry Seddon. Seddon was evasive when confronted, but then revealed to the shocked Vonderahe that all of Miss Barrow's monies and properties had now passed to him. Eliza Barrow had been a woman of substantial means: she owned a public house in Camden, along with an adjacent barbershop, and also had an extensive shares portfolio. Seddon told him that Mrs Barrow had signed over all of these assets in return for an annual allowance, which following her death, due to 'epidemic diarrhoea', had now expired. Vonderahe, who had taken an instant dislike to Seddon, reported his suspicions to the police and in due course investigations were made.

Miss Barrow had been taken ill on 1 September 1911; a doctor was called and he visited her several times before she died. The cause of death had been given as acute enteritis. To detectives examining Seddon's financial dealings, it seemed Miss Barrow's sudden death had proved to be a stroke of luck, and on 15 November the body of Eliza Barrow was exhumed.

The post-mortem was performed by pathologist Bernard Spilsbury, and finding no sign of any disease, he conducted further tests, this time finding traces of arsenic. On 4 December, Seddon was arrested at his home and charged with the murder of Eliza Barrow, and in the following month, his wife was also arrested and the two were jointly tried at the Old Bailey in March 1912.

Mr Justice Bucknill presided over the ten-day trial, which featured the most famous counsel of the day doing battle in the courtroom. Richard Muir outlined the prosecution's case, and said that Seddon worked as the District Superintendent for the London & Manchester Assurance Company, and that Eliza Barrow had gone to live with the Seddons in July 1910. For a fee of 12s a week, she rented several rooms in the house at Islington, and according to Seddon, in October 1910, a number of shares in India Stock were transferred to him in return for an annuity of two guineas per week. When Seddon subsequently sold this stock, it realised over £1,500, and with this money he purchased a number of properties in Mile End which he rented out, yielding him a healthy income.

Seddon also claimed that in March 1911, Miss Barrow had again approached him about a number of financial matters, and as a result, they came to an arrangement whereby she signed over the Camden Town public house and the adjoining barbershop in return for another annuity, this time for £1 per week for life.

Muir suggested a motive: he stated that by the summer of 1911 Seddon had acquired all of Miss Barrow's property, and although he had income coming in, he was obliged to pay out over £3 a week to the lonely old spinster renting rooms in his house. He alleged that Seddon and his wife had poisoned Eliza Barrow in order to free themselves from paying out the weekly monies. Muir suggested that Seddon had reasoned that the longer Miss Barrow stayed alive, the more it would cost him.

Evidence showed that there had been a large number of arsenic-laced flypapers in the house. Seddon's wife admitted that several of these had been scattered around Miss Barrow's room. There was also a bowl of flypapers soaking beside her bed, and the eminent defence counsel Marshall Hall offered the suggestion that the victim may have accidentally consumed the poison, either through drinking the liquid or inhaling the fumes over a long period of time.

Tollington Park, Islington – where Eliza Barrow died. (Author's collection)

Frederick Seddon – whose greed led him to the gallows. (Author's collection)

At the conclusion of the trial, Margaret Seddon was found not guilty and released; Frederick Seddon was found guilty of murder and sentenced to death. Seddon and the trial judge were both Masons and had met in the past at various events. As the black cap was placed on the judge's wig, Seddon made the Masonic brotherhood sign, which required fellow Masons to help each other. In passing sentence, Mr Justice Bucknill tearfully acknowledged the sign, but added that all members of the brotherhood respected the law and, however much he regretted it, he must nevertheless condemn Seddon to death. The assets Seddon had coveted and which had led him to commit the callous murder were disposed of as he awaited the hangman.

Seddon's remains were interred in a felon's grave at Pentonville in an adjacent plot to those of Dr Crippen, who had faced the hangman at Pentonville just eighteen months previously. By a strange coincidence, Eliza Barrow's final resting place had been a plot at Islington cemetery, just a matter of yards from the grave of Belle Elmore, the victim of Dr Crippen.

21

MURDER AT FENCHURCH STREET STATION

❖ *Edward Hopwood, 29 January 1913* ❖

In the spring of 1907, after only one year of marriage, 29-year-old Florence Alice Bernadette Silles found herself widowed with a baby son. She went to live with her sister in Ilford, and adopting the name Flora Dudley, attempted to make ends meet by working as a music hall

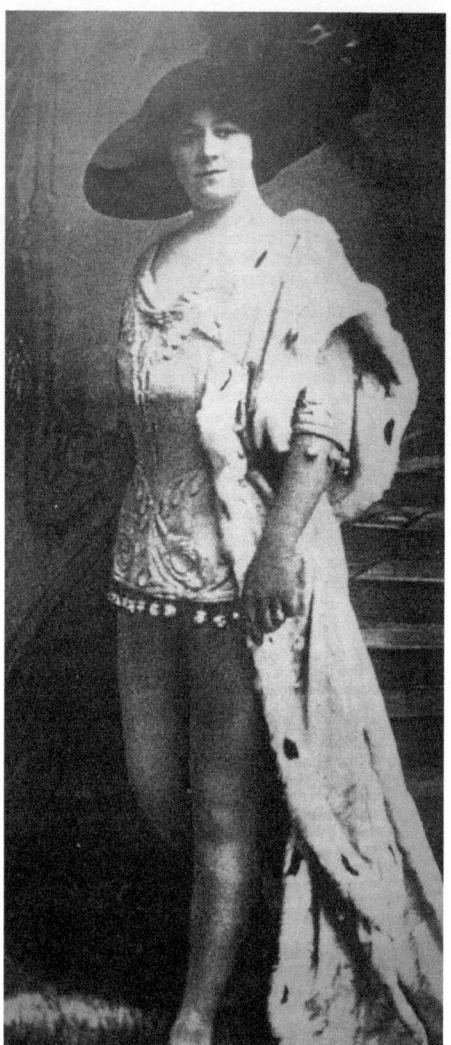

Music hall star Flora Dudley – shot dead on the concourse at Fenchurch Street station.
(T.J. Leech Archive)

artiste. Struggling to get by and forced to work her way up from the bottom of the bill, her luck seemed to change when she met Edward Hopwood in May 1912.

Flora was staring in a pantomime at Manchester Tivoli when she met Hopwood, who told her he was helping to finance a new play, and she seemed perfect to be cast as a principal actor in the forthcoming production. Hopwood said he was the managing director of a company named 'Commerce Limited' and claimed to be a wealthy bachelor. In reality, Hopwood was a 45-year-old married man with three children; his company was in dire trouble and he was in great financial difficulties.

Less than four months later, on 13 September, a letter was received at Ilford addressed to Hopwood. Over the summer Hopwood had used this as a business address on a number of occasions, but suspicious that he had not been honest with Flora, her sister opened the letter and realised Hopwood's true financial situation. Faced with this revelation, Hopwood claimed it was all a misunderstanding, blaming the company secretary for the perilous state of affairs and promising to resolve the situation.

On 26 September, Hopwood purchased a gun in Brighton, and later that day, he arranged to meet Flora in London. Two days later, Hopwood and Flora spent the evening in the West End before taking a taxi-cab, directing the driver to head towards Fenchurch Street station. As they reached the station concourse, the driver heard a loud bang followed by a scream. Pulling into the kerb, thinking that he might have a puncture, the driver climbed out to inspect the tyres. At that moment, the door opened and Flora Dudley collapsed into his arms, moaning that she had been shot.

As the driver and passersby tended to the stricken woman, a further two shots rang out from inside the taxi. Hopwood had placed the barrel of the gun to his temple and fired. In his haste to pull the trigger, the barrel slipped and the gunshots proved not to be fatal, merely wounding the side of his head. He was soon well enough able to be nursed back to health, unlike Flora, who died from her wounds later that evening.

At his trial, Hopwood did not deny killing Flora Dudley but claimed it had been a terrible accident. As they headed back to the station in the taxi, Flora told him she knew his promises for a better life were false, and that she had decided they should part. Hopwood said he had then pulled out his gun and made to shoot himself. Flora pleaded with him not to be foolish, and during the struggle the gun went off accidentally, fatally wounding her.

His version of events failed to convince the jury, who stated that while Hopwood may well have intended only to commit suicide that night, they believed he had committed murder once Flora told him their romance was over.

22

OVERCOME WITH JEALOUSY

❖ *Henry Longden, 8 July 1913* ❖

Twenty-seven-year-old typist Alice Catlow More worked for the East and West Society of China, an organisation with offices on New Oxford Street, whose aim was to promote trade between England and the Far East. Alice had lived for a time in Leeds with a butcher named Henry Longden, who, at 52 years old, was almost twice her age, before the pair moved to London in the summer of 1912.

Less than a year later, the relationship between the pair had become fraught. Although Longden was undoubtedly in love with Alice, he constantly ill-treated her, and the more she tolerated it, the worse his treatment towards her seemed to become. Alice decided she could take it no longer, and this realisation coincided with her becoming friendly with a man named Silva, a customer at her place of work.

When Longden returned home from work on 16 March 1913, a row broke out because Alice had not lit the fire. This time, instead of letting Longden ill-treat her, she packed her bags and moved into lodgings. Convinced that the reason she had left was because she had embarked on an affair with Silva, Longden confronted him in the street outside the offices on New Oxford Street.

'You are the man who has induced this lady to leave my home!' he shouted. Silva denied the claims, and so Longden turned to Alice. 'Then I will deal with you later!'

On the following afternoon, Longden attacked Alice on Taviton Street as she made her way to her lodgings in St Pancras. As Alice staggered down the street bleeding heavily from a gaping neck wound, Longden followed a few paces behind, holding a large butcher's knife. When Alice slumped to the floor dead, Longden turned the knife on himself, but failed in his attempt to take his own life.

Charged with wilful murder, Longden appeared before Mr Justice Rowlatt at the Old Bailey on 2 June. Defence counsel claimed the murder was unpremeditated and was a result of extreme provocation. There was no doubt of the prisoner's guilt, and the jury took just a short time to return their verdict, although adding a strong recommendation to mercy.

At Longden's subsequent appeal, the panel agreed with the judge's remark that he had been overcome with jealousy when he carried out the murder, but in view of his previous bad character, and his ill treatment of the victim, they quickly dismissed the appeal.

23

THE CELLAR CEMETERY

❖ *Frederick Albert Robertson, 27 November 1913* ❖

The procession to the gallows was slow, the prisoner's wooden leg making an eerie tapping sound that echoed down the prison corridor as they made their way to the execution chamber. Throughout his time in the condemned cell, the prisoner had given no explanation or made any confession to the crime that had horrified the country. As the condemned man took his place on the trapdoors, hangman John Ellis held back a moment in case the prisoner wished

Frederick Robertson.

Frederick Robertson took the secret of his horrific crime to the grave. (T.J. Leech Archive)

to make a last minute confession, but seeing he had no intention of speaking, Ellis placed the noose around his neck and walked to the lever. Seconds later, the truth of what had happened that fateful day five months earlier were taken to the grave.

The terrible smell coming from the drains was enough for the new lodger in the top floor flat at 12 Saratoga Road, Clapton, to demand the landlord fix the problem. On the morning of Friday, 25 July 1913, a neighbour, Joseph Lidden, who carried out repairs for the landlord, called at the flat, and after checking the drains, could find nothing wrong, but he too could detect a foul smell coming from somewhere in the house.

Lidden let himself into the vacant ground floor flat, where the smell intensified. He lifted a loose floorboard, and in the recess below, he discovered the badly decomposing body of a small child. Beside that was the body of another child. Holding his handkerchief to his mouth, Lidden fled from the house and summoned the police.

When detectives began their investigations, they found that there were in fact three bodies in the shallow grave. Their identities were not difficult to discover. The flat had been empty since the departure of the previous tenents, Frederick Robertson, a 26-year-old metal worker, his wife Lily, and three young children: 2-year-old twins Nellie and Freddie, and 10-month-old daughter Beatrice. Robertson had taken over tenancy in early June, and had handed the keys back on 12 July.

Police investigations soon revealed that Robertson's wife had been admitted into Homerton Hospital on 24 June, and her husband had told her the children, who had initially been looked after by family friends, were now being cared for by the Salvation Army.

Robertson was arrested at the junction of Shepherdess Walk and City Road, north London. His tell-tale limp gave him away, and with Robertson's description circulated across the metropolis, Divisional Detective Inspector Haigh of J Division watched the man pass, and then approached and tapped him on the shoulder.

'Is your name Robertson?' he asked. Told it was, Haigh said he was arresting him for the murder of his three children. At that, Robertson burst into tears. 'Don't take hold of me. I will come quietly,' he said, as they walked to the police station.

Robertson killing the children and, although his claims that they had been left with the Salvation Army were easily disproved, he then admitted that he had merely abandoned them outside the Homerton workhouse, as he couldn't cope with looking after them. Asked to explain how the bodies had come to be found under the floorboards at the house, he could give no satisfactory explanation. Robertson kept up claims that they couldn't be his children, but the fact that the bodies were of three children of similar age to his own was just too much of a coincidence.

An inquest was held a few days later, where cause of death was thought to have been asphyxiation. The saddest sight was Lily Robertson, an intern some seven weeks in the local hospital and still a sick woman, accompanied by a nurse, barely comprehending the horror of losing her three babies and the arrest of her husband.

Robertson's three-day trial took place before Mr Justice Lush at the Old Bailey in October, where the prosecution put forward a likely motive. Evidence was given that Robertson had become romantically involved with 18-year-old Gertrude Flude, who worked at the same factory as Robertson. It was alleged that he had tried to get rid of the children, whom he saw as an obstacle to starting up a new relationship. He had first taken them to the local workhouse and, when they refused to accept them, he had chosen to take their young lives.

His defence put forward a plea that the children had died of meningitis and that all the accused had done was dispose of the bodies. It was a futile claim. Although the bodies were too badly decomposed for cause of death to be clearly determined, the evidence against Robertson was too strong to suggest any other verdict than wilful murder.

24

LOST IN TRANSLATION

❖ *Lee Kun, 1 January 1916* ❖

On the night of Saturday, 9 October 1915, a disturbance took place at a house on King Street, Poplar. A Chinese sailor had entered the house and accused one of the tenants of having stolen from him. The tenant, known locally as Swanny, was alleged by the sailor to have been swindling him out of a sum of £4 10s a month for most of the previous year. There was a scuffle which ended with the Chinese man bundled out into the street.

One week later, 27-year-old Lee Kun returned to the house and asked to speak to 34-year-old Elsie Goddard, another of the lodgers there. Elsie was a divorcée who had shared a house with Kun at Pennyfields, Poplar, until their relationship floundered, and she left him and moved in to King Street with the new man in her life, Swanny, a Russian sailor.

Also residing at the house was a friend of Elsie's, Harriet Wheaton. Elsie and Harriet were sitting in her front room when Kun entered and said he wanted to speak to Elsie. He took her gently by the arm and led her out into the back yard, from where seconds later, Harriet Wheaton heard the sounds of a struggle. She rushed into the yard and saw Kun holding a knife, which he then proceeded to thrust repeatedly into Elsie, killing her instantly.

Harriet picked up a broom handle and attempted to beat him off, bravely holding the enraged Kun at bay until neighbours, alerted by Elsie's screams, rushed in and subdued the killer.

Kun stood trial before Mr Justice Darling at the Old Bailey in November. He claimed that Elsie Goddard, whose real name was Clara Thomas, had taken some money from him and refused to pay it back. He had gone to the house to speak to her about repaying him and they went into the yard, where she had produced a knife and attempted to stab him. Kun said that he had tried to stop her, and in the ensuing struggle, she received fatal stab wounds. It was a weak defence, and the jury took just a short time to find him guilty as charged.

Lee Kun appealed on the grounds that the evidence at his trial had been presented in English and, although the prisoner had resided in England for several years, his

Sent to the Gallows.

Sarah Thomas had been living with a Russian sailor, and she also associated with Lee Kun (27), a Chinese seaman. After a quarrel the woman remarked, "Since he has been away I have married a Russian, and I don't want to have anything more do with him."

On the day following that statement Lee Kun was seen repeatedly stabbing the woman

LEE KUN.

Lee Kun hanged on New Year's Day, 1916. (T.J. Leech Archive)

grasp of the language was still very poor. His counsel argued that although he had had proper representation, the fact that the evidence had not been translated meant that he had not been able to fully comprehend proceedings. This, they claimed, should invalidate the trial, as it had been unfair.

Counsel pointed out that Mr Justice Darling, on hearing the verdict, had not asked the accused if he had anything to say before sentence was passed, and had merely gone ahead and donned the black cap. When Darling realised his mistake, he recalled Kun to the dock, and, although the prisoner was now in shock and unable to fully understand the question, then asked him if he had anything to say!

The appeal was rejected; the court felt that all the evidence had been translated for Kun at the police station when he was first remanded at the subsequent police court and at his trial for murder. Although some of the subsequent evidence may have been lost in translation during the Old Bailey trial, they claimed it had not differed substantially from that heard at the original hearing. They ended by stating that although the trial may have been slightly flawed, there was no substantial miscarriage of justice, certainly not enough to necessitate a retrial.

25

IN THIS DREADFUL PLACE

❖ Roger David Casement, 3 August 1916 ❖

Dublin-born 51-year-old Roger David Casement was a former member of the British Consulate, knighted in 1911 for his work in exposing atrocities in Africa and South America. Although Casement had been a patriotic Briton early in his life, the traumatic experiences of witnessing human rights abuses in the Congo and Peru led him to become anti-Imperialist and, shortly after receiving his knighthood, he retired from the government to concentrate on supporting the cause of Irish nationalism.

On 15 October 1914, shortly after the outbreak of the First World War, Casement went to Germany, where he stayed in Berlin for eighteen months, trying to persuade the German government to support an Irish rebellion against British rule. He also visited PoW camps in the hope of convincing Irish prisoners to enlist in a brigade he was forming to fight on the German side. Prison guards physically abused those prisoners who did not support Casement.

With an uprising planned for Easter Sunday 1916, Germany agreed to assist the Irish rebels by sending a shipment of arms. Unbeknown to the Irish, these arms were, in the main, obsolete and useless weapons captured on the Russian front. Learning this, Casement sent a warning that the weapons were faulty and not to use them. This message was intercepted by British agents who traced and seized the shipment. On the following day, 20 April, a German submarine sailed into Tralee Bay. Casement rowed ashore and was immediately placed under arrest.

Casement was taken to the Tower of London, pending trial at the Old Bailey in June. As a British subject who had conspired with His Majesty's enemies in a time of war, Casement was charged with high treason. The national press did much to stir public opinion, printing extracts from Casement's diaries. These private papers had been leaked by the government and revealed Casement to be a homosexual. In Edwardian days, this was enough for the last of his sympathetic former colleagues to turn against him. Found guilty and sentenced to death by Lord Chief Justice Reading, Casement was returned to the condemned cell at Pentonville. As he awaited the hangman, it was announced that he had been stripped of his knighthood. A large crowd cheered when the notice of execution was posted on the prison gates, shortly after Casement had walked bravely to his death.

Roger Casement – hanged for treason.
(Author's collection)

Casement's grave in Glasnevin Cemetery, Dublin.
(Crime Picture Archive)

In Ireland, Roger Casement was respected as a hero who had fought and died for Irish independence. His last request was that his body should not be left 'in this dreadful place' and that it should be returned to his native Ireland for burial. The request was denied, and Casement was buried in the felons' graveyard close to the execution shed.

In February 1965, then Prime Minister Harold Wilson gave permission for Casement's body to be exhumed and returned to Ireland, where it was buried in Dublin's Glasnevin Cemetery.

26

THE DAMNING LETTER

❖ *William James Robinson, 17 April 1917* ❖

Although I tell you now I am quite guilty of the crime…it was not done for robbery it was simply unfortunate. I took him for somebody else whom I'd had a row with on the previous day. I had no intention of killing him, but I do not look for sympathy for I don't deserve it! (Letter written by William Robinson in the condemned cell, 8 March 1917)

Several customers watched as the handsome 26-year-old Canadian soldier, Alfred Williams, and his pretty companion, Maggie Harding, finished their drinks and headed for the door in the Sussex Stores tavern in Upper St Martin's Lane, Soho. It was almost closing time and as he finished his pint, Walter Rhodes was about to head for home when he noticed two men quickly down their drinks and follow the Canadian out of the door. Their rapid movements attracted the attention of several other customers and when, moments later, they heard the sound of glass breaking and a scream ring out, they hurried to the door.

The Canadian was lying on the ground, blood oozing from a wound to his throat; the girl bending over him, cradling the stricken soldier in her arms as his life ebbed away. The two men that had followed them outside were nowhere to be seen.

Among those drinking in the tavern were a couple of off duty special constables who were able to give detectives investigating the murder a description of the attackers, and within days, 26-year-old William Robinson, a messenger, and 24-year-old newspaper packer John Henry Gray were taken into custody.

At the trial before Lord Chief Justice Coleridge at the Old Bailey in March, Maggie Harding told the court that as they left the tavern, the two men had approached them and Robinson had picked a fight, during which he smashed a bottle against the wall, stabbing the jagged edge into the soldier's throat. Other drinkers, including Walter Rhodes, identified Robinson and Gray as the two men seen following Williams and Miss Harding out of the pub.

Robinson and Gray protested their innocence, claiming that it was a case of mistaken identity, and that they were in another part of the city when the murder took place. The two-day trial ended with Robinson being found guilty of murder and sentenced to death; Gray was convicted of manslaughter and sentenced to three years imprisonment.

Returned to the condemned cell at Pentonville, Robinson, who had been invalided out of the army following an horrific leg injury that had left him with a pronounced limp, penned a letter to his victim's girlfriend in which he claimed that the attack had been due to a case of mistaken identity, and that the sentence was justified. A prison warder read it in the course of his duties and noted the contents before it was forwarded to the Home Office, and a copy made.

In the letter, Robinson also wrote that on the night before the murder, he had been in another pub where he had argued with some Canadian soldiers, and when he saw Williams, he mistook him for one of the men he had argued with and attacked him on the spur of the moment.

The reality was slightly different. Robinson had been in the public house at the time Williams had been given more than £20 by a fellow soldier for safekeeping, while he went out on the town to enjoy his last day of leave before they travelled across to France.

An amazing series of events then occurred. Gray's conviction was quashed on appeal. Robinson then lodged an appeal that his sentence should likewise be revoked. However, the letter he had penned, that 'damned letter' he later referred to it as, was produced to show that in Robinson's case, the sentence was just and the appeal was therefore rejected.

27

'BLODIE BELGIUM'

❖ *Louis Marie Joseph Voisin, 2 March 1918* ❖

It seemed a curious place to dump a parcel and so, climbing over the railings on Regent Square, Bloomsbury, Thomas Henry went to investigate. Recoiling in horror, he found himself looking down on the torso of a woman minus a head, arms and legs, and wrapped in a cotton sheet. Next to it was another parcel; this one contained the severed legs of the same corpse, wrapped in a sack. Of the head and arms there was no sign.

It was 8.30 a.m. on Friday, 2 November 1917 and, within minutes of the gruesome discovery, detectives had launched a murder enquiry. Pathologist Bernard Spilsbury examined the remains and stated that whatever had caused the death had also drained the body of blood, and as there were no tell-tale marks on the body parts he examined, he suspected that cause of death had probably been a throat or head injury. As Spilsbury examined the body parts, Detective Inspector Wensley led a team of officers in examining the other clues. The limbs had been wrapped in a white cloth sack stamped 'Argentine La Plata, cold storage.' The fabric was a type of sacking used to wrap meat, and since the body had been skilfully dissected, detectives believed the killer might be a butcher. The cotton sheet used to wrap the torso bore a distinct red cotton laundry mark '11 H,' and scribbled on a scrap of brown paper were the words, 'Blodie Belgium'.

Wensley worked out that the parcels must have been placed in the square sometime between 6.15 a.m. and 8.30 a.m., when they were discovered. It had rained during the night, and as the parcels were dry on the upper surface, they must have been deposited after it had stopped raining at 6.15 a.m.

It was the laundry mark that set the investigation moving at a pace. It was traced to a French woman, Emilienne Gerard, who lived on Munster Square, near Regent's Park, and when detectives visited Munster Square, they learned from the landlord that Emilienne Gerard and her husband Paul had taken out a tenancy on the house on 3 April 1916. Paul Gerard had subsequently joined the French Army, and was currently in his native land on

Louis Voisin. (Author's collection)

active service. A search of Emilienne's home unearthed a number of interesting items, including traces of blood, and an IOU for £50 which was lying on the table. Signed by one Louis Voisin, it gave his address as 101 Charlotte Street, London.

This was a vital clue. Detectives learned that Voisin was a butcher, and that Emilienne had been his housekeeper. Emilienne Gerard had last been seen alive at her home on the evening of 31 October 1917. The capital had been suffering bombing raids from German Zeppelin airships at the time, and on that particular night, the raid had been one of the heaviest.

Louis Voisin was a 51-year-old Frenchman and, when questioned, he claimed to have been at home all night on 31 October. His alibi was supported by his live-in lover, Berthe Roche. Investigations led the police to a neighbour, who claimed to have seen Berthe washing a blood-soaked shirt on 1 November. Voisin was asked to write the words 'Bloody Belgium' on a sheet of paper. Three times he wrote out the phrase, and each time he spelt it 'Blodie Belgium'.

Asked to account for his movements on 2 November, Voisin said he had been working at Smithfield until 7.45 a.m. Workmates, however, told police he had gone off duty at 6.30 a.m. A search was made of the basement at Charlotte Street, and it was immediately clear that this was where the murder had taken place. There were large quantities of bloodstains in the doorway, and in a sawdust-filled barrel, detectives found the missing head and arms of Emilienne Gerard.

Both Voisin and Roche were charged with murder, and at the Old Bailey before Mr Justice Darling in January 1918, the prosecution suggested that there had been a relationship between Emilienne and Voisin, and that Roche had taken her place in his affections. On the night of the murder, Emilienne, fearful of the Zeppelin raid, had gone round to Voisin's flat, where a jealous Roche had attacked her.

Voisin told the court that on the morning of 1 November, he had gone to Emilienne's flat and found her dead. Believing the killer was trying to frame him for the murder, he had panicked and tried to conceal the crime by dumping part of the body in the square, and hiding the other parts in his basement until he could think straight.

The cellar at Charlotte Street, where the head of Emilienne Gerard was found in the wooden barrel.
(Author's collection)

There was little evidence to convict Berthe Roche of murder, and on the second day of the trial the judge directed the jury to find her not guilty. Instead, she was charged with being an accessory after the fact, held over until the next sessions.

On the third day, it took the jury just fifteen minutes to find Voisin guilty of murder. His execution, fixed for 26 February 1918, was postponed for a week until the case against Berthe Roche had been heard. Duly convicted on the lesser charge, she was sentenced to seven years imprisonment. Within months, she was diagnosed as insane, and died a year later.

28

A MURDEROUS RAMPAGE

❖ *Henry Beckett, 10 July 1919* ❖

Private 320903 Henry Beckett had been released from another stay in prison, on the condition that he enlisted in the army. In the summer of 1916, he joined the Suffolk Regiment and, following the armistice, he was demobbed. Needing somewhere to stay when he arrived back in London, he was introduced by his sister to the Cornish family, who had a house in Forest Gate.

Forty-three-year-old Alice Cornish was the sister of Beckett's stepfather, and, although the family link was slight, they were eager to help the returning war hero and offered him a room until he could sort himself out. Initially the family warmly welcomed 36-year-old Beckett, and he even became friendly with a neighbour, a widow named Mrs Sparks. But it was soon to turn sour. Word reached Alice and her husband, Walter, that Beckett was an habitual criminal with a record of violence. Beckett was confronted with this news, and during an argument with Alice Cornish, he was asked to leave. Beckett packed his meagre possessions and went to stay with Mrs Sparks.

On the morning of 28 April, Beckett left Mrs Sparks's and went to a public house. Wandering back after lunchtime closing, he found himself passing the Cornish house on Stukely Road. Alice Cornish was alone at the time, but when she saw Beckett pass, she called out to him and they continued their previous quarrel. Beckett lost his temper, and picking up a poker, he struck Alice about the head, knocking her unconscious. He then carried her into the garden shed, where he battered her to death with an axe, finishing off the job by sticking a large fork into her throat. He then stripped the body of any jewellery, and unable to remove a wedding ring, he casually chopped off the finger and removed the gold band.

He then set off on a murderous rampage. The next person to come home was 6-year-old Marie Cornish. She skipped up the path to the house and, finding Beckett in the kitchen, she turned to go into the lounge and was struck on the head with a hammer. Beckett hit her several more times until he was satisfied she was dead. He then picked her up and threw her down the cellar steps. Fifteen-year-old Alice was the next to arrive home. She was battered with the same hammer as her younger sister and also thrown into the cellar.

Walter Cornish arrived home from work later that afternoon, and was angered to find Beckett drinking tea in the kitchen. They exchanged words before Beckett then struck him over the head with an axe. Cornish fought bravely but was no match for the

Private 320903 Henry Beckett. (T.J. Leech Archive)

DESPERATE FIGHT TO SAVE BECKETT.

EXPERTS' APPEAL FOR SPECIAL INQUIRY GRANTED BY HOME SECRETARY.

Henry Perry, alias Beckett, may yet be saved from the gallows. The life of the man who murdered the four members of the Cornish family has been fought for by mental experts of the highest calibre, who contend that Beckett, as an epileptic subject, could not be held responsible for the brutal deeds.

Following an appeal before the Lord Chief Justice, Mr. Shortt, the Home Secretary, announced that Beckett's mental condition would be made the subject of a special inquiry.

Beckett's plight made newspaper headlines.
(T.J. Leech Archive)

former soldier, although he was able to push open the back door where his cries for help were heard by a neighbour who rushed to fetch the police.

Leaving Cornish in a heap on the kitchen floor, Beckett fled the scene, his clothes, hands and face all heavily bloodstained. Walter Cornish was taken to hospital where he died two days later, having been able, however, to tell police the identity of his attacker.

Four days later, with Beckett being the subject of a major manhunt, a special constable saw a strangely dressed man walking along Barking Road, East Ham. He was stopped and recognised as Beckett, and when searched, he still had in his pocket the ring he had brutally cut from his first victim.

Beckett stood trial at the Old Bailey before Mr Justice Darling in May and pleaded insanity. He claimed to have been captured and tortured by the Turks during the war and to have also received head wounds and shrapnel injuries, which resulted in his hearing voices urging him to do bad things.

The fact that he had stolen items of jewellery during the killing spree suggested that the acts hadn't simply been carried out in a moment of madness, and he was duly convicted of wilful murder.

THE SEPARATION ORDER

❖ *Thomas Foster, 31 July 1919* ❖

On the morning of Wednesday, 11 June 1919, neighbours were awoken by the sounds of a fearsome argument coming from the home of Thomas and Minnie Foster at Stainsbury Street, Bethnal Green. It had been a tempestuous fifteen years of marriage that had borne six children, but throughout their married life, Thomas, who worked as a chain maker, had been a heavy drinker and, when drunk, was often violent towards his wife.

As neighbours went to investigate, Thomas Foster ran out of the house, and as he made to escape, a female neighbour was able to stop him, and others held onto him until a policeman arrived. When the officer entered the house, he found Minnie lying on the bed, clutching her youngest child in her arms. Although the child was unhurt, Minnie was dead, her throat savagely cut by the bloodstained razor found lying on the mantelpiece. There were also a number of wounds on her arms where it appeared she had tried to fend off her attacker.

Tried before Mr Justice Avory at the Old Bailey just a fortnight after the murder, Foster claimed he had killed his wife because she had led an immoral life. This was shown to be untrue as all the evidence suggested, besides being a faithful wife, Minnie Thomas was a decent, hardworking woman and a good mother to their children.

Foster's defence claimed he was insane at the time of the murder and that there was a history of insanity in the family. He had been sober at the time of the attack and the prosecution could find no motive other than his anger at the separation order his wife had issued a few weeks before, which she retracted when he offered to change his ways.

30

HOUSE OF SIN

❖ *Frank George Warren, 7 October 1919* ❖

In April 1919, 26-year-old Lucy Nightingale left her native Liverpool following a quarrel with her husband and travelled down to London, moving in with 66-year-old Henry Ball, a retired butcher, at 13 Prah Road, Finsbury Park. Ostensibly his housekeeper, she was in fact working for Ball as a prostitute, using the house for business purposes.

On Tuesday, 29 July, Ball walked into the police station and announced that he had found the body of his housekeeper in one of his bedrooms. Once police confirmed his statement, Ball was questioned further – and he told a fascinating tale.

For the last few months, his wife had been an inmate in a nearby asylum, and on the previous afternoon he had gone to visit her. But before setting off, he had met two sailors in the Blackstock public house who were friends of his housekeeper. He named them as 18-year-old Harold Horatio Morgan and 41-year-old Frank George Warren.

Ball said that Morgan had spent the Monday night with Lucy, and that he and Warren planned to see her again that Tuesday evening. He claimed that he had arrived home at 9.30 p.m., and after going out for a drink, he returned and fell asleep downstairs. Waking in the early hours, he had called out for Lucy. When he received no answer, he went to her room where he found her bound and gagged on the floor. She had been strangled.

Right: *Lucy Nightingale*.
(T.J. Leech Archive)

Far right: *Frank Warren*.
(T.J. Leech Archive)

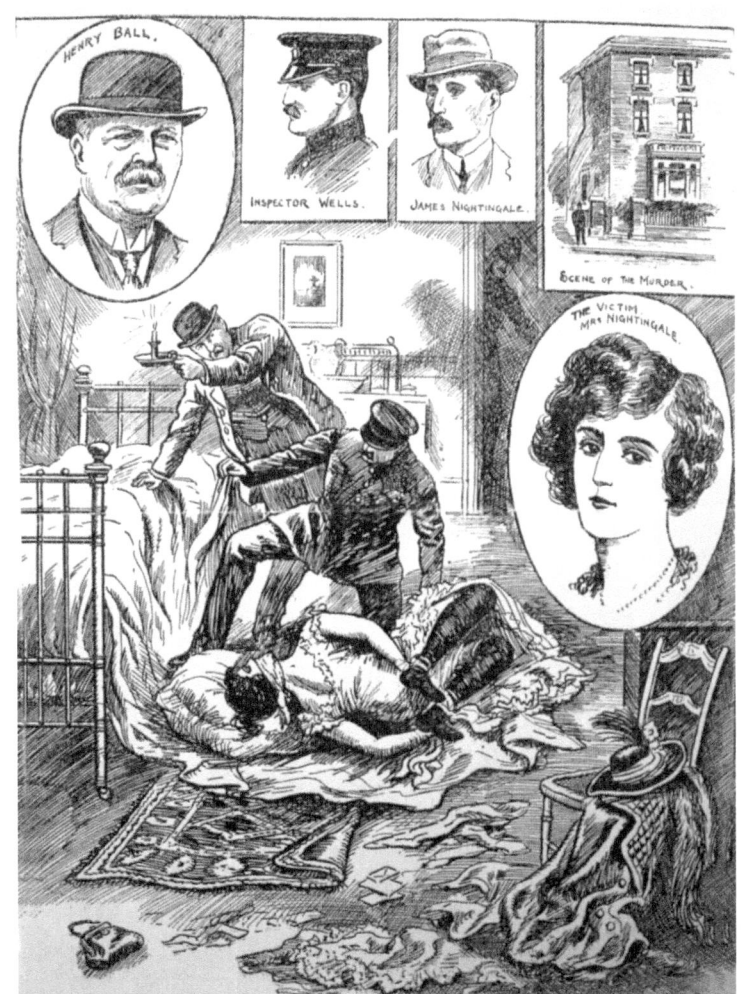

The Illustrated Police
News *depicted the discovery
of Lucy Nightingale's body
on the front page*. (T.J.
Leech Archive)

Ship's cook Warren, and Morgan, a steward from South Wales, were quickly traced. Both were already wanted by the police for having absconded from their last ship and for having taking with them large quantities of whisky and cigarettes from the stores. When questioned by detectives, they each gave a different version of events.

Warren, who lived in Harringay, said that Morgan had called at his house in a rage, claiming that a woman had done him out of 20s, and that he meant to take his revenge. At Morgan's request, Warren had accompanied him to Prah Road, where Morgan had killed Lucy.

Morgan's tale was somewhat different. He said that he and Warren had gone to the house, and Lucy had suggested that they stay the night. She wanted to spend the night with Warren, and it was arranged that Morgan should share a room with Ball. Not long afterwards, he heard screams coming from Lucy's room, and soon after Warren came rushing down the stairs shouting for Morgan to grab his coat.

Police initially charged all three men: Ball with being an accessory after the fact, while Morgan and Warren were charged with murder. Before the case reached the courts, charges against Ball, who was also accused of running a house of sin, were dropped. Morgan and Warren stood trial before Mr Justice Darling at the Old Bailey on 18 September.

The prosecution found several discrepancies in Warren's version of events, the main one being that when he returned to Harringay on 29 July, he had in his possession three rings which he gave to his girlfriend. These were identified as belonging to Lucy Nightingale. This seemed to clear Morgan, and on the following day, the jury retired and found Morgan not guilty. Warren was found guilty as charged.

31

THIS AFFAIR...

❖ *Arthur Andrew Clement Goslett, 27 July 1920* ❖

> This affair is all through her. She alienated my affections from my wife and she has been the instigation to this murder. (Statement by Arthur Goslett following his arrest)

When officers from Scotland Yard interviewed Captain Arthur Goslett, shortly after the discovery of his wife's body in the River Brent near allotments at Brentmead Place, Golder's Green, he appeared to be a loving husband, devastated at her sudden and tragic death. On Sunday, 2 May 1920, the body of Evelyn Goslett had been found floating face down in the river. Close by, at the bottom end of Western Avenue, officers found signs of a struggle, along with traces of blood on the grass leading down to the riverbank.

A check on her recent movements found that at 8 p.m. the previous night, Evelyn had taken supper with her two lodgers, Marjorie Orell and Daisy Holt, and a short time later, she left the house. She was never seen alive again. Captain Goslett, who had been out during the evening, had returned home around 10.30 p.m.

On the following morning, maid Constance Hanrahan found Goslett making a cup of tea in the kitchen, and he told her his wife had not come home. This was the main topic of conversation around the breakfast table as the lodgers congregated that morning. Jules Mear, Evelyn's son from a previous marriage, knew that his mother had arranged to meet Goslett on the previous evening, but agreed to go to his grandfather's to see if she had gone there instead.

When police arrived at the house with news that his mother's body had been found in the river, Jules told the police of the planned rendezvous. When interviewed, Goslett seemed shocked at the news, but soon broke down and confessed that he had killed his wife, giving a full account of what had happened. He said that on the morning of 1 May, he had asked his wife to meet him that night, at 9.15 p.m. outside the Prince Albert pub. Goslett told her he was thinking of buying a new house and wanted her to look at it with him. They met as arranged, and as they walked along the riverbank, he pulled out a tyre lever which he had concealed in his pocket and struck her several times on the back of the head. As Evelyn slumped to the ground, Goslett bent down, kissed her hand and, after begging her forgiveness, pushed her into the river and returned home.

A post-mortem had found that Evelyn Goslett had still been alive when she was thrown into the water and that the cause of death was due to drowning. When asked why he had committed the crime, Goslett told a remarkable tale. He claimed that their lodger, Daisy Holt, whom he had bigamously married, had forced him to do it, and that having returned home after killing his wife, he had spent the night in bed with Daisy.

Although Daisy Holt strenuously denied the entire story, it was to form

Captain Goslett under arrest. (Author's collection)

part of Goslett's defence when he stood trial at the Old Bailey before Mr Justice Shearman on Tuesday, 22 June 1920. Two marriage certificates were produced in court. The first, dated 12 June 1914 was for his marriage to the murdered woman; the second, dated 7 February 1919, under the alias Arthur Godfrey, was for his marriage to Daisy Ellen Holt. Daisy had been pregnant at the time, and shortly after the wedding, she gave birth to a child, whereupon her husband confessed that his real name was Goslett and that he was already married.

Telling her that he was in an unhappy marriage, Goslett had come up with a scheme. He told Daisy she could pretend to be the widow of his brother killed in the war, and she could stay at his house in the guise of a lodger. Daisy Holt had seemingly agreed to this deception. Gradually though, Daisy grew unhappy at her situation and began to pressurise Goslett to resolve the situation, if need be, by murdering his wife, threatening to expose him as a bigamist if he refused.

Daisy Holt told a very different tale. She admitted marrying the defendant, and to bearing him a child which she had since given up; however, shortly after coming to live in the Goslett household, Daisy's identity was revealed to Goslett's wife. Instead of making a scene, Mrs Goslett told Daisy that although she could not agree to her living at the house any longer, she would try to arrange somewhere for her to live. Daisy said that Goslett had murdered his wife in the hope that he could continue to live with her. She denied that she had spent the night in bed with him following the murder but confessed that they had been intimate several times while she had lodged at the house.

Goslett's fate was never in doubt, but if the jury believed his version of events, then Daisy Holt should have been beside him in the dock facing the same murder charge. The jury found that Daisy had played no active role in the murder, and Goslett alone was convicted. No charges were made against Daisy Holt.

THE BLACK FAST MURDER

❖ *Marks Goodmacher, 30 December 1920* ❖

The Jewish Day of Atonement has several names. Known as both the Black Fast and Yom Kippur, it falls on the tenth day of Tishri, the seventh month of the ecclesiastical year and the first of the civil year. Occurring in either late September or early October, it is the culmination of the observance of the Ten Penitential Days and is the most sacred of Jewish holidays. It is also a day of confession, repentance and prayers for the forgiveness of sins committed during the year, and is the day on which an individual's fate for the ensuing year is thought to be sealed. Twenty-four-year-old Fanny Zetoun effectively sealed her fate on Atonement Day 1920, when she failed to resolve a quarrel with her father that had torn the family apart.

Fanny Zetoun had started married life living in her father's house in the East End, and for a short time the arrangement was to everyone's satisfaction. Soon though, 50-year-old Marks Goodmacher, an orthodox Jewish tailor, began to interfere in the life of his daughter and son-in-law. He started to abuse Fanny verbally and physically while her husband was at work and, on one occasion, tried to force himself on her.

Eventually, Fanny became pregnant and when her father was told, he became enraged to the extent that he threatened to 'rip up her belly.' Fanny and her husband announced that they were leaving and found a place of their own on nearby Grove Street. Goodmacher

Fanny Zetoun – killed by her father.
(T.J. Leech Archive)

Black Fast Murderer Marks Goodmacher – the first man to be hanged by William Willis. (T.J. Leech Archive)

The Illustrated Police News' *depiction of the Black Fast Murder.* (T.J. Leech Archive)

Hangman William Willis. (Author's collection)

was distraught to be left on his own and pleaded with Fanny and her husband to return. His requests were to no avail, and as they tired of his pleading, they took to avoiding places he was likely to be. The rift between them grew but Goodmacher, realising that Yom Kippur would soon be here, knew it would give him the chance to resolve the situation. Atonement Day came and went with no word from his daughter, and Goodmacher was enraged. On Thursday 23 September, when Fanny's husband returned home from work, there was no reply when he called out to his wife. When he went upstairs to the bedroom, however, he was greeted by an horrific sight.

The room was a scene of carnage: money and jewellery lay strewn across the floor, and on the bed lay his wife with her throat horribly slashed. She was clearly dead, and found beside her, slumped in a chair, was her father, also with a throat wound. Fanny Zetoun was beyond help, but her father's wounds were mostly superficial. He was treated in hospital and made a full recovery.

Marks Goodmacher was convicted at the Old Bailey before Mr Justice Darling on 18 November, when his plea of insanity was dismissed, and he was hanged on 30 December 1920, on what proved to be the busiest day in modern times for executions. That morning, three men were executed in different prisons across the country. With the only two experienced executioners, John Ellis and Thomas Pierrepoint, already engaged at Birmingham and Leeds respectively, the prison commissioners needed to promote an assistant to carry out the execution at Pentonville. William Willis, an assistant of fourteen years, was entrusted with the responsibility and carried out his duties to everyone's satisfaction.

THE FRAUDSTER

❖ *Frederick Alexander Keeling, 11 April 1922* ❖

Frederick Alexander Keeling didn't see any harm in the little deception. After all, having bravely fought long enough for king and country, he had earned his little 'pension', and the extra £4 a week certainly came in handy.

Fifty-four-year-old Keeling worked as a plasterer and had been separated from his wife for several years. By November 1921, he was living with Ada Haines in a lodging house on St George's Road, Tottenham. Living in the same house was Emily Dewberry, and when she learned that Keeling was still claiming a married man's pension, extra money he was not entitled to, she took it upon herself to report the matter to the pensions office.

An investigation was held, and in due course a warrant was issued against Keeling. He was arrested and bailed, to appear at a further hearing in which Emily was to be called as a witness. They were due to appear in court on 24 November, and when neither appeared at the hearing, police officers were sent to investigate. Receiving no reply when they knocked on the door of Emily Dewberry's room, they forced the door and discovered her body partially hidden under the bed. Beside it lay a hammer bearing the initials F.K.

Keeling was on the run for over a fortnight before he was tracked down. Police had kept surveillance on Ada Haines and watched her movements, and when she met Keeling in a public house, he was placed under arrest. He denied the murder, claiming that a stranger must have killed Emily, and backing up his alibi, Ada Haines testified that Keeling had hardly left her sight on the day of the murder. In her opinion, he could not possibly have had time to commit the murder.

At the trial before Mr Justice Darling in March 1922, the prosecution's case was that Keeling's hammer was the murder weapon; blood had been found on his clothing; and there was a strong motive of revenge against the victim for reporting him for his fraudulent pension claim.

Fraudster Fred Keeling's crime sketched in the Illustrated Police News. (T.J. Leech Archive)

KEY WITNESS

Getting away with murder is never easy, less so if there are witnesses; and if the key witness is a serving police officer, then the chances of escaping justice are almost non-existent. On the evening of Saturday, 14 January 1922, a police sergeant, standing on a bridge overlooking the River Lea, saw a young couple walking along the towpath towards him. He watched them pass below and walk away into the distance. He was preparing to head back to his beat, when the officer heard a splash. Moments later, he saw the young man return to the bridge alone. He made his way up to the roadway and, as he did so, the officer approached him and asked where his companion had gone?

Unaware that he had been watched from the bridge, the young man told the sergeant that he was mistaken and there had been no one with him. At this, the officer asked the man to accompany him back down the towpath until they reached the place where he had seen the couple approach. When they reached the spot, they saw the body of the woman floating in the water. The woman, identified as 25-year-old Margaret 'Madge' Evans, was pulled from the water but found to be dead. The man, who gave his name as Edmund Tonbridge, a 38-year-old warehouse clerk from Walthamstow, was taken into custody.

From then until his Old Bailey trial before Mr Justice Darling in March, he gave various accounts of what had happened. Tonbridge said he had known the woman for several years, and in November 1920 they had had a child together, for which he had given her 15s a week until the child was adopted.

Edmund Tonbridge under arrest. (T.J. Leech Archive)

Relieved that the financial burden was now lifted, Tonbridge said he was angered when Madge told him she was once again pregnant. She talked of marriage, and arranged to meet him at Clapton railway station close to her home on Gunton Road that Saturday evening. They then went for a walk along the banks of the River Lea.

What happened next was open to conjecture. Tonbridge said that rather than agree to her request of marriage, he pulled from his jacket a letter from a man named George Andrews, in which it was claimed that Andrews was the father-to-be and, moreover, that he was also the father of her first child, the one for whom Tonbridge had paid out maintenance monies for several months.

While walking together, Tonbridge had told Madge that he had a small bottle of potassium cyanide in his pocket, which he had just purchased from a Walthamstow chemist to use in his hobby of photography. He claimed that when faced with the truth, Madge had stopped to light a cigarette and had reached into his pocket, snatched the acid and gulped it down. She had then collapsed and fallen into the river. An autopsy had confirmed that death was due to cyanide poisoning.

While this seemed to suggest suicide, detectives constructed a case of murder against Tonbridge. At his trial, the prosecution said that Tonbridge had told the girl he had some medicine in the bottle which would help terminate her pregnancy, and as they were walking, he tried to get her to swallow it. Bruises on her face suggested that she had resisted before he had forced the poison into her mouth. The letter from Andrews was found to be a forgery which Tonbridge himself had written.

The one-day trial ended with the jury finding Tonbridge guilty of the brutal murder, and he was sentenced to death.

Official notice of the execution of Edmund Tonbridge. Instead of the usual time of 9 a.m., for some unknown reason he was hanged at 12.15 p.m. (Author's collection)

WHISPERS ON THE STAIRS

❖ *Henry Julius Jacoby, 7 June 1922* ❖

Detectives investigating the murder of Lady Alice White needed answers to three questions:

1. How did the murderer gain access to the hotel?
2. How did he leave?
3. How was he such an expert or so lucky to have left no possible clue behind?

Initially it was believed that Lady White had been murdered by a thief intent on stealing her jewels, but the fact that nothing had been taken, there was no sign of forced entry, and the reception, manned twenty-four hours a day, confirmed that no suspicious persons had come and gone from the hotel.

Wealthy widow, Lady White was a long term guest at the Spencer Hotel in Portman Street, and occupied room 14, which was, in effect, a suite of four inter-connecting rooms. On the morning of Tuesday, 14 March 1922, a chambermaid, receiving no reply to her knock, let herself into the room and discovered Lady White lying in her bed. She had been badly beaten, and the pillow and blankets were soaked in blood. So severe were her injuries that part of her brain was visible through the fractured skull, and, being too poorly to be moved, Lady White was tended to by doctors in her hotel bed, as Scotland Yard detectives began their investigations.

Lady White had spent the previous evening playing bridge with her friends and had retired to bed at around 11 p.m. She died from her injuries in the early hours of the following morning, and the case became a murder hunt. As there were no signs of forced entry into the hotel room, investigations focused on the members of staff.

One vital clue seemed to emerge from the early round of interviews, when 18-year-old pantry boy, Henry Jacoby, told detectives he had heard strange whisperings on the stairs close to his basement bedroom in the early hours of Tuesday morning. Jacoby said that he had mentioned this to the night porter, and although they had searched the corridors and basement, they found nothing. He then went back to his bedroom, and learned about the attack on Lady White when he came on duty. Although this statement seemed to support the initial thought that it was the work of a burglar, Jacoby's story sounded a little too rehearsed, and police decided to investigate his background before eliminating him from the list of suspects.

Before starting work at the hotel three weeks previously, Jacoby had lived in a lodging house, but left suddenly following a report that some money had been stolen. With evidence now linking Jacoby to that theft, he was brought into custody, where he was further questioned about the murder of Lady White. After initially denying the crime, he then admitted responsibility for the attack, but denied murder.

Jacoby claimed that on hearing voices, both he and the night porter had searched the corridors. Failing to find any sign of intruders, however, he had returned to bed. He said that soon after, he again heard the voices, and this time he had gone into an adjacent room, where workmen had left an assortment of tools, and picking up a hammer and torch he had gone to investigate. Approaching room 14, he again heard voices, and seeing the door slightly open, he entered and was confronted by a figure he believed was an intruder. He struck out with the hammer. When he shone the torch, he realised that he had struck the old lady, and fearful for the consequences, he had gone back to his room, washed the hammer and replaced it before retiring to bed.

THE MURDER OF LADY WHITE.

PANTRY BOY'S ALLEGED PREMONITION.

HENRY JACOBY, the 18-year-old pantry boy, again appeared at the Marylebone Police Court yesterday, charged on his own confession with the wilful murder of Lady (Alice) White, widow of Sir Edward White, at Spencer's Hotel, Portman-square, on March 14. At the previous hearing Jacoby had applied to the magistrate for defending counsel, but Mr. Leycester said he had no power to grant the request. Yesterday he was represented by Mr. Lucien Fior, barrister. Mr. Charles Wallace prosecuted for the Director of Public Prosecutions.

Evidence was given of the statement made by Jacoby while under arrest, which was read by Mr. Wallace at the previous hearing.

Mary Parker, domestic servant, said she met Jacoby on March 11, with her step-sister, Edith Corcott, a waitress at Spencer's Hotel. On March 13 she went with Jacoby to the Metropolitan Musichall. When they came out Jacoby said:—" You may think me a fool, but I have a feeling that something is going to happen." Later on he repeated the statement, and said he thought it had something to do with Spencer's Hotel.

A further remand for seven days having been ordered, Mr. Fior stated that at the next hearing he should ask leave to recall some of the police officers for cross-examination. He had only received the depositions in the case the previous night.

Above left: *The* Illustrated Police News *depicted the murder of Lady White on the front page.* (T.J. Leech Archive)

Above right: *Newspaper headline following the death of Lady White.* (T.J. Leech Archive)

Left: *Pantry boy Henry Jacoby.* (Author's collection)

On the strength of this testimony, Jacoby found himself before Mr Justice McCardle at the Old Bailey on 28 April, charged with wilful murder. After listening to all the evidence, the jury retired to consider their verdict. They then asked the judge if they could return a verdict of manslaughter if they believed that Jacoby had not intended to kill, but he directed them that, even if he had only intended to inflict grievous bodily harm, there could be no verdict of manslaughter.

Believing the prosecution's version of events, that Jacoby had entered the room with the intention of committing theft, but had resorted to murder when he was disturbed, the jury returned a guilty verdict but added a strong recommendation for mercy on account of his youth.

An appeal was dismissed, and when the Secretary of State discussed the case with the trial judge, he concurred that age alone was not enough to spare a brutal killer from the gallows.

36

THE NEWLY-WEDS

❖ *William James Yeldham, 5 September 1922* ❖

As William and Elsie Yeldham exchanged their wedding vows at Braintree Registry Office on Saturday, 20 May 1922, they were hiding a dreadful secret. Just three days earlier, they had carried out the brutal assault and robbery of a man in Epping Forest and then used some of the proceeds of their crime to pay for their nuptials. Even as they made their way to the registry office, they had seen a report that the victim had since died in hospital and a murder hunt was underway.

Twenty-three-year-old William Yeldham lived in some outbuildings on Highland's Farm near Ilford, run by his grandfather. He was mainly unemployed, although he did a little work on the farm at times, preferring instead to live off the immoral earnings of his wife-to-be, Elsie. Yeldham had originally tried to get 22-year-old Elsie off the streets, and had found her a place to live on the farm, sharing what meagre income he had had with her. Desperate to put food on the table, but not wanting to work for it, he stole a bicycle which he sold for a small sum, only to be arrested and sentenced to six months in gaol for the theft.

With Yeldham behind bars, Elsie returned to prostitution, and when released, Yeldham again tried to get her to stop, while reluctantly accepting that it was the only way either of them could make any money.

One regular client of Elsie's was George Stanley Grimshaw, a 54-year-old decorator from Walthamstow. In the spring of 1922, Elsie came home with a seven-guinea gown, which Grimshaw, a married man, had bought for her. This show of extravagance probably cost him his life.

On Wednesday, 17 May, Elsie boarded a bus with Grimshaw and headed for the relative privacy of Epping Forest where they often went to 'do business'. They sat together on the upper deck, Grimshaw unaware that Yeldham had followed them and was sitting below. They alighted at Higham's Park, a quiet part of Epping Forest, and Yeldham followed a short way behind, hiding in a holly bush as Elsie and Grimshaw sat down on the grass beside a lake. As Grimshaw slipped his arm around Elsie's waist, Yeldham crept from the bushes and rushed up to him, splitting his skull with a heavy spanner he had taken from the farm.

As the older man slumped to the ground mortally wounded, Yeldham told Elsie to go through his pockets. They removed his watch and wallet which contained over £15, before walking away from the victim, casually tossing the spanner into the River Ching. The body was discovered on the following day, and although Grimshaw was still alive when the ambulance was summoned, he was certified dead on arrival at Whipps Cross Hospital.

Newly-weds William and Elsie Yeldham.
(Author's collection)

Investigations into the dead man's friends and acquaintances eventually lead police to Elsie, and when officers went to Ilford to find her, they learned that she had recently married and moved away. The newly-weds were soon located in Braintree, and when confronted they immediately broke down and confessed.

Jointly tried at the Old Bailey before Mr Justice Shearman on Wednesday, 19 July, they gave varying accounts of what had happened on the day of the murder. In one version, Yeldham said he had become jealous when Elsie had told him she was meeting her sister when he knew she was going to meet Grimshaw. He had followed her, and in a jealous rage had battered his love rival.

The prosecution claimed that it was a joint enterprise and that Grimshaw had been selected because they knew he would be carrying a large amount of money. They also claimed that the couple had married in haste, so that the new Mrs Yeldham was now no longer legally obliged to testify against her husband.

The jury found both William and Elsie Yeldham guilty of murder, and both were sentenced to death. Their joint appeal was heard on 21 August, but it was quickly dismissed. On the following day, however, it was announced that the sentence on Elsie Yeldham had been commuted to life imprisonment on account of the fact that she had acted under the influence of her husband-to-be.

37

DO SOMETHING DESPERATE

❖ *Frederick Edward Francis Bywaters, 9 January 1923* ❖

It was not really the happy marriage that she yearned for. Still only in her mid-twenties, Edith Thompson did not feel ready to accept that life was a humdrum routine of work and dull domesticity, and was looking for a little excitement and passion in her life. Her husband, Percy, was a steady and staid man, but although they had a pleasant family home in Kensington Gardens, Ilford, Edith was not content with her lot.

Then, in the summer of 1921, it all changed. Into her life came Freddie Bywaters, a handsome 18-year-old merchant seaman. Bywaters was a friend of Edith's younger sister, Avis, and had just returned from a four-month voyage to Australia. He was invited to join Avis

and the Thompsons on a short holiday to the Isle
of Wight, and the Thompsons both took an instant
liking to the young sailor, so much so that when
they returned to Ilford, Percy invited him to lodge
with them until his next voyage.

Soon, Edith and Bywaters became lovers. They
kept their affair a secret, but on Monday, 1 August,
Edith and her husband had a blazing row, which
ended when Percy slapped his wife. Bywaters
stepped in and stopped him. A few days later, the
Thompsons again quarrelled, and this time discussed
separation. Bywaters asked Percy if he would grant
his wife a divorce. He refused and told the younger
man to leave his house.

Bywaters went back to sea that summer, and over
the next year, he and Edith kept up their affair when
he was in London, and by mail when he was at sea.
Edith settled back into her unexciting marriage,
but regularly wrote long and rambling letters to
Bywaters pouring out her heart and feelings. She
enclosed newscuttings relating to murder trials and
even hinted that she had tried to kill her husband
by poisoning him and putting broken glass in his
food.

*Freddie Bywaters stands between Percy and
Edith Thompson.* (Crime Picture Archive)

On Saturday, 23 September 1922, Bywaters
returned from sea, and during the next week or so,
arranged several less than clandestine meetings with
Edith. They lunched together in cafés close to her
place of work, and strolled in parks and along the
Thames. By now they were both very much in love.

On 3 October they met for lunch, and when Edith
finished work, Bywaters was waiting for her. Edith
told him that she had to hurry home as she and her
husband had tickets that evening for the theatre. At
midnight, after leaving the West End by train, Percy
and Edith arrived at Ilford station and set off on foot
up Belgrave Road. As they reached the intersection
with Kensington Gardens, a man appeared from
the shadows, pushed Edith to one side and stabbed
Percy Thompson to death. As Edith screamed and
shouted, the attacker fled into the night.

The murder weapon was soon found in a drain
in nearby Seymour Gardens, and although Edith
had recognised the overcoat worn by the attacker
and knew that Bywaters had killed her husband,
she initially claimed not to know the identity of
the assailant. Detectives soon learned from Percy's
brother that Edith had been 'carrying on' with
a chap called Bywaters, and later that day, he was
visited by police.

Bywaters' cabin on his ship was searched, and
detectives found a number of letters, all written by

Freddie Bywaters. (Author's collection)

NO REPRIEVE IN THE ILFORD CASE.

HOME OFFICE DECISION.

Double Execution on Tuesday.

PARENTS STUNNED.

From Our Own Correspondent,
London, Friday Night.

The fate of the Ilford couple, Frederick Bywaters and Edith Thompson, was sealed late this afternoon, when the Home Office made the following announcement:—

The Secretary of State, after careful consideration of all the circumstances, is unable to advise interference with the due course of the law in the cases of Frederick Edward Francis Bywaters and Edith Jessie Thompson, who were convicted of the murder of Percy Thompson.

It is stated that Mr. Bridgeman, the Home Secretary, who is primarily responsible, came to his decision after consultation with his colleagues in the Cabinet.

The arrangements for the execution are in charge of the Under-Sheriff for Essex. Bywaters will be executed at nine o'clock on Tuesday morning, in Pentonville Gaol, and Mrs. Thompson at Holloway.

Judging by the common trend of conversation the decision of the Home Secretary came as a surprise. It was clear the idea was abroad that the authorities

PREVIOUS EXECUTIONS OF LOVERS.

Within recent years there have only been two couples who have been hanged on the same charge.

In January, 1903, Joseph Taylor and Mary Daly were executed for the murder of the woman's husband, John Daly, at Kilkenny and on 29 December, 1903, John Gallagher, a miner, and Emily Swann, were executed at Leeds for the murder of the woman's husband, William Swann.

The Leeds case had many points of similarity with the Ilford crime, for Mrs. Swann—like Mrs. Thompson—was not alleged to have taken any part in the actual killing of her husband.

Mr. Bridgeman, the Home Secretary.

LAST WOMAN TO BE HANGED.

It is more than 15 years since a woman was hanged in Great Britain. The last to suffer this fate was Mrs. Rhoda Willis, baby farmer and murderess, convicted under the name of Mrs. Leslie James, and executed in Liverpool in Cardiff Gaol on 14 August, 1907.

The following is a list of the women hanged in the past 22 years, with the places of execution:—

1890, 22 December.—Mary E. Wheeler (otherwise Pearcy) for murder of Mrs. Hogg, Newgate.

1894, 2 April.—Margaret Walber, for murder of husband, Liverpool.

1896, June 10.—Amelia Dyer, the baby farmer, Newgate.

1899, 19 July.—Mary Ann Ansell, murder of sister, St. Albans.

1900, 9 January.—Louisa Masset, murder of son, Newgate.

Mrs. Thompson.   Bywaters.

Above and below: Newspaper headlines on the Ilford Murderers. (T.J. Leech Archive)

ILFORD EXECUTIONS TO-DAY.

FINAL APPEAL UNSUCCESSFUL

The execution of Mrs. Thompson and Frederick Bywaters for the Ilford murder will take place this morning.

Mr. F. A. S. Stern, Mrs. Thompson's solicitor, endeavoured on Sunday night to persuade the Home Secretary to postpone her execution, travelling to Minsterley, near Shrewsbury, to see Mr. Bridgeman at his country house. Mr. Stern informed a Press representative yesterday that he arrived at about 11 p.m., when the house was in darkness, but eventually obtained an interview with the Home Secretary, and drawing his attention to a statement in a Sunday newspaper as to an alleged confession by Bywaters, asked if he would postpone the execution while inquiries were made. Mr. Bridgeman replied that it was only a repetition of what Bywaters had already stated, but promised to consider the matter.

The Home Office issued the following official announcement last evening:—
The Home Secretary states that after full consideration of all the representations made to him, he regrets that he finds no grounds for departing from his decision in the cases of Frederick Edward Bywaters and Edith Jessie Thompson.

Edith, which suggested a motive. One in particular was to the point:

Yes Darlint, [sic] you are jealous of him and I want you to be – he has the right by law to all that you have the right to by nature and love – yes darlint be jealous, so much so that you will do something desperate...

Bloodstains found on Bywaters' coat were enough for him to be taken into custody, and unaware that her lover was at the station, Edith was invited down to help with enquiries. Seeing Bywaters in the interview room, she broke down and confessed: 'Why did he do it? I did not want him to and must tell the truth.' It was nearly forty-eight hours after the murder when, for the first time, she admitted seeing Bywaters scuffle with her husband. When further letters from Edith were found in Bywaters' cabin, several of which included references to poisoning her husband, police decided to charge both with wilful murder.

The trial of the 'Ilford Murderers' took place before Mr Justice Shearman at the Old Bailey in December. The prosecution alleged that Bywaters had killed Percy Thompson, incited by Edith, thus making her equally guilty of murder. Letters found in Bywaters' possession satisfied the jury that even if she had been unaware of the method, time and place Bywaters would carry out the murder, Edith was fully supportive of this act, and therefore was morally as well as legally guilty.

Even as sentence of death was passed, Bywaters maintained that it was his doing alone and that Edith hadn't had anything to do with the death of her husband. A newspaper campaign resulted in almost a million signatures asking for a reprieve, but despite these protestations, it was announced that there would be no reprieve for either Bywaters or Thompson.

No woman had been hanged in Great Britain since the summer of 1907. Thompson was the first of three women sentenced to death in two days at the Old Bailey in December 1922 and, although the other two were both quickly reprieved, there was to be no mercy in the case of Edith Thompson. The lovers were both hanged at 9 a.m. on 9 January 1923. Bywaters walked bravely onto the drop at Pentonville; Edith Thompson had to be dragged in a petrified stupor to the execution chamber at nearby Holloway Gaol.

There was no doubt that Frederick Bywaters was guilty of a brutal murder, and although many believed her fatal letters were merely the fantasised ramblings of a lovesick woman, they were enough for the prosecution to believe she was in league with the killer. It is believed by many that, rather than murder, Edith Thompson was hanged for adultery.

THE WOMAN IN THE CAB

❖ *Bernard Pomroy, 5 April 1923* ❖

On Monday, 5 February 1923, 22-year-old domestic servant Alice Cheshire asked her employer if she could have the evening off, as her fiancé planned to take her to the theatre. In the company of her young man, Bernard Pomroy, a 25-year-old shop assistant from Hemel Hempstead, they left her workplace at West Hampstead and headed for Leicester Square. As they walked out the door, watched by Alice's friend and workmate Gladys Payne, Pomroy called out to her: 'Say goodbye properly, in case she does not come back again!' Gladys laughed at what she took to be a weak joke. As it turned out, it was a fateful prophecy.

Leaving the theatre shortly after 11 p.m., the couple hailed a taxi and told the driver, Herbert Golding, to take them to Watford. Arriving at Watford, Pomroy then directed the driver to return to London and gave the address of Templewood Avenue, Hampstead, where Alice worked. They arrived there at about 1.30 a.m.

The house was in darkness when they approached, and telling the driver that they would not be able to gain entry without disturbing the occupants, Pomroy instructed him to head back towards Leicester Square. As they approached Swiss Cottage, Golding heard the woman give a short cry, but with no further noise or any sign of a struggle, he ignored it and concentrated on driving. Arriving at Leicester Square, the cabbie slowed down and awaited further instruction. Pomroy told Golding to drive to the police station. When they arrived at Vine Street police station, Pomroy leapt out of the cab and rushed inside. As he did so, the driver could see his

fare's hands were heavily bloodstained. More worryingly, the female passenger lay slumped on the back seat. Inside the police station, Pomroy shouted that he had just killed his girlfriend, and that her body and the knife used were on the back seat of the taxi-cab outside. Alice Cheshire had suffered horrific throat wounds and was hurried to hospital, where she died from her injuries a few hours later.

At his Old Bailey trial on 1 March, events leading up to the death of Alice Cheshire were unveiled. By January 1923, Pomroy and Alice Cheshire, both of Hemel Hempstead, had known each other for three years and, although Alice had found a position in service in London, they had recently become engaged. Any plans they may have made for a future together were shattered when, on Sunday, 4 February, Alice's sister, Mabel, dropped a bombshell on their father by telling him that she was pregnant and that the prospective father was Bernard Pomroy, her sister's fiancé. The girls' father spoke at length with Pomroy, who said that he would go to see Alice on the Monday night, although he knew she was due back home on the Tuesday. Pomroy was

Bernard Pomroy. (T.J. Leech Archive)

determined not to wait and contacted Alice, telling her he was coming to London on the following day, and invited her to the theatre.

Pomroy refused to offer any defence or employ counsel to speak on his behalf. The trial became a formality, and before sentencing him to death Mr Justice Horridge drew attention to a statement made by the prisoner's brother regarding the accused's mental state. Pomroy had lost the use of his arm during the war, and his disability had left him depressed and irritable.

An appeal looked again at claims of Pomroy's insanity, but it was quickly rejected, and he was hanged two months to the day after the brutal murder.

39

THE GUILTY SECRET

❖ Rowland Duck, 4 July 1923 ❖

One wonders how many times Rowland Duck cursed his situation as he counted down the days in the condemned cell at Pentonville, waiting for his appointment with the hangman. If only he had resisted the advances of his lodger, it could all have been so very different.

Twenty-five-year-old Duck lived with his wife and three children in Cambria Street, Fulham. He had been badly injured during the First World War, blown up when his trench suffered a direct hit and, the trauma of seeing comrades killed left him shell-shocked and prone to epileptic fits. Unable to hold down a steady job, he was forced to do casual labouring jobs, and in order to supplement the family income, Duck and his wife took in a lodger, 18-year-old Nellie Pearce. Nellie earned her living as a prostitute and on occasions, possibly when she was short of rent money, Duck became one of her customers.

Events took a turn for the worse in the spring of 1923. Mrs Duck had now learned of her lodger's occupation and gave Nellie notice to quit the house. Duck initially managed to placate his wife, and she agreed that Nellie could stay until she could find new lodgings. Around this time, Duck discovered he had contracted gonorrhoea from Nellie. He confronted her and told her to pack her bags. She refused, saying she still had nowhere else to go and threatened to disclose his infidelity if he insisted she move out.

On 2 May, Duck came home drunk and quarrelled with his wife over the lodger. Mrs Duck demanded that Nellie be thrown out on the following day, as she seemed to be making no effort to find new lodgings.

In the early hours of the following morning, Duck went into Nellie's bedroom, and as she slept, he cut her throat with a knife. After wrapping the body in blankets and pushing it under the bed, he then left the house and walked around for an hour before approaching the desk sergeant at Walham Green police station and confessing to having killed the woman.

In a busy May Assizes, Duck was one of five people facing a murder charge when he appeared before Mr Justice Swift in May at the Old Bailey. There was no attempt to deny that Duck had killed Nellie Pearce; the defence pleaded guilty but insane. His counsel claimed that the trauma he had suffered during the war had left him emotionally scarred, highly nervous and with an uncontrollable homicidal impulse. His mother gave evidence that, since his wartime injury, even the slightest amount of drink would send him 'a bit funny' and that he would have to be held down until he was calm.

The medical board which was held while Duck was awaiting trial had found nothing to suggest that he was insane, and the prosecution's motive, that he had killed the girl to stop her revealing his guilty secret, was enough for the jury to take less than an hour to find him guilty of murder.

'NOT PLAYING THE GAME'

❖ *George William Barton, 2 April 1925* ❖

Despite relations between his wife and her sister being often strained and less than harmonious, the same wasn't so with George Barton and his sister-in-law. So much so, that when his wife died, 59-year-old widower George Barton and his deceased wife's younger sister, 38-year-old Mary Palfrey, soon embarked on a relationship. They began to spend most evenings out together at public houses and music halls and had even started to take family holidays at Mary's brother's house in Norfolk. Mary had herself been widowed in 1917, and as their romance flourished, a date of 5 February 1925 was set for their wedding.

They spent the weekend of 17 January with Mary's brother in Norfolk, and returned to her home at East Ham, London, on the Monday. Barton worked as a blacksmith and had a house at Dulwich, but spent most nights at Mary's house. On the morning of Tuesday, 20 January, Barton left to go work, but when Mary's son, Edward, returned home at lunchtime, he found his mother's body on the floor of the kitchen. Her throat was cut and she had been battered with a piece of heavy iron pipe.

Three days later, Barton's son, Albert, received a postcard from his father asking for forgiveness for what he had done. Barton claimed he had committed the crime after Mary

George Barton. (T.J. Leech Archive)

Hangman Robert Orridge Baxter – chief executioner at Pentonville between 1925 and 1935. (Tony Homewood)

had made disparaging remarks about Barton's deceased wife. He ended the note by saying that he planned to flee the country. Instead, on the following day, 24 January, Barton gave himself up to the police. He told them he had read about the death of his fiancée in the papers, but claimed he had no knowledge of carrying out the crime. However, in a second statement later that day, Barton admitted killing Mary. He said jealousy was the cause, and that he killed her because she was 'not playing the game'. With a date set for their impending marriage, Barton expected his bride to be faithful, but she had told him that a sailor would often visit after he had gone to work. She had then made some remarks about his previous wife and, in a rage, he had picked up the iron pipe and struck her on the head. As she slumped to the floor, he picked up a razor and cut her throat.

Barton was convicted at the Old Bailey before Mr Justice Avory on 26 February. Asked if he had anything to say before sentence was passed, Barton remarked: 'I am sorry I am not Ronald True, as then I would be sent to a convalescent home to dig up the garden for the rest of my life!' (Well-to-do True had been found guilty but insane of a brutal murder three years earlier.) As the judge passed sentence of death, Barton derisively snarled: 'And may you be hung tomorrow!'

41

CAUGHT RED-HANDED

❖ *William John Cronin, 14 August 1925* ❖

It was during a visit to his sister, who rented a first floor flat at 126 Old Church Street, Stepney, that William Cronin first met Alice Garrett. Forty-year-old Alice had recently been widowed, and although ship's fireman and coal trimmer Cronin was fifteen years older, they soon began a relationship and he moved into Alice's flat. In the summer of 1925, Cronin had heard from his sister that while he was away at sea, Alice Garrett would entertain other men in the house, and on Friday, 12 June, Cronin accused her of cheating on him. Neighbours heard the couple quarrelling, followed by Alice crying out, 'Murder!' As neighbours hurried to investigate, Cronin rushed out into the street and tried to flee. Inside the house, Alice Garrett was lying dead on the floor, her head almost severed from her body. Cronin still held the bloodstained razor and, as passers-by tried to detain him, he slashed out, injuring one of them before he could be subdued.

Tried at the Old Bailey before Mr Justice Swift, Cronin claimed he was innocent of the murder, which had taken place while he was asleep and had been carried out by someone else, who had since fled the area. This was despite being caught red-handed with the murder weapon after fleeing the house, leaving the victim still warm and oozing blood on the floor. The jury did not even bother to leave the box before finding Cronin guilty as charged. 'Thank you, Sir. I am very glad that you have sentenced an innocent man to death,' Cronin told the judge, after sentence of death was passed on him.

Cronin was no stranger to the court at the Old Bailey. In September 1897, he had stood trial for his life, following an incident in Limehouse. A quarrel had broken out between a number of pickets at the docks, and a man named Cuthbert who was accused of breaking the strike. It was alleged that during the scuffle, Cronin had entered Cuthbert's house and had struck his baby daughter with a shovel, fatally wounding her.

Cronin had denied the crime, and, as further witnesses testified that the child may have been struck accidentally during the affray, the charge was reduced to manslaughter and Cronin received seven years' imprisonment, serving the first part of his sentence at the fearsome Newgate Gaol. All told, he had served four terms of imprisonment for both theft and assault, before he culminated his criminal career with murder.

PRIME SUSPECT

It didn't take detectives long to work out who the prime suspect was. They were investigating the murder of Francis Rix, butler to Sir George Lloyd, the High Commissioner of Egypt, whose imposing residence was situated on Charles Street, Mayfair. Early on Sunday morning, 7 June 1925, a maid noticed that Rix hadn't collected his cup of tea from outside his room. She knocked on his door and entered. The butler was still in bed, and opening the curtains, she recoiled at the sight. Rix's blankets were soaked with blood and a large bloodstained axe lay on the floor beside the bed.

Robbery was soon found to be the motive, as items of money and jewellery were missing, and at the top of the list of suspects was 18-year-old Arthur Henry Bishop. Until recently, Bishop had been employed as a pageboy at the house, but in February, Rix had dismissed him when his work had failed to reach the standard expected. Although he didn't want to override his butler's decision, Sir George Lloyd had given Bishop a good reference and found him a position with a friend across the city.

Bishop had taken the new job the commissioner had found for him, but within a matter of days had absconded, stealing a bicycle, some silver and a sum of money. He had spent two nights in the city with a prostitute until his money had run out. He had then called at the house in Mayfair.

On the morning after the murder, Bishop approached an off-duty policeman who was tending his garden on the outskirts of Shoreham, Kent. Holding out a newspaper, he told the startled officer, 'I am Bishop – the man wanted for this murder…You had better take me in.'

Bishop was asked to wait while the officer changed into uniform before escorting him by omnibus to the police station at Sevenoaks. A search of his clothing revealed several items that had belonged to Rix and he then made a full confession.

Bishop said that he had gained entry through a basement window and, finding the axe, he had picked it up. He made his way to Rix's room and entered. As he tiptoed across the room, he thought Rix had stirred, and without waiting to find out, had swung the axe and struck him on the head, killing him instantly. He had then searched the room and stolen what property he could find.

Tried before Mr Justice Swift at the Old Bailey, Bishop could offer no reason for the crime other than that he was insane. It was found that, after committing the murder, he had returned to the prostitute he had spent the previous days with and used what little money he had stolen to pay for her company for another night. With the money gone, he had caught a bus out to Shoreham where he read about the crime in the paper and learned that he was the prime suspect.

Eighteen-year-old Arthur Bishop – the youngest man to be hanged at Pentonville. (T.J. Leech Archive)

THE NIGHT-TIME DANDY

❖ *Eugene de Vere, 24 March 1926* ❖

Although christened Ewen Anderson Stitchell, the 25-year-old Scots-born tailor and air force veteran preferred to use the rather more sophisticated and cosmopolitan sounding alias of Eugene de Vere. He had left his home at Renfrew in the latter days of the First World War, joining the Black Watch until after the Armistice, when his father was able to secure his discharge. It was then that he became an air-force cadet, but not long into his service he was invalided out when a blister, caused by his new boots, became septic and so badly infected that doctors had to amputate his leg below the knee.

Moving to London, he then began a new life. Posing as a wounded officer, de Vere took to begging on the streets. In order to highlight his disability, he would remove his false leg, roll up his trouser leg and stand on crutches. Accompanied by a barrel organ or accordion, he would sing sombre ballads and hymns, frequently earning a respectable sum of £2 or £3 a day.

In contrast to his daytime activities, by night de Vere became a night-time dandy and something of a gigolo. Sporting a fine quality dress suit, he graced many of the West End bars and clubs, using his charms to great effect. Then, in the summer of 1925, he met 17-year-old Polly Walker.

Polly lived with her parents at 58 Arlington Road, Camden Town, a short distance from where de Vere had a room. From the moment he met her, de Vere became infatuated, although it seems she did little to encourage his advances. Eugene de Vere was also an intensely jealous man. Several times he almost came to blows with anyone he caught chatting to Polly, and when, at a Christmas party, a young man offered to take Polly for a ride on his motorcycle, de Vere made such a fuss that Polly had to turn down the offer. When he heard that the same young man had requested her company at a dance, de Vere threatened to beat him if he continued to pursue Polly.

On New Year's Eve, Polly's mother took de Vere to one side and warned him of his behaviour. She said that Polly was upset by his constant pestering and unwelcome advances and if he persisted, she would have no option but to send her daughter away to stay with relatives, and then he would see no more of her.

When he returned home, de Vere was enraged. He barely slept that night, mulling over what Polly's

Eugene de Vere, dressed as a night-time dandy. (T.J. Leech Archive)

mother had said, and, determined to sort the matter out once and for all, he left his lodgings early the next morning. He let himself into Polly's house and sat in the kitchen. A short time later Polly came downstairs in her dressing gown and demanded to know what he was doing there. There was an argument and Polly called him a beast and bit him on the finger. He chased her through the kitchen and followed her upstairs, where he attacked and killed her. He then stole some jewellery, which he later pawned, and fled the capital.

A neighbour had heard Polly's screams, but did not go to investigate, and it wasn't until her father returned home at lunchtime that her body was discovered. Entering her room, he found her lying partly beneath her bed. A bloodstained poker lay on the bedroom floor, alongside a pair of heavy tongs. Polly had been battered about the head, and a silk stocking was tied tightly around her throat.

Polly Walker – strangled by Eugene de Vere.
(T.J. Leech Archive)

Detectives had little doubt who the main suspect was. Fleeing London, de Vere had walked about thirty miles to Hitchen, Hertfordshire, where he checked into the Acacias, a temperance hotel on Station Road. He spent the night at the hotel, and on the following morning, while he went out to purchase a newspaper, the proprietor was struck by the likeness of the new guest to the photograph of the man wanted for the murder in Camden. He was arrested later that morning.

Before Mr Justice Salter at the Old Bailey, de Vere claimed that he had been provoked into committing murder. When he was arrested, he had a bite mark on his finger, which he claimed had spurred him into carrying out the attack. Evidence was also introduced to show that de Vere was mentally unstable and that on one occasion, when Polly had refused his offer of a date, he had attempted to poison himself.

Clarifying the law on provocation, Mr Justice Salter told the jury that even if the bite was the catalyst for the murder, such a small bite could hardly be an excuse for a vicious beating and strangulation, and for the jury to consider a reduced charge of manslaughter. Finding insufficient provocation, the jury duly returned a guilty verdict.

44

JOE THE PAINTER

❖ *Johannes Josephus Cornelius Mommers, 27 July 1926* ❖

Forty-three-year-old Johannes Mommers had left his native Holland and moved to England just prior to the outbreak of the First World War in 1914. Having served his adopted homeland until the Armistice, he settled at Thundersley, Essex, and found work as a house painter. In 1919, he made the acquaintance of the Pionbini family, and although he was at the time happily married, he developed a fondness for the eldest daughter, Augusta Violette, at the time aged just 16.

Johannes 'Joe the Painter' Mommers.
(T.J. Leech Archive)

In the coming years, that affection grew into a more serious romance and the couple began to meet in secret whenever possible. It appears that Augusta was keen for Mommers to end his marriage and for them to set up home together, but whenever she raised the issue, he would try to change the subject and stall her.

On the evening of 7 May 1926, the couple went for a walk together and ended the evening drinking in a local pub. At closing time, they walked back to Augusta's house, where they sat for a while in the kitchen. Suddenly, Augusta's sister, Olive, heard a scream. She woke her mother and they went downstairs to investigate; Augusta was lying on the kitchen floor, bleeding profusely from an horrific throat wound.

'Oh mummy, save me, save me!' she cried out before losing consciousness. She died within the hour.

Mommers was the immediate suspect, having been with Augusta prior to her receiving the fatal injuries. He denied that he was responsible and claimed the wounds must have been self-inflicted. He handed the police a razor, stating that he had found Augusta with it in her hand and had taken it from her and put it into his pocket before he left the house and walked home. Mommers' clothing was taken away for examination, and when bloodstains were discovered, he was charged with murder.

At his trial before Mr Justice Shearman at Essex Assizes on Wednesday, 16 June, the court debated whether Augusta's death had been murder or suicide. The prosecution claimed Mommers was jealous of Augusta and killed her because she rejected his advances. His defence counsel argued that Augusta had committed suicide by cutting her own throat after Mommers had refused her pleas to leave his wife and be with her. They offered strong medical evidence which suggested that if Mommers had murdered Augusta, it would have been reasonable to expect to find wounds on her hands or arms where she had tried to fight off her attacker. Pathologist Dr Bronte could find no such wounds, and stated that the direction and position of the cut were consistent with suicide. A Harley Street surgeon also testified that Augusta's wounds were more consistent with suicide than murder. Despite this, the jury chose to believe the prosecution's version of events and duly returned a verdict of guilty.

Mommers' execution was carried out amid a petty feud between the hangmen. Long serving executioner William Willis, whose first visit to Pentonville had been two decades ago, was angry at being engaged only as an assistant to the recently promoted executioner, Robert Baxter. There was bad blood between the two men, as Willis had seen the promotion of Baxter as a threat to his earning capacity, and although he accepted the engagement, he did so begrudgingly.

The prison governor noted later that at this execution, Willis appeared callous and cold-blooded, and when he saw Mommers at exercise on the day before, it was felt that the assistant hangman viewed the prisoner with 'a wanton bloodlust'. On the morning of the execution, Willis, whose conduct was described as being overbearing and pompous, failed to strap the prisoner's legs on the drop, possibly in an attempt to discredit Baxter. This merely resulted, however, in the governor reporting the incident to the Home Office, and after a career lasting twenty years, Willis was sacked as an executioner.

45

THE GRUDGE

❖ *Hashan Khan Samander, 2 November 1926* ❖

Work was well underway aboard the SS *China* as she prepared to depart Tilbury docks. It was 10 a.m. on Friday, 9 July 1926, and Indian sailors Aslam Khan Zardad and Khannar Jung Baz had not long come off watch and returned to their cabin. Baz, who worked as a fireman on the steamer, was soon asleep, while Zardad, having just put down his book to get some sleep, was lying on his bunk when he heard the door creak open and someone tiptoe inside.

He recognised the man as 36-year-old Hashan Khan Samander, and as Zardad pretended to sleep, Samander crept into the cabin, paused for a moment, and then quickly left. Moments later, he returned, and again quickly exited. Samander then made a third visit and this time, Zardad noticed he was carrying a large knife in his hand. Zardad had no time to react before the intruder rushed straight at Baz's bunk and plunged the knife through the sheets. As Baz cried out, Samander plunged the knife twice more, fatally wounding the sailor. He then crept out into the corridor and hurried away. Zardad jumped from his bunk and followed Samander into the second engineer's cabin, where the alarm was raised.

At Samander's trial before Mr Justice Wright in September, Samander strenuously denied committing the murder, simply claiming it was a case of mistaken identity. The court heard that there had been a long history of animosity between Baz and Samander. They had signed on to the SS *China* at Bromley, and they had then been transferred together to the SS *Kalyan*, before returning to the SS *China*. It was on 9 May, while they were serving on the SS *Kalyan*, that trouble between the two first broke out. After a quarrel, Baz attacked Samander with a pair of scissors, wounding him in the arm. Twenty-three-year-old Baz was taken before the captain and fined two days' pay. The relationship between the two had soured since and resulted in Samander taking his terrible revenge.

Samander denied being the man who had entered the cabin, and said that at 9.30 a.m. on the morning of the murder, he saw two men board the SS *China*. He said that as he spoke to one of the men, the other said that he needed to use the toilet and headed off towards Baz's cabin. The main prosecution evidence was the testimony of eyewitness Aslam Zardad, and the jury believed he was telling the truth, that Samander bore a grudge against Baz, and duly returned a guilty verdict.

46

THE CARRIAGE

❖ *James Frederick Stratton, 29 March 1927* ❖

The suburban train chugged slowly out of Hackney Central station. In the last carriage, the only two occupants were quarrelling. As the train approached a set of signals adjacent to Graham Road, the train halted and a man leapt from the carriage and ran down the line towards the engine. Fireman Walter Tidd, on the footplate, saw the man approaching and asked him what he thought he was doing. To his great shock, the man replied that he had just killed his girl.

With blood streaming from a cut to his hand, the man said his name was James Stratton, and as the fireman accompanied him back to the carriage, he told Tidd, 'I hope she is dead, or it

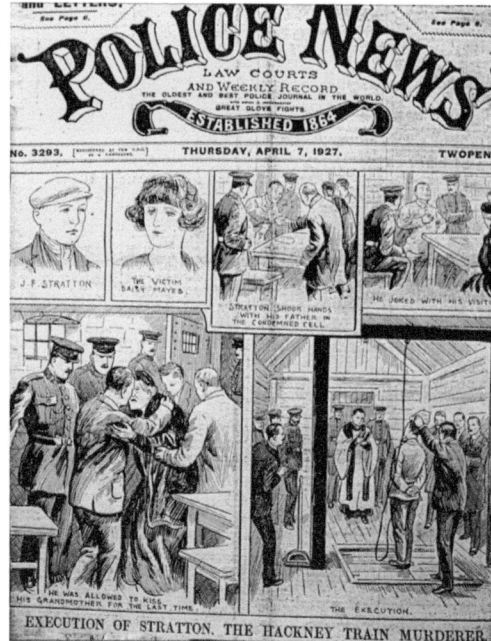

EXECUTION OF STRATTON. THE HACKNEY TRAIN MURDERER.

The killer and his victim. (T.J. Leech Archive)

The execution of James Stratton as depicted by the
Police News. (T.J. Leech Archive)

will mean ten years for me.' The scene in the empty carriage was horrific. Twenty-five-year-old Daisy Dorothy Mays was slumped in her seat, covered in blood, and, realising she was beyond help, Tidd escorted Stratton along the line to Hackney station, where he locked him in the stationmaster's office while he went to fetch a policeman.

Meanwhile, the train had moved along to Dalston Junction station, where police surgeon, Dr Barlow later examined the body and found that Daisy had been struck with a blunt instrument and then stabbed repeatedly.

At his trial before Mr Justice Branson at the Old Bailey on 10 March, Stratton pleaded guilty to the charge, and for the benefit of the jury, the events that led to the murder were explained. Daisy Mays was an attractive girl, who shared a house with her brother and sister on Grinstead Road, Deptford. For over seven years, she had worked as a typist and had been friendly with Stratton, who worked as a warehouse packer at the same firm.

Stratton, who lived with his grandmother in Hackney, said that he and Daisy had enjoyed a good relationship until Christmas Day 1926, when she told him their relationship was over. Stratton begged her to reconsider and the two met up occasionally while she pondered her true feelings for him.

On Sunday, 20 February 1927, Stratton arranged a date with Daisy, but she failed to turn up. After waiting for over an hour, he travelled to Deptford to find her, only to discover that she was out with another man. On the following day, they arranged to meet up at Liverpool Street station at 7.30 p.m. Stratton finished work early, and as he left his lodgings to meet Daisy, he put a knife in his pocket along with a shoemaker's iron last, wrapped up in a piece of rag. This time Daisy was waiting for him as arranged, and after a quick drink in a local pub, he asked her why she had stood him up on the previous evening. A quarrel ensued when he accused her of being involved with another man. It was while they were travelling home on the train that she told him that they had no future together and she no longer wished to see him again. At that, he struck her with the iron last, before pulling out his knife and inflicting twenty-four wounds to her head and upper body. When arrested, Stratton told detectives that he had been waiting for the opportunity to 'do her in' since Christmas Day. The verdict was a formality and just thirty-six days after the murder was committed, Daisy Mays was avenged.

IN A BLUE FUNK

❖ *John Robinson, 12 August 1927* ❖

It takes either sheer panic or ice cool nerve to commit a murder directly opposite a police station; more so if the room in which one commits the murder is directly overlooked by the said station offices. The case that was to lead to a Lancashire-born soldier making the short walk to the gallows began on 10 May 1927, when workers in the left luggage department of Charing Cross railway station noticed a foul smell coming from a wicker trunk. A check through the records showed that it had been deposited three days before, and as the smell was making conditions in the office unpleasant, the police were called in to investigate.

An officer forced the lock to reveal five brown paper parcels. Examining the first, detectives found it contained parts of a human body. The other parcels yielded similar contents, and in due course, the dissected, decomposing remains were sent for examination by pathologist Sir Bernard Spilsbury who was able to give detectives, under the leadership of Chief Inspector George Cornish, quite a bit to go on. Spilsbury was able to state that the cause of death had been asphyxia; that the victim – a woman – had been dead for about a week, and that the presence of small bruises around the neck suggested that she had probably been unconscious before being strangled.

Aside from the medical leads, there were other clues inside the trunk; one of which was a pair of ladies knickers with the name P. Holt sewn inside. Mrs Holt was traced, identified the underwear as belonging to her and suggested to detectives that they must have been stolen by one of her servants, going as far to name her as Minnie Alice Bonati.

Minnie Bonati was last seen alive on 4 May, which concurred with Spilsbury's estimation of the approximate date of death. A second-hand dealer from Brixton came forward after reading a report of the case and the mysterious trunk. He identified it as one he had sold a week before. A taxi driver also came forward, telling detectives he had picked up a fare with a similar trunk and taken him to Charing Cross station. He had been hailed by a man standing in the doorway of an office block at 86 Rochester Row, directly opposite the police station.

At the Rochester Row offices, police learned that one of the tenants, 36-year-old John Robinson from Leigh in Lancashire, had not been seen for several days, neither there nor at his lodgings. They did, however, find a telegram addressed to Robinson at the Greyhound Hotel, in Hammersmith. This was a vital link, as an old duster had also been found in the trunk with the word GREYHOUND sewn into it. This led police to Mrs Robinson, who said she had bigamously married John Robinson, and though they were no longer together, she said they kept in touch from time to time. At her next meeting with her 'husband,' Cornish accompanied her and questioned Robinson about the suspected murder.

Robinson strenuously denied having anything to do with the death of Minnie Bonati, and when he was placed in an identity parade, neither the taxi driver nor the Brixton shopkeeper picked him out. Despite this, Cornish was convinced he had his man. He arranged another search of the offices at Rochester Row, and this time they found a bloodstained matchstick in the folds of a wicker basket. There was also a crack in one of the windows and a dent in the fender around the fire, which suggested violence had taken place there.

Robinson was taken into custody for further questioning, and although Cornish had very little evidence against him at this stage, the suspect cracked and confessed. He made a statement in which he claimed that Minnie had propositioned him at Victoria Station. He took her back to the office where an argument ensued. They fought and Minnie fell backwards, banging her head on the fender. Robinson had then panicked and fled, returning on the

Minnie Bonati. (Author's collection)   *John Robinson.* (Author's collection)

The trunk Robinson used to conceal the body of Minnie Bonati. (T.J. Leech Archive)

following morning expecting to find her gone. Instead, to his horror, she lay where she fell: the blow had killed her. Panic stricken, Robinson decided to dispose of the body. He said he had bought a knife to dismember Minnie and the trunk to conceal the body in.

Throughout his trial at the Old Bailey in July before Mr Justice Swift, Robinson maintained that he was innocent of murder. He admitted being responsible for her death, along with dissecting and disposing of the body – everything except the intention to kill. When asked why he did not go straight to the police, he bowed his head and claimed, 'I was in a blue funk and did not know what to do.' Professor Spilsbury supplied the crucial evidence that destroyed Robinson's testimony. He claimed that Minnie Bonati had been asphyxiated after a violent assault, and death could not have come as a result of a fall as Robinson had maintained. This was enough for the jury, and on the third day of the trial, they took just one hour to find Robinson guilty of wilful murder.

48

DEATH ON A COUNTRY ROAD

❖ *Frederick Guy Browne, 31 May 1928* ❖

A postman on his rounds, shortly after sunrise, made the gruesome discovery. It was Tuesday morning, 27 September 1927, when the post van trundled slowly through the fog that enveloped the country road between Ongar and Romford. By the side of the road the postman spotted a figure lying prone on the grass, and on closer inspection, saw that it was local bobby PC George Gutteridge. He had been shot twice in the neck, and with what seemed a gruesome callousness, the killer had also fired a bullet into each eye.

Detectives suspected that the officer had been killed while challenging a motorist who had stolen a car a few hours earlier from a doctor's house in Billericay. The car was later found abandoned in Brixton, and in the foot well was the cartridge from a Webley revolver, the same type of bullet that had been used to murder PC Gutteridge.

Despite massive press coverage the hunt for the killer continued into the New Year, when Frederick Browne, a 49-year-old mechanic, was arrested on suspicion of stealing a car. As Browne's garage was close to where the doctor's car was dumped, police searched his premises and found a Webley revolver. Ballistics expert Robert Churchill confirmed that it was the murder weapon.

Browne was an ex-con, a petty thief and known associate of William Patrick Kennedy, an ex-soldier who claimed to be a former member of the IRA. Known as 'Two Gun Pat', Kennedy was tracked down and arrested in Liverpool. Under interrogation, he admitted being with Browne in the stolen car when PC Gutteridge had flagged them down and asked to see a driver's licence. Browne was unable to satisfy him that he was the owner of the car, and as Gutteridge took out his notebook and made to note the registration, Browne shot him.

Browne and Kennedy stood trial together before Mr Justice Avory at the Old Bailey in April 1928. Despite Kennedy's claims that he was not responsible for the officer's death, as the law stood, both were equally to blame, and the five-day trial ended when both were sentenced to death.

Fearing a disturbance if the two met on the scaffold, the Home Office decided that they should be hanged at different prisons. Kennedy was hanged at Wandsworth, while at the same minute, Browne walked to the gallows at Pentonville.

Frederick Guy Browne. (T.J. Leech Archive)

PC George Gutteridge. (T.J. Leech Archive)

ESSEX POLICEMAN SHOT.

BAFFLING CRIME.

MURDERED ON NIGHT PATROL.

The Essex County Police, with the assistance of officers from Scotland Yard, are engaged in investigating what appears to be one of the most baffling crimes that have occurred in recent years. Early yesterday morning the body of Constable George William Gutteridge, of the Essex County Constabulary, stationed at the village of Stapleford Abbots, was found on the road at a 'lonely point between Passingford Bridge and the village. He had been shot through the head. Two bullets of the revolver or automatic pistol type were found near the body. It is believed that four shots were fired at close range, and the indications are that one or two shots were fired while the constable lay on the ground. Beside the body were found Gutteridge's helmet and his notebook. In his hand was a pencil. Apparently the constable had been about to make some notes when he was assailed. The theory is that a motor gang, whom the policeman may have sought to stop for travelling without lights, may be concerned in the outrage. But last night the police had but slender clues on which to work.

The murder of PC Gutteridge made headlines across the country. (T.J. Leech Archive)

THE 'DRUMMER'

❖ *Frederick Stewart, 6 June 1928* ❖

On the afternoon of Thursday, 9 February 1928, Alfred Webb, the occupier of Flat 3, Pembridge Square, a luxury Bayswater flat, returned home to find an intruder inside. Whoever had gained entry had done so by breaking a glass panel in the door, and once inside, had put the chain on the door, preventing anyone else gaining entry while they went about their housebreaking.

Through the broken glass in the door, a figure could be seen moving about, so Alfred told his son, Clifford, and friend Frank Sweeny, who were accompanying him back to the flat, to go and find a policeman. They descended the stairs and had barely reached the front street when a shot rang out. Clifford Webb rushed back inside, passing a man hurrying from the flats and heading off up the street. Racing upstairs, he found his father lying mortally wounded outside the front door to the flat, a bullet wound over his left eye.

Alfred Webb died in hospital the following day. A search of the area soon revealed the murder weapon; a Browning automatic pistol which had been thrown into a nearby garden.

The police learned that on the day of the murder, a stranger had been seen knocking on doors of houses and flats in the area. In police slang, he was 'sounding the drum'; knocking at doors looking for empty houses. If the knock was answered, he would ask the householder an innocent question, such as 'does so and so live here?' It was learned that on the day of the

Pembridge Square, Bayswater, at the time of the murder. (T.J. Leech Archive)

Housebreaker Frederick Stewart. (Author's collection)

murder a man had been calling in the neighbourhood, and at one of the houses he had asked to see the chauffeur. Asked where he was from, the caller said he was from Warwick Garage.

Detectives were unable to find a Warwick Garage, but one of the team knew of a Warwick Mews, a haunt of 28-year-old petty thief and 'drummer' named Frederick Stewart. Stewart, who fitted the vague description given of the man seen fleeing the flat following the murder, was found to be living in Southend, where he was arrested two weeks later.

Tried before Mr Justice Avory at the Old Bailey on 18 April, Stewart told an implausible story. He admitted that he had burgled the flat but claimed that the shooting of Alfred Webb was accidental. He claimed he had been disturbed by Webb returning home and that the older man had punched him in the face. This caused his hand to jerk and the gun went off. He claimed that he had not been aware that he had shot Webb until reading about the crime in the following day's newspaper.

Medical evidence contradicted this, stating that the natural reaction to being struck in the face would be to loosen the grip, thus dropping the gun rather than pulling the trigger. Crucially, there was no evidence of any powder burns on the body of the gun as there would be if it had been discharged as Stewart claimed. This suggested that the gun had been fired from a distance and ruled out its going off accidentally during a scuffle.

Following conviction, Stewart was sentenced to hang on Derby Day. Being a keen gambler, Stewart asked for his execution to be put back a day so that he could discover the result of the Derby. His request was refused. As he was led to the gallows, he told hangman Robert Baxter to have a bet on Felstead, an unfancied long shot. Whether the hangman heeded this tip is unknown, but Felstead galloped home a 33 to 1 winner.

50

ALIAS MR DENNIS

❖ Frank Hollington, 20 February 1929 ❖

Pretty domestic servant Annie Hatton had been courting John Dennis since they had met in Victoria Park early in 1928. Seventeen-year-old Welsh-born Annie was a domestic servant who had moved to London and found work looking after the two young children of Nathan Markovitch and his wife, who ran a butcher's shop at 17 Loddiges Road, Hackney. The family lived above the premises, and it was here, on the night of Saturday, 17 November, that Annie Hatton was found dead in the kitchen. Her feet had been bound together; a tablecloth tied around her head, and several rooms had been ransacked. The cause of death was suffocation.

Markovitch told detectives that he had taken his wife to the theatre and they had left home at 8 p.m., returning about three hours later. Annie had been at the house looking after the young children. He also said that Annie had, until recently, been courting a man named John Dennis, but had ended the relationship when, after a quarrel, he had struck her in the face, leaving her with a bloody nose. With no signs of forced entry into the house, detectives reasoned that Annie had known her assailant.

Concentrating their efforts on her boyfriend, detectives eventually discovered that Dennis was a 25-year-old plasterer from Bethnal Green, whose real name was Frank Hollington, a married man with a young child. It took twelve days before he was tracked down, but shortly before midnight on 29 November, he was arrested at home, and under questioning admitted that he had used the alias 'John Dennis' in the hope his wife wouldn't find out about the affair. He admitted that he had been responsible for Annie's death, but claimed that it was accidental.

The story of their relationship and the events that led to murder was told in the Old Bailey on 14 January 1929, when Hollington stood before Mr Justice Humphreys. Frank said that he had first met Annie in Victoria Park, where she often took the children. They struck up a conversation and after several casual meetings, she agreed to go out with him. Their short courtship had ended abruptly when he saw her talking to another man, and in the quarrel that followed, he lost his temper and hit her.

Mrs Markovitch testified that a few days before her death, Annie had been overheard on the telephone apologising for failing to keep a date, and rearranging it for Wednesday, 14 November 1928. Hollington admitted that he had made the call, and when she failed to turn up on the Wednesday at the Empress Picture Palace as arranged, he went looking for her. Unbeknown to Annie, he saw her in the company of another man.

Hollington said that on the night of Annie's death, he had gone to visit her. They were in the kitchen talking when he asked her why she had failed to turn up on Wednesday. She told him that a girlfriend had asked to see her, as she wanted to talk about some problem. He accused her of

Frank Hollington, alias Mr Dennis, under arrest. (T.J. Leech Archive)

lying, and when she lied to him again, he lost control and punched her. As she fell to the floor, Hollington struck her again, this time rendering her unconscious. Fearing what he had done, he decided to tie her up and make it appear that a robbery had taken place by removing a few items off the mantelpiece. He was adamant that she was alive when he left and had only discovered she had died when he had read it in the newspapers.

The prosecution contested this claim about the robbery, saying that if Hollington, alias Mr Dennis, believed Annie was still alive when he left the flat, then he must have known that any attempt at faking a robbery would have been futile, as she would have revealed his identity once she had regained consciousness. The jury agreed, and despite the defence offering a plea of guilty of manslaughter, they found him guilty of wilful murder.

51

A FAMILY MATTER

❖ *William John Holmyard, 27 February 1929* ❖

By the age of 25, William John Holmyard, an army bandsman in the East Lancashire Regiment, had served his country with distinction in many parts of the Empire, and on returning from India in November 1928, had decided to apply for a discharge.

He signed his papers on 5 November and returned to his native London, lodging with his parents in Pimlico. Holmyard's father was a drunken layabout, who acted as a bookies' runner for a number of street gamblers, including his own father, William Holmyard Senior, who lived

William Holmyard – hanged for the murder of his grandfather. (T.J. Leech Archive)

next door at 37 Tachbrook Street, Pimlico. Although well past retirement age, the 72-year-old grandfather, a wealthy widower, still ran his own furniture business, and supplemented his income by acting as a bookmaker.

On Friday, 7 December 1928, the old man was found badly injured in the small office at the rear of the premises. He had been battered around the head with a pair of heavy tongs that lay bloodstained between the body and the hearth. Once police inquiries had eliminated any of the customers who had laid bets with Holmyard, attention turned to his grandson, who had been seen entering the premises on the afternoon of the attack, was known to be short of money, and who police learned from papers found in the office, had borrowed money from his grandfather.

At the police station, Holmyard admitted that he had struck his grandfather in self-defence following a quarrel. He said that following his discharge, he had borrowed £7 from his grandfather to tide him over until he could find a job. Over the next few days, he had repaid some of the loan, but had then borrowed further sums until the debt stood at £17. Holmyard had called to see his grandfather. He was annoyed that the loan, which he had hoped would be kept secret, was now known to his father, who in turn was now pestering his son for beer money. A fierce argument broke out and Holmyard picked up a pair of copper fire irons and struck his grandfather, whom, despite his age, was a burly, well-built six-footer.

Although he claimed it was self-defence, Holmyard was charged with wounding and held in custody. Things took a more serious turn when, on the following Monday, William Holmyard Senior died from his injuries. The charge was now one of wilful murder.

At his Old Bailey trial before Mr Justice Humphreys in January 1929, Holmyard maintained that he had acted in self-defence after his grandfather had picked up a heavy chair and swung it at him. Fearing for his life, he picked up the tongs and lashed out. Critically, when asked by the prosecution how many times he had struck the old man, the prisoner said twice, admitting that he had struck a final blow as the old man lay on the ground. This was the crucial point in the case and effectively destroyed any chance of a lesser verdict of manslaughter through self-defence.

52

A HEAD FULL OF JEALOUS IDEAS

❖ *Alexander Anastassiou, 3 June 1931* ❖

It was probably no more than just a bit of harmless chat, but within a few hours it was to have fatal consequences, with one person dead and another arrested, charged with wilful murder. On the afternoon of Thursday, 26 February 1931, 22-year-old Cypriot waiter, Alexander Anastassiou, was laughing and joking in his native language with several waitresses at the

Piccadilly Hotel in the West End where he worked, when he was confronted by his fiancée Evelyn Holt, who had decided to call on him on her way home from work. Although she was unable to understand much of what they were saying, his manner and the waitresses' giggling made Evelyn suspect he was being too friendly with his young colleagues and she was not pleased.

The pretty 23-year-old from Shepherd's Bush worked as a waitress in a Lyons Corner House a few blocks from the Piccadilly Hotel and had been dating Anastassiou since the previous December, 1930. Their courtship had moved at a pace and within weeks they had become engaged. Despite Evelyn's anger at seeing her fiancé seemingly flirting, Anastassiou soon won her over, and when he finished work, they went to the cinema, and after supper in a nearby café, returned to his rooms at 65 Warren Street, off Tottenham Court Road.

At 11.30 p.m., Anastassiou's landlady, Lena Ballerini, heard screams and a loud thud from upstairs. Hurrying to investigate, she found his door locked. As another tenant rushed to fetch the police, the landlady banged on the door. Police Constable James Murphy was passing when he was summoned to the scene, and after several minutes of knocking and demands that the door be unlocked, it slowly opened.

PC Murphy entered the room and found Evelyn Holt lying dead on the floor with a gash in the back and several to the front of her neck. Anastassiou was standing by the wall when he suddenly made to grab the bloodstained razor lying on a nearby table. PC Murphy had noticed him eyeing the razor and was able to place him under arrest before he could pick it up.

On Monday, 27 April, Anastassiou stood before Mr Justice Swift at the Old Bailey. Speaking through an interpreter, the Cypriot offered a not guilty plea and gave his version of the events that led to the death of his fiancée. He said that the quarrel they had had earlier on the afternoon of her death had been the last straw. Although they had been engaged for several weeks, he had begun to have second thoughts once he discovered she possessed a jealous and angry streak that led to her shouting and screaming at him whenever he so much as smiled at another woman. 'Her head was full of jealous ideas,' he told the court.

Anastassiou said that on their returning to his room, he told her that he was intending to emigrate to America and that he was ending their engagement. Evelyn did not take the news well and burst into tears. As she prepared to go home, Evelyn had asked to borrow a comb, and when he opened a drawer to hand her one, she spied his razor. As she went to return the comb, she pulled out the razor and threatened him, adding that she had friends at work that would hurt him for stringing her along.

He said she then rushed at him, they struggled and eventually he overpowered her, but during the process, she received the fatal wounds. 'I did not know what I was doing,' he told the court, implying either self-defence or insanity.

Prosecuting, Eustace Fulton referred to a statement the prisoner had made when arrested in which he had claimed, 'I wanted to touch her but she not let me...' This seemed to imply another motive; maybe he was angry at having his amorous advances spurned. Wounds on Evelyn hands and arms, probably inflicted when she tried to defend herself, suggested he had attacked her, and although Anastassiou also had wounds on his neck, these were mainly scratches made by fingernails and supported the theory that she had tried to fight him off.

Summing up, the judge said it was for the jury to decide if they believed it was a case of wilful murder or whether the crime was committed in self-defence, which could reduce the charge to manslaughter. 'I did not intend to do it,' Anastassiou claimed, as sentence of death was passed on him.

Like most convicted killers, Anastassiou chose to appeal although the vast majority of appeals were quickly dismissed. Anastassiou's appeal took place on Monday, 18 May, and the court was packed to capacity, not for the Cypriot, but for those wishing to witness the appeal scheduled for later that morning of William Wallace, a bespectacled, mild-mannered man accused of the brutal murder of his wife in Liverpool, a case which had divided opinion since it had hit the headlines earlier that year. Anastassiou's appeal was based on the fact that the judge had been unfairly biased in his summing up and was quickly dismissed. As the Cypriot waited to be returned in the cells below, Wallace took his place in the dock and was sensationally acquitted on the following day, by which time Anastassiou was back in the condemned cell at Pentonville.

There was one other point of interest in this case. Cypriot Dr Angelos Zemenides, who had acted as interpreter in court during Anastassiou's trial, was shot dead near his home in Hampstead in January 1933. His killer was never brought to justice.

53

THE KILLING OF 'PIGSTICKER'

❖ *Oliver Newman & William Shelley, 5 August 1931* ❖

Forty-five-year-old Herbert Ayres lived in an area close to railway sidings at Scratchwood, near Edgware. Resembling a shanty town, Scratchwood was a community of crudely built huts, converted railway carriages and shacks, populated by a transient group of homeless refugees and casual workers who mostly worked as railway labourers, or down the nearby sewers. Usually referring to each other by nicknames, they were constantly in trouble with the police and were feared and mostly despised by the local community.

On 1 June 1931, the body of Herbert Ayres, known as 'Pigsticker', was discovered in a shallow pit beneath a smouldering pile of rubbish. Sir Bernard Spilsbury was called in and was soon able to confirm the victim had died as a result of repeated blows to the head, and had been dead for approximately three days.

The Scratchwood shanty town where 'Pigsticker' was killed. (Author's collection)

A key witness was traced; Jack Armstrong had been living at the camp at the time of the murder and claimed the killers were two tramps, 61-year-old Oliver Newman and 56-year-old William Shelley, known as 'Tiggy' and 'Moosh.' The two lived in a rather grand hut for the area, although it was nothing more than a timber shack covered with tarpaulin. Both worked a few miles from the shanty town and would only return home after drinking themselves into a stupor in the nearby pub.

Armstrong told police that while sleeping on the floor of the men's hut, he had heard a quarrel and then saw them attacking Ayres. He later saw the body of Pigsticker being carried towards the dump where it was later discovered. Fearful for his own safety, he left the camp on the following day.

Newman and Shelley were quickly picked up and did not deny killing Ayres. On the contrary, they claimed they were justified in their actions because 'Pigsticker' had repeatedly stolen food from their hut. The first time they had caught him, they give him a stern warning and a beating; on the second occasion they had killed him.

Their trial before Mr Justice Swift at the Old Bailey on 25 June was memorable

Oliver Newman and William Shelley on the gallows.
(T.J. Leech Archive)

mainly for a comical outburst from the dock. As the defence challenged Armstrong's evidence as to the time he had seen the prisoners attacking the victim, he was asked if there had been a clock in the hut. 'There was but there isn't now,' he told the court. 'Why is that?' counsel asked. 'Because I have it here,' he said to much laughter in the gallery, withdrawing it from his pocket. 'Look, Tiggy,' Shelley called out, to further laughter, 'He's gone and pinched our clock!'

When the inevitable death sentence was passed and Newman and Shelley were asked if they had anything to say before sentence was carried out, Newman spoke up: 'Yes, it should have happened twenty years ago!'

54

THE SHIP'S MATE

❖ *William Harold Goddard, 23 February 1932* ❖

The story was plausible enough. On the morning of Monday, 30 November 1931, 25-year-old William Goddard walked into Ipswich police station and confessed that he was responsible for the death of Charles William Lambert, his skipper on board the barge *Speranza*, moored at Woolwich.

On the previous Saturday afternoon, Goddard had asked the captain if there was any mail for him. Fifty-seven-year-old Lambert told him there were two letters, one of which was from his fiancée. What angered Goddard was the disparaging way the captain had referred to his girl as he threw the letter at him.

Taking exception to what he had heard, Goddard punched Lambert in the face. Goddard said he was horrified to see the captain fall backwards in a heap and tumble down the stairs leading to his cabin. In shock, he hurried after Captain Lambert, only to find him back on his feet and now brandishing a hammer. Lambert had a look of rage on his face and was threatening to 'do for' the younger man.

Goddard told police that he had managed to wrestle the hammer from Lambert, but that during the scuffle the skipper had injured his neck and slumped to the deck. When Lambert didn't respond when asked if he was alright, Goddard panicked and fled the boat. Several hours later, he went back to check if the captain had moved. Whatever the truth of what had happened thus far, it was then undermined by what Goddard said next. Instead of seeking medical help or calling the police, he had simply removed the stricken man's watch and chain in the hope that, when the body was discovered, police would think he had died during a robbery.

When detectives questioned Goddard, his version of events was soon found to be untrue. When they boarded the barge, they found the body as described, but, crucially, Goddard had made no reference to the rope knotted around Lambert's neck. A pathologist later found that the cause of death was strangulation.

Goddard then offered the explanation that he had tied the rope around the captain in an effort to drag him onto the deck. He argued that as it had been foggy that evening, and he could have thrown the body overboard if he had wanted to disguise his crime.

Goddard was tried before Mr Justice Finley in January 1932. The court heard that when the accused had made his original testimony at Ipswich, he had admitted striking Lambert with the hammer and had also claimed that after doing so, he had had to 'finish him off' to keep him quiet.

William Goddard never denied being responsible for Lambert's death, but maintained it was accidental and, at worst, he should be convicted of manslaughter. The fact that he had stolen the dead man's watch and other items, which he had subsequently pawned, convinced the jury to side with the prosecution's version of events and return a guilty verdict.

55

THE FRIGHTENED WOMAN

❖ Maurice Freedman, 4 May 1932 ❖

Maurice Freedman was already a married man when he began courting Annette Friedson in the summer of 1930. Although he had deserted his wife, the ex-policeman now earned a living as a gambler and moneylender, and had neglected to mention his past, which only came to light in October 1931, when someone told Annette's family about him.

The family didn't approve of Annette's boyfriend and took steps to actively discourage her from continuing the relationship. When she confronted him about his wife, they quarrelled, and from then on the relationship became strained. They continued to go on dates but these often ended in arguments, and eventually matters came to a head on Saturday, 23 January 1932, when, following another row, she told him their relationship was over. Freedman was enraged, and when it became clear she wasn't going to change her mind, he became aggressive and threatening towards her. In an effort to pacify him, Annette agreed to a meeting on the following day and Freeman went away. Annette had been frightened by his outburst and decided not to make the rendezvous on the following day, although she knew that by standing him up, Freedman would be even angrier.

Bloodstains on the stairs show where Annette Friedson died. (T.J. Leech Archive)

Annette became a frightened woman. On Monday afternoon, as she left work, she saw Freeman loitering across the road but managed to avoid him seeing her leave. Fearful that he may cause trouble, she asked her brother to escort her to work.

For over twelve years Annette had worked as a typist for H.R Munns & Co., an export firm at 103 Fore Street, close to Moorgate station. On the Tuesday morning, her brother saw her onto a tram which would take her to the door of her workplace. At 9.30 a.m., the body of Annette Freidson was found on the staircase in the office block. Her throat had been cut and a trail of blood on the stairs led to where she had been attacked.

There was only one suspect, and 36-year-old Freedman was arrested at his lodgings in Oakfield Road, Clapton, that same evening. He admitted that he had been present when she died but denied it was a case of murder. He told detectives he had gone to the offices and waited for Annette to arrive. Freedman and Annette argued, and he asked her if they were to continue their romance. When she said no, he took a razor from his pocket and pressed it against his own throat.

He claimed he had no intention of harming either himself or Annette, but simply wanted to scare her into changing her mind. He said that Annette had reached out and tried to prevent him slitting his own throat, and in the ensuing struggle, the razor had accidentally been drawn across her throat. He had panicked when she had collapsed, bleeding profusely from the deep gash to her neck.

Freeman stood trial before Mr Justice Hawke on 9 March. The prosecution dismissed his story of an accident and claimed it was a brutal murder carried out because Annette had ended their relationship. Surely, the prosecution said, if Freedman's account of events was true and her injuries had been accidental, he would have tried to obtain medical assistance rather than fleeing the scene and concealing the murder weapon beneath the seat of a bus.

THE NEPHEW

There was a ring on the doorbell of the flat on Blackstock Road, Finsbury Park, and tenant Elizabeth Kerswell heard her neighbour greet the visitor. She heard a man's voice and then the woman who occupied the top floor flat, Elizabeth 'Betts' Standley, asked, 'Are you coming up for a few minutes, Jack?' It was just after 9.30 a.m. on Saturday, 4 March 1933. At noon, one of Betts Standley's lodgers arrived home from work and found her body partly hidden beneath her bed. She had been beaten about the head, stabbed several times, and a length of flex was knotted around her neck. From the state of her clothing, it appeared as though it had been a sexual attack.

Forty-four-year-old Mrs Standley had been living with her husband and two lodgers on the top floor at Blackstock Road, following the sale of her house a few months earlier. With the proceeds of the sale, she had purchased a coffee stall at King's Cross for her husband and the remainder, well over £100, she carried around with her in her handbag. The money was now missing.

Detectives learned that she had also lent a sum of money to her nephew, Jack Puttnam, and with the neighbour mentioning that the visitor had been called Jack, Puttnam became the prime suspect. Thirty-one-year-old Puttnam ran a printing business with his brother, and in the previous months, had borrowed several sums from his aunt which she had been pressing him to repay.

Taken in for questioning, Puttnam claimed he had not seen his aunt for weeks. Detectives knew he was lying as they already knew she had visited him at his home in Wood Green a few days before her death. Despite this, they released Puttnam on bail while their investigations continued. A bus conductor came forward to say that on the morning of the murder, he had been stuck in traffic when he saw a man rush from the house on Blackstock Road. He told police he would recognise the man again and was able to identify Puttnam in an identity parade.

Satisfied that they had their man, on 24 March, detectives charged Puttnam with murder. He now made a detailed statement admitting he had gone to his aunt's home that morning to resolve the issue over the money and to ask for more time to repay it. They began to quarrel, and during the argument, he had picked up a meat skewer and stabbed her. He had then tied the flex around her neck and arranged her clothing to make it look like a sexual assault.

When Puttnam stood trial before Mr Justice Hawke, he retracted the confession, saying he had lied to police because his alibi for the time of the murder would have implicated his brother's wife, with whom he was having an affair, and with whom he had spent the morning his aunt was murdered. He said that he only confessed because the arresting officers threatened to reveal details of the affair to his brother if he didn't.

The evidence against Puttnam was strong. There were bloodstains on his clothes and items stolen from his aunt's home were found in his room. Detectives also disproved his claim that he had picked up the skewer in the heat of the moment and stabbed her with it by showing that the murder weapon was, in fact, a printer's gimlet which Puttnam had taken with him.

Puttnam's father also reluctantly admitted in court that his son had asked him to provide a false alibi for the morning of the murder, and although the missing money was never recovered, Puttnam was convicted of the murder of his aunt.

57

SHOTS IN THE KITCHEN

❖ *Varnavas Loizi Antorka, 10 August 1933* ❖

The kitchen at the Bellometti Restaurant on Soho Square was a hive of activity. It was Friday lunchtime, 12 May 1933, when head chef, Cypriot Boleslar Pankorski, demanded that silver service waiter, Varnavas Antorka, a fellow Cypriot, put some plates into the gas stove to warm. It was a reasonable enough request and in the stressful, busy kitchen, the chef's orders were barked out with little thought for politeness.

Antorka did not respond, and when, a few minutes later, Pankorski saw that the job still hadn't been done, he threatened Antorka with the sack. 'If you don't do it, you must finish now!' he roared at him. Antorka was not intimidated and retorted that he would finish him first. At that, the chef told Antorka to get out of the restaurant. Cook Zacharias Panagi witnessed the exchange of words and watched as Antorka picked up his coat and stormed out into the street.

An hour later, waiter William Summers saw Antorka in a corridor at the back of the restaurant. As Pankorski walked down the stairs, he found the sacked waiter lurking at the bottom. Antorka rushed at the chef and shouted at him: 'You gave me the sack, you bastard. Take me back or else I'll shoot you!' Moments later, a shot rang out, and as other waiters hurried into the kitchen, further shots were fired, one of which wounded a kitchen porter in the leg. Pankorski slumped to the floor, killed by the first shot.

Tried before Mr Justice Humphreys at the Old Bailey at the end of June, 31-year-old Antorka was described as a quiet, inoffensive man of good character. He had come to England in 1928 and, unable to speak a word of English, he quickly taught himself the language and found work at the Soho restaurant.

His defence claimed that he had only pulled out the gun to frighten the chef into giving him his job back. The prosecution countered by claiming that Antorka had committed murder in revenge for being sacked, and by first returning home to collect the gun, it showed premeditation, and it was therefore wilful murder.

58

THE NE'ER DO WELL

❖ *Robert James Kirby, 11 October 1933* ❖

A sound at the door disturbed the household in Valence Circus, Dagenham. Slipping on his dressing gown, Charles Kirby opened the door to be confronted by his brother, Robert. Following Charles down the stairs was their mother, to whom Robert Kirby announced solemnly: 'I have done Gracie in.'

Charles Kirby got dressed and went to fetch a policeman. He told him of his brother's confession to murder and accompanied him to the home of 17-year-old Grace Newing, who lived in nearby Stevens Road. There they found the young girl lying on the floor, strangled by a cord. Also present was another police officer, summoned by the distraught girl's mother, Rosina, who had discovered the body a short time before.

At the Old Bailey before Mr Justice Swift in September, it was learned that 26-year-old Kirby had been courting Grace Newing for three months and that she had become pregnant by him. Although described by members of his own family as a 'ne'er do well' and something of a layabout, Kirby was still welcome at Grace's parents' house, where he had committed the murder.

At 8.45 p.m. on the night of Thursday, 6 July 1933, Kirby had called at the house on Stevens Road and waited in the kitchen with her mother for Grace to return home from her job in a confectionary shop. As Kirby and Mrs Newing sipped tea and chatted, her young son was fiddling with a piece of cord. Leaving Kirby alone in the kitchen, Rosina retired for bed at 10.45 p.m., and heard Grace enter around 11.30 p.m.

Rosina told the court she had just drifted off to sleep when she heard sounds of a disturbance from downstairs. By the time she had slipped on her gown and ventured down the stairs, Kirby had fled and Grace lay dead on the kitchen floor. Tied tightly around her neck was the cord her son had been playing with earlier in the evening.

Kirby made a statement following his arrest in which he claimed that Grace had, 'asked me to do it and I did her the favour!' He refused to go into the witness box and simply reiterated she had asked him to kill her.

Following conviction, Kirby told doctors assessing his medical condition that he had strangled her because she had refused to have sex with him that night.

59

SUSPICIONS

❖ *Harry Tuffney, 9 October 1934* ❖

There, inside the handbag, was the letter. Quickly scanning the contents, he saw, as he suspected, that it was from Sydney, and it confirmed his worst fears. Not only did the letter mention arrangements for a date on the following day, but there were also references to a flat they were planning to move to. Harry Tuffney's suspicions were confirmed and his heart was broken.

At 8.30 a.m. the following morning, Saturday, 30 June 1934, 36-year-old motor mechanic, Tuffney walked into Marylebone Lane police station. 'I've killed my girl,' he said coldly told the desk sergeant, adding with almost comical irony, 'I've had my head over the gas ring since about 4 a.m., but it was no use.'

Tuffney then made a statement explaining his actions. He said that he had a room at 75 Star Street, Paddington, and had been courting a fellow tenant, Edith 'Kate' Longshaw, whose room was across the hall. He said that they had been courting for a while and when he had proposed marriage, she had accepted. He then learned from friends that she had been seeing other men, one in particular, Sydney Briggs, who had just left his wife.

Tuffney said that on the previous afternoon, Edith had asked him to repair her handbag after the strap had broken. Completing the task, he then rummaged through the contents looking for proof of her infidelity, and there in one of the pockets was the letter. Convinced that Edith was about to end the relationship, he decided that if he could not have her then no one else would.

Tuffney went to a local hardware store and paid one and three pence for an axe. Later that evening, when he returned the handbag, he asked Edith if she planned to leave him. She denied she had any such plans and asked him to spend the night with her. He waited until she fell asleep before going to his room, collecting the axe and striking her once on the head. So severe was the blow, the blade was embedded into her head right up to the shaft.

He then returned to his room and tried to take his own life by gassing himself. He took a number of cushions which he laid on the floor next to the gas ring. He then turned on the gas, lay on the floor and waited to die. By sunrise the aroma of gas had filled the air, but Tuffney was still very much alive. He had then presented himself at the police station.

Before Mr Justice Atkinson at the Old Bailey, Tuffney's only hope of escaping the gallows rested on his plea of insanity. The defence claimed there was a history of insanity in the prisoner's family: his mother had died in a mental hospital in 1928, one brother had been diagnosed insane, another had died in an asylum as a child, and an aunt had also died in an asylum. But the medical board that examined Tuffney following his arrest could find no signs of insanity, and the prosecution's version of events, that he had killed Edith because his fiancée was about to leave him, was enough for the jury to return a guilty verdict.

60

TO GET ON IN THE WORLD

❖ *John Frederick Stockwell, 14 November 1934* ❖

On Tuesday, 7 August 1934, cleaners arriving on duty at the Eastern Palace cinema, Bow Road, East London, made an horrific discovery. As the others busied themselves in the stalls and foyer, Nellie Earrey climbed the stairs to the circle and upper balcony. Moments later, her screams had the others rushing up the stairs. Dudley Hoard, the 40-year-old manager, and his wife, Maisie, had a flat above the cinema, and access was via a door at the rear of the circle. As Nellie had entered the upper foyer, she had stumbled across the body of Hoard, lying in a pool of blood in the doorway to his apartment. As one cleaner rushed to fetch the police, Mrs Earrey entered the flat and found Mrs Hoard, badly wounded with serious head injuries.

Dudley Hoard died from his injuries in hospital, but his wife soon recovered and was later able to give police a detailed statement. Chief Inspector Fred 'Nutty' Sharpe took over the investigation and pieced together what had happened. The previous day had been a bank holiday and the cinema safe would therefore have contained the takings since Saturday afternoon, which would have been a considerable sum.

As there were no signs of a forced entry to the premises, Sharpe deduced that the killer had either hidden on the premises after the previous night's programme or had been known to the victim. Mrs Hoard was able to make a statement on the following morning. She claimed that shortly after they had retired to bed, they were woken by someone ringing the doorbell. Her husband went to investigate and admitted the visitor. She remembered little else before waking up in hospital.

The clues soon fell into place. One of the employees, 19-year-old John Stockwell, an attendant

John Frederick Stockwell.
(Author's collection)

at the cinema, did not turn up for duty on the following day. Tuesday, 7 August had been his day off, so he had not been questioned that day, but when his absence was noted on Wednesday, further inquiries were made. The discovery of a bloodstained axe, hidden on the premises, further supported the fact it was an 'inside job', as an intruder would have either left with the axe or casually discarded it next to the body, rather than hiding it in a store cupboard.

In addition, Stockwell was missing from his lodgings at Bromley-by-Bow, and on the following day, his description and photograph were published in the national press. Stockwell's fiancée contacted the police with a letter she had received from her boyfriend bearing a 'Lowestoft' postmark, in which he claimed he had fled as he was known to the police for a previous crime. He had failed to disclose this to his employers and he was afraid that if he were fingerprinted, he would lose his job.

Detectives travelled to Lowestoft, where the suspect's clothes had been found on the beach. The local police had received a letter from Stockwell in which he admitted the attack on Hoard, but claimed that he had not meant to kill anyone and that he planned to drown himself. He closed the letter by asking if the money in his savings' account could be given to his fiancée.

Stockwell was traced to Yarmouth, where he had booked into the Metropolitan Hotel under the name Smith. He aroused the suspicions of the manager when he signed the register and gave his address as Luton, Hertfordshire. Knowing Luton was in Bedfordshire, the manager contacted the police and the guest was identified as John Stockwell and placed under arrest.

Stockwell's father had been killed in the First World War, and ten years later, his mother had passed away. From that date he had been passed from one relative to another, constantly getting into trouble until, at the age of 16, he was eventually thrown out into the streets.

Stockwell was visited by his fiancée on the day before his execution and their meeting made a pitiful scene. Broken-hearted by her lover's brutal crime, she wept as he told her, 'They finish things off at nine o'clock tomorrow. I can't imagine what made me do it, except that I wanted money to get on in the world.'

61

A LITTLE CLANDESTINE BUSINESS

❖ Charles Malcolm Lake, 13 March 1935 ❖

The Westminster Poor Law Institution on Fulham Road, Chelsea, was a refuge for the homeless. Housing almost 1,400, it provided food and shelter, but under strict conditions. Residents could not come and go as they pleased; they had to ask permission before leaving the premises and were expected to wear a uniform, work hard, and maintain discipline and good behaviour for fear of being thrown back onto the streets.

George Hamblin and George Harvey were both residents at the institution. Hamblin acted as an unofficial bookmaker, a practice which was strictly against the rules, and Hamblin had use of a small room, B77, where he conducted his clandestine business, making a little extra money through taking small bets from the other residents.

On the evening of Friday, 26 October 1934, 49-year-old George Hamblin was discovered battered to death in room B77. In the midst of the hundred or so bloodstained betting slips that were littered around the body, there lay a bloodstained hammer.

Police investigations soon found that one resident had been seen behaving in a suspicious manner that same evening. At 5 p.m., George Harvey, one of Hamblin's regular customers, had asked for a 48-hour pass out of the institution, and when he handed in his work uniform at the end of his shift, the shirt was missing. Before he could be questioned about the missing shirt, however, Harvey had already left in order to visit his girlfriend, where he stayed for two days as the murder enquiry progressed.

When Harvey returned to the institute, he was immediately arrested and charged with murder. A search of his property revealed over £3 in cash, but what was more telling was a postal order for one and sixpence made out in the name of Hamblin. Harvey claimed that he had known nothing of the murder until he had read about it in the newspaper on Saturday evening. Explaining how he had come to be in possession of £3, he claimed to have earned it from the other residents by selling tea at one or two pennies a cup. Offering police a potential motive for the crime, he said that Hamblin had confided in him that he was being blackmailed.

Harvey's girlfriend told police that on the night before the murder, he had taken her to the cinema and told her that he had lost a large amount of money on a horse. On the following night, when they had again visited the cinema, his behaviour had seemed a bit strange. A search of the lavatories at the cinema unearthed Harvey's work shirt splattered with blood, along with two ready-reckoners as used by bookmakers, and a cash pouch, recognised as having belonged to the murdered man.

When he was tried before Mr Justice Atkinson at the Old Bailey in January 1935, the evidence against Harvey was strong. Witnesses testified that he had been seen to enter the storeroom with Hamblin half an hour before the latter was found dead, and this, together with the evidence found at the cinema, which Harvey was known to have visited after the murder, was enough to convince the jury of his guilt.

Before he stood trial, the prisoner admitted that George Harvey was not his real name, but asked that his real name not be revealed in court. He explained that his mother was very ill and the shock of finding her son on a murder charge might be too much for her. This was agreed, but once the death sentence had been carried out, his real name was revealed as Charles Malcolm Lake. His execution also marked the first appearance outside the prison of wealthy abolitionist, Mrs Violet van der Elst, protesting against capital punishment.

62

LAST MINUTE EVIDENCE

❖ *Allan James Grierson, 30 October 1935* ❖

Maxine Gann waited at Marble Arch and watched each approaching car, hoping it would contain her boyfriend, car salesman Allan James Grierson. He had arranged to pick her up at 1 p.m. and take her for a drive to Torquay, where he was to take a car to show a client. As the minutes turned into an hour and he still hadn't appeared, Maxine resigned herself to the fact that there had been a change of plan and she returned home.

Arriving back at the rented flat she shared with her mother at Gloucester Road, near Regent's Park, she was shocked to find the door locked and no sign of her mother. She prepared herself for another long wait, but when there was still no sign of her mother by 4 p.m., she became alarmed and called on a neighbour, a builder, who forced entry into the flat. It was immediately clear that something was amiss: a suitcase half full of silver lay on the sitting room floor, clothes were scattered across the bedroom floor and the door to her mother's room was locked. The builder picked the lock and there, lying in a pool of blood, was 63-year-old Louisa Berthe Gann. She had been battered several times with a flat iron.

On the following morning, Sunday, 22 June 1935, she died from her dreadful head injuries, as detectives, led by Chief Inspector Len Burt, searched for their prime suspect, Allan Grierson. Maxine Gann told police she had met Grierson at a club in Hammersmith nine weeks earlier.

Allan Grierson.
(Author's collection)

She said that her mother's friend, Dorothy Riley, had wanted someone to look after her flat while she was away, and she and her mother had moved into the flat, where they were joined a few days later by Maxine's new boyfriend who was currently homeless, having returned to England from Australia a few weeks earlier.

Within days, Grierson had fled, taking with him a number of items, which he later pawned. He had then contacted Maxine and apologised for stealing from the house, returning a pawn ticket for the missing items. He told her he had found a job and was hoping to sort himself out. He ended by begging her for a second chance.

With his request granted, he had then promised to make amends by taking them on a trip to Torquay. He arranged to meet Maxine at Marble Arch, after which he would collect her mother and they would head for the coast.

Twenty-seven-year-old Grierson was the son of a Southampton solicitor, and the police hunt for him was given widespread publicity, including an announcement on the BBC, and, as the search continued, a photograph was issued to the press. He was eventually traced to Weybridge, where he had taken lodgings. When his landlady saw a photograph in her Sunday paper that looked uncannily like her lodger, she contacted the police and Grierson was arrested on 1 July, after making a failed attempt to jump from a window as detectives burst into his room.

Grierson goes to the gallows. (T.J. Leech Archive)

Although there was a great deal of circumstantial evidence linking him to the murder, when Grierson stood trial before Mr Justice Porter in September, the prosecution's case was far from clear-cut. Grierson had already admitted to Maxine that he had stolen items from the house before the murder, and his fingerprints were legitimately all over the house. Without a witness to place him at the murder scene, it seemed he would escape justice.

In the end, it took some late evidence to secure a conviction. One of the items found to be missing was a silver cruet set, and Maxine Gann knew that it had been in the house on the morning of the murder. On the eighth day of the trial, the cruet was traced to a local pawnbroker, who recognised Grierson as the man who had pawned it on the afternoon of the murder.

This last minute evidence proved fatal for Grierson; the jury needed just thirty minutes to find him guilty of the horrific murder. His execution was the last carried out by Robert Baxter. After twenty years as a hangman, Baxter's eyesight had deteriorated to the extent that he was noticeably clumsy and uncertain in placing the rope around Grierson's neck. His name was deleted from the short list of qualified hangmen on the following day.

63

ON LOVERS' LANE

❖ *Leslie George Stone, 13 August 1937* ❖

On the morning of Monday, 12 April 1937, a railwayman on his way to work discovered the body of a young woman on the Firs, a deserted lane at Leighton Buzzard, Bedfordshire. The woman was naked apart from a topcoat and pair of gloves, and the cause of death was strangulation, evidenced by her own black silk scarf knotted tightly around her neck. Removed to a local mortuary, she was identified as 23-year-old Ruby Anne Keen, who lived in nearby Plantation Road, and who was engaged to a member of the local police force. Despite her lack of clothes, there had been no sexual assault, but bruises and cuts on her face indicated that she had fought desperately against a possible rapist or sexually-motivated killer.

Valuable forensic evidence was gathered at the scene. Although there were footprints around the body, there had been so much movement during Ruby's struggle for survival that most were smudged and unable to give up an adequate cast. Crucially though, the killer had more than likely knelt beside his victim to knot the silk scarf around her neck; this had yielded two perfect imprints and plaster casts were taken.

There was to be a startling development as the murder enquiry began: a policeman's fiancée had been murdered, and as detectives sifted through the witness statements, it seemed more and more likely that the killer was a policeman. A witness came forward to say he had seen Ruby on the previous evening close to where she was found murdered. She had been killed in a quiet part of the town, know locally as 'Lovers' Lane,' and the witness had seen her at 10.30 p.m. on Sunday night in the arms of a man, whose face he couldn't see, but who was wearing a dark blue tunic and trousers, similar to those worn by policemen.

Ruby had been an attractive young woman whose good looks and bubbly personality attracted a host of male admirers. Her fiancé was the immediate suspect, but he had been on duty the previous night and therefore had an alibi, and so the net was cast wider and one name soon headed the list.

Soldier Leslie Stone had first met Ruby Keen in 1931. He lived in the small hamlet of Heath and Reach a mile from Leighton Buzzard, and the two had seemed destined to marry until, the following year, his unit was posted overseas to Hong Kong. To begin with, the couple had corresponded regularly, but gradually Ruby's letters dried up and finally stopped.

Above left: *Leslie Stone*. (Author's Collection)

Above right: *Ruby Keen*. (Crime Picture Archive)

Left: *Hangman Tom Pierrepoint returned to Pentonville for the first time in twenty-four years to hang Leslie Stone*. (T.J. Leech Archive)

By the time Stone was discharged from the army in December 1936, Ruby had become engaged to the policeman, but when Stone and Ruby met up again on 4 April 1937, they arranged to have a drink for 'old times' sake'. A week later, Stone met Ruby in the Golden Bell. He was wearing a new blue serge suit with highly polished buttons. They drank in several public houses around the town and were last seen at 10 p.m. walking towards the Firs, a popular local spot for lovers.

Soon after the body was discovered, Stone spoke to detectives, saying he had heard of the murder and wanted to make a statement in order to prove his innocence. He went on to say he had left Ruby outside the Stag Hotel just after 10 p.m. This, officers knew, was a lie: two regulars at the Stag, who knew Ruby, had followed the couple out of the pub and had been behind them as they made their way down the Firs.

It was to be a vital development. Stone's false statement immediately drew attention to him and he was questioned further. Detectives also learned he had been wearing the new blue suit on the night Ruby was murdered, and when it was examined under a microscope, it was found to be a perfect match to the casts made at the murder scene.

Although the suit had been cleaned vigorously around the knees, small grains of soil found under microscopic examination were the same type as the soil around the murder site, and a single piece of fibre found stuck to the lining of Stone's jacket was a perfect match to the slip Ruby had been wearing.

Tried before Lord Chief Justice Hewart at the Old Bailey on 29 June, Stone initially denied any involvement in the murder, but on the second day, he changed his story and confessed that he had accidentally killed Ruby. He claimed that they had gone down 'Lovers' Lane' where they had quarrelled after she refused to leave her fiancé and rekindle their romance. She had then hit him, and in the heat of the moment, he had grabbed her scarf, accidentally choking her.

As they deliberated a verdict, the jury asked the judge for guidance on a point of law. They asked whether Stone was still guilty of murder if he had killed Ruby while attempting to rape her. Told that he was, it took the jury less than half an hour to seal his fate.

64

THE CORONATION DAY MURDER

❖ *Frederick George Murphy, 17 August 1937* ❖

To celebrate the Coronation of King George VI on Wednesday, 12 May 1937, the country was granted a two-day public holiday. Most shops and offices closed for the duration, and when they reopened on the Friday morning, Stanley Wilton, a salesman, had just arrived for work at Harding's furniture store, 22 Islington Green, London, when he was handed a letter by Ethel Marshall, the girlfriend of Frederick Murphy, the odd-job man at the store, which read:

> Don't get frightened. There is a dead woman in the cellar at number 22 and you can believe me Stan, it's nothing to do with me, but you know what the police will say.

Wilton locked the shop and went down to the cellar to investigate. The derelict room was not used by the shop and all was in darkness. Turning on the light, Wilton at once noticed a large tin trunk and a bundle of clothes covered by a royal blue overcoat. He lifted the coat and discovered the body of a woman.

Wilton called the police. PC Wood was the first to arrive, and confirming there was indeed a body in the cellar, he called for assistance. Divisional Detective Inspector Salisbury headed the

Odd-Job Man Told Girl of Discovery

PART of a statement attributed to the accused was quoted as follows--" I did not do her in, but I admit I handled the body "--when Frederick George Murphy appeared at the North London court this week charged with the murder of Rose Field. The woman's body was found covered with paper behind a tin trunk in a cellar beneath a furniture shop in Islington Green. Post-mortem by Sir Bernard Spilsbury showed that death was caused by manual strangulation.

Mr. Gwatkin, appearing for the Director of Public Prosecutions, said that Murphy, who had been employed as an odd job man by Mr. Marsh, a furniture dealer, had a key to the premises where the body was found.

Murphy was told that the shop would be closed on Coronation Day and the following day, and that he would not be required till May 14.

The accused lived with a Mrs. Ethel Marshall in a furnished room in Colebrook-row, Islington.

On May 11, Murphy went with a lorry-load of furniture to Eastbourne, returning at 4-30 a.m. on Coronation Day.

He, the lorry-driver and another man went into a nearby cafe, and afterwards the accused went in the direction of his home.

AT NUMBER 22

On May 14, when the shop opened for business, Murphy was not there. He

Rose Field.

Rosina Field, murdered by Frederick Murphy.
(T.J. Leech Archive)

Frederick Murphy, hanged at Pentonville by Alfred Allen. It was Allen's only senior engagement at the prison and the last time he worked as a hangman.
(T.J. Leech Archive)

murder enquiry and quickly established that the body was that of Rosina Field, a 49-year-old prostitute known as Rosie, and that she had been strangled.

A hunt was launched for 53-year-old Irish born Frederick Murphy, 'Mick' to his friends. Murphy was well-known to the police. He was short and stocky, balding and truculent, with a long criminal record, and in 1933 he had been charged, but acquitted due to lack of evidence, for the murder of prostitute Katherine Peck, who, quite coincidentally, was also known as Rosie.

Murphy was only at liberty for twenty-four hours, during which time he made a failed attempt to hang himself under a railway bridge, and on the following morning, he handed himself in at Poplar police station. He told detectives that he had gone into the furniture store on 13 May to do some cleaning. He said he had panicked when he discovered Rosie's body because, with his past record, he felt he would be blamed for her death.

Detectives had already amassed evidence against Murphy and knew that he was not telling the whole truth. A number of witnesses testified that they had seen Murphy enter the furniture store on Coronation Day in the company of a woman. One witness stated that, although he had not seen the woman's face, he had noticed that she was wearing a vivid blue coat.

With Murphy's admission that he had discovered the body, and witness evidence showing he had been with the woman the last time she was seen alive, he was sent for trial at the Old Bailey at the end of June.

Murphy's alibi was weak and was soon proved to be a pack of lies. The court heard how Murphy had told his girlfriend he had found the body in the cellar and had taken her to the shop to show her the body, telling her he was going to bury it. He had then penned the note, asked her to hand it to his employers, and made plans to flee the area.

After deliberating for less than an hour, the jury found Murphy guilty as charged, and trial judge Lord Chief Justice Hewart asked the prisoner if he had anything to say before sentence was passed. Leaning forward on the front of the dock, Murphy began an angry tirade blaming the detectives for 'stitching him up'. He accused DDI Salisbury of perjury and said that the detective had told Murphy that if he admitted hitting the woman and concealing the body, the charge would be reduced to manslaughter. He then turned to the judge and berated him: 'You could not give a good word for me…you told the jury I was a liar…it's about time committing perjury in this court was put a stop to!'

Murphy's diatribe lasted several minutes, during which time the judge's clerk stood patiently with the black cap in hand waiting to place it on Hewart's wig. Murphy finally stopped to draw breath and the judge signalled for his black cap and sentenced the prisoner to death.

65

SELF FIRST, SELF LAST, SELF ALWAYS

❖ *John Thomas Rodgers, 18 November 1937* ❖

On the afternoon of Wednesday, 25 August 1937, railway steward Ivan Chamberlain left his home in Green Lane, Northwood, Middlesex and reported for duty at Euston station. Chamberlain worked for the LMS railway in the restaurant car, and as the railway operated express services up to the north of the country and into Scotland, he often spent nights away from home. Chamberlain had been married to his 25-year-old wife, Lily, for just over a year, and their home was a one-room apartment adjacent to the Northwood Hotel, where Lily worked as a barmaid. Ivan Chamberlain was not due back in London until the following day. Lily finished her shift that evening and arrived home a few minutes before 11 p.m.

When she failed to turn up for work the next day, one of her colleagues called round to see what the reason was for her absence. The door to the flat was unlocked, and entering, he was horrified to find Lily lying dead on the floor. Clad only in her nightdress, she had been badly beaten, but cause of death was later found to be asphyxiation due to strangulation.

Lily wasn't the only member of staff who had not reported for work on that Thursday morning. Liverpool-born John Rodgers, a barman at the hotel, had been off-duty the previous afternoon, but was due on duty that day for the lunchtime shift. Rodgers had a room at the hotel, but had not spent the night there. Was his disappearance just a coincidence?

A description of Rodgers appeared in newspapers, stating that he was wanted for questioning by detectives in relation to the murder of Lily Chamberlain. One of these reports was seen by someone who knew Rodgers, and spotting him at Golders Green station, he kept him talking while the police were sent for.

Once in custody, Rodgers told detectives he had spent the previous afternoon in Ruislip, but arriving back too late to gain entry into the hotel, he had decided to call on Lily to see if she would put him up. He knocked on the door but received no answer. He saw that the door was slightly ajar so he entered, only to find Lily lying on the floor badly injured, but still alive. He tried to revive her, and in the process got some blood on his clothes. So far, the tale seemed plausible, but the next part was too much for detectives to believe.

Rather than seek medical assistance for his injured colleague, Rodgers claimed he had panicked, believing that police would think him responsible for the attack. Instead, he found some of her husband's clothes and changed into them, leaving the house and fleeing to Southend, disposing of his bloodstained trousers in a wood on the way to the station and throwing his bloodstained shirt off the pier. Asked why he had not tried to summon help, Rodgers replied coldly, 'With me it is self first, self last and self always.'

Far left: *John Thomas Rodgers*. (Author's collection)

Left: *Lily Chamberlain*. (T.J. Leech Archive)

CERTIFIED COPY OF AN ENTRY OF DEATH   GIVEN AT THE **GENERAL REGISTER OFFICE**

Application Number W008332

REGISTRATION DISTRICT			Islington					

1937 DEATH in the Sub-district of Barnsbury   in the Metropolitan Borough of Islington

Columns:—	1	2	3	4	5	6	7	8	9
No.	When and where died	Name and surname	Sex	Age	Occupation	Cause of death	Signature, description and residence of informant	When registered	Signature of registrar

CERTIFIED to be a true copy of an entry in the certified copy of a Register of Deaths in the District above mentioned.

Given at the GENERAL REGISTER OFFICE, under the Seal of the said Office, the ....day of................

DXZ 795713   See note overleaf

CAUTION: THERE ARE OFFENCES RELATING TO FALSIFYING OR ALTERING A CERTIFICATE AND USING OR POSSESSING A FALSE CERTIFICATE ©CROWN COPYRIGHT
WARNING: A CERTIFICATE IS NOT EVIDENCE OF IDENTITY.

Rodgers' death certificate. (R.M. Rodgers)

Throughout his trial at the Old Bailey before Mr Justice Charles, Rodgers maintained his innocence, claiming his version of events was the truth. The prosecution countered this, claiming Rodgers' account was untenable. The jury deliberated for two and a half hours before finding Rodgers guilty of murder.

Rodgers had had a hard life. He had spent time in a borstal for stealing and had several other convictions for theft. It was also discovered, following sentence, that when Rodgers was aged 4, his mother had been charged with the murder of his father. Convicted of manslaughter, she had served five years.

Rodgers had protested his innocence so vehemently that members of his family believed a miscarriage of justice had taken place when he was hanged, and his brother, so disgusted by the English judiciary, emigrated to Canada shortly after the execution. What they didn't know was that a few hours before he was led to the gallows, Rodgers confessed that he had gone to Lily's house, knowing her husband was away and hoping to have sex with her. When she refused his advances, he had beaten her with an iron bar before sexually assaulting and then strangling her.

MISTAKEN IDENTITY

❖ *Udham Singh, 31 July 1940* ❖

On the afternoon of Wednesday, 13 March 1940, a joint meeting between the East India Association and the Royal Central Asian Society took place at the Tudor Rooms, Caxton Hall, Westminster. Led by Brigadier General Sir Percy Sykes, the debate was primarily on the state of affairs in Afghanistan, and beside him on the platform were a number of other distinguished guests, including Sir Michael O'Dwyer, former Lieutenant Governor in the Punjab.

Proceedings concluded shortly after 4 p.m., and as the crowd, which had numbered over 150, began to break into small groups, a well-built, middle-aged Asian man approached the stage down the central passageway, withdrew a revolver and fired six shots in rapid succession into the group on the platform.

Three of the speakers received minor injuries, but O'Dwyer was hit in the heart and kidney and died immediately. The gunman pointed the weapon at the crowd as he headed for the door, shouting, 'Make way!' He was overpowered before he could reach the door.

Identified as Udham Singh, a 37-year-old Sikh extremist, the gunman gave his address as Mornington Crescent. When Singh was questioned as to the motive, detectives realised the shooting had been a case of mistaken identity. Although O'Dwyer had served as Lieutenant Governor of the Punjab during the 1919 Amritsar riots, which had been quelled with fearsome brutality, the general responsible was one General Dyer. Singh had noted Dyer in his diary as O'Dyer, and believed that the speaker was the General.

Sir Michael O'Dwyer – assassinated by Udham Singh in a case of mistaken identity. (T.J. Leech Archive)

Udham Singh. (T.J. Leech Archive)

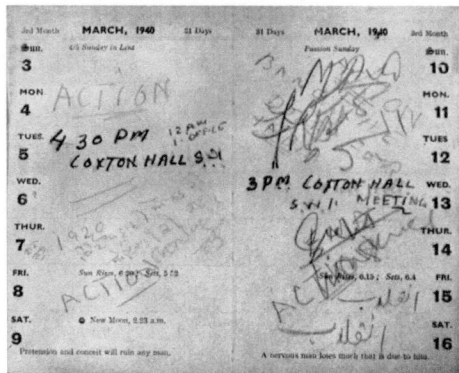

Udham Singh's diary. (Crime Picture Archive)

Singh went on a forty-day hunger strike before his Old Bailey trial in June. His defence was that the shootings were accidental and that his intention had been to fire the gun at the ceiling, in order to frighten those in attendance. The testimony of the arresting officer, that Singh had said, 'Only one dead? I thought I could have got more,' and the fact he had fired six shots and made six hits, destroyed his defence.

The case bore many similarities to that of Madar Lal Dhingra in 1909 (see Chapter 12), and like Dhingra, Singh paid with his life on the scaffold. The hangman was Stanley Cross, who was making his debut as chief executioner. It was noted on the official record of execution that Cross seemed incapable of working out the drop, and although he planned to give a drop of 7ft 1in, when it was measured an hour after the execution, it was shown that Singh had received a drop of just 6ft 6½ ins.

67

OPERATION SEA LION (1)

❖ *Carl Meier & Jose Waldburg, 10 December 1940* ❖

'We are divided from England by a ditch just 37km wide and we are not even able to get to know what is happening there!' declared Adolf Hitler, shortly after the commencement of the Second World War. During the summer of 1940, under the code name 'Operation Sea Lion', Germany began to formulate plans to invade the British Isles. The main purpose was to test the lie of the land before a fully-fledged assault was mounted, and so a number of low-grade agents were sent with the primary task of amassing and reporting back any information that might facilitate the invasion.

The spies selected had been coerced into working for the German Intelligence (*Abwehr*), normally after having committed some indiscretion that had brought them to the attention of the authorities. With just a few hours of training, they were likely to last only a short time in the field, but the mission would serve several purposes. For one, it would gauge the strength of the British counter-espionage teams, and any information sent back was better than none at all. With reassurances that they would be rescued during the forthcoming invasion, the spies set out in a small fishing boat for the Kent coast under the escort of two German minesweepers. The boat contained four would-be agents; three Dutch and one German.

In the early hours of 3 September, they transferred to two small dinghies and set off in pairs for the English coast. In their possession they had a wireless set and an elementary cipher system. The first pair landed near Dymchurch before dawn and made their way inland. Their boat was soon spotted by members of the Somerset Light Infantry who were patrolling the coastline, alert to the threat of an invasion. A hundred yards further along the beach, they found a figure crouching in the reeds. He gave his name as Charles van den Kieboom, a 25-year-old Dutchman. Keiboom had a Japanese mother and had marked oriental features. He claimed he was a refugee and that he had rowed to England, having fled the Nazis in his homeland. His story was initially accepted and he was taken in for further questioning.

A short time later, soldiers made another discovery on the beach. First, they picked up another Dutchman hiding in the bushes. He gave his name as Sjoerd Pons, also claiming to be a refugee, and as before, his story was accepted, only to be seriously questioned later, when, further along the beach, a suitcase containing a wireless and battery cells convinced the authorities the two men were spies.

The other pair fared marginally better. At around 10 a.m., a man in his mid-20s entered a public house at Lydd and ordered a glass of cider. The landlady was suspicious that a young man would be ignorant of the strict English licensing laws and alerted her husband, who immediately contacted the police. The man was duly questioned and asked for his permit pass, as Lydd was in a prohibited area and access in was strictly monitored. Unable to produce the document, he was taken into custody where he gave his name as Carl Meier and, as the others had, claimed he was a Dutch refugee.

The fourth member of the party, 25-year-old Jose Waldburg, the only German and a professional spy with two years' training, stayed at large a further twenty-four hours, and during that time he sent three messages back to his controllers. In French, the first message read:

ARRIVED SAFELY. DOCUMENT DESTROYED. ENGLISH PATROL 200 METRES FROM COAST BEACH WITH BROWN NETS AND RAILWAY SLEEPERS AT A DISTANCE OF 50 METRES. NO MINES AND FEW SOLDIERS. UNFINISHED BLOCKHOUSE NEW ROAD. WALDBERG.

A second message was sent a few hours later:

MEIER PRISONER ENGLISH POLICE SEARCHING FOR ME. AM CORNERED SITUATION DIFFICULT I CAN RESIST THIRST UNTIL SATURDAY IF I AM TO RESIST SEND AEROPLANES WEDNESDAY EVENING 11 O'CLOCK AM 3KM NORTH ARRIVAL LONG LIVE GERMANY. WALDBERG.

Spy Jose Waldberg. (T.J. Leech Archive)

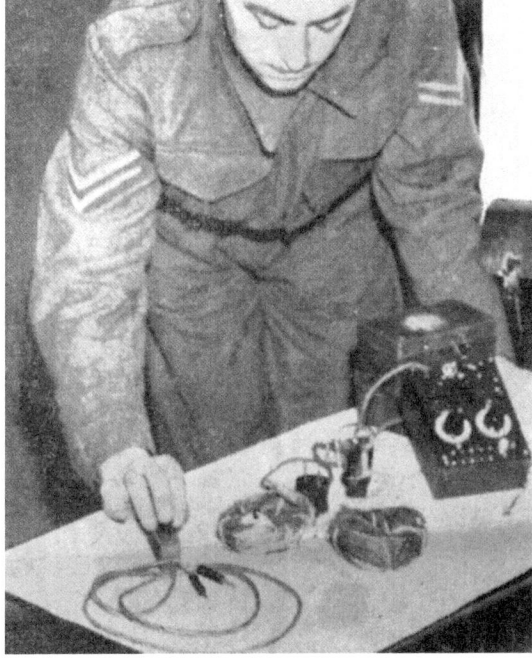

Waldberg's radio. (TNA:PRO)

A third message again repeated much of the second, but claimed there were sounds of machineguns near the 'reservoir painted red.' Waldberg was taken into custody, where he was confronted with the messages that had been intercepted and charged with treachery.

Tried at the Old Bailey before Mr Justice Wrottersley in November, Keiboom and Pons both vigorously protested their innocence and claimed they had only carried out the mission in order to escape the Nazis. Meier admitted he had been lured into spying with the promise of large financial inducements; Waldberg claimed he was actually French and had been blackmailed into carrying out the mission, as the Germans were holding his family hostage.

The arrests and subsequent trial had been held 'in camera' (in secret) so that the Germans would not be alerted to their capture, but the failure to receive any communication beyond the three messages sent by Waldberg would surely have alerted them.

Much to the surprise of the prosecution, Pons was acquitted, only to be re-arrested as an illegal alien and detained; the other three were found guilty and sentenced to death. Neither Meier nor Waldberg appealed against conviction and were hanged side by side three weeks later.

68

OPERATION SEA LION (2)

❖ *Charles van den Kieboom, 17 December 1940* ❖

Having been convicted at the Old Bailey alongside Meier and Waldberg (Chapter 67), Kieboom launched an appeal on the grounds that he was blackmailed into spying, but it was quickly dismissed with the panel claiming it was the most obvious excuse for an espionage charge.

Like the first two spies executed one week earlier, he was hanged by Stanley Cross, now carrying out his third execution, and as with the other two, his skill was called into question when it was noted he had trouble working out drops. Cross never officiated as a chief executioner again.

69

THE FIRE OF THE UNDERWORLD

❖ *Antonio Mancini, 31 October 1941* ❖

In the spring of 1941, as the Battle of Britain was being fought in the skies high above the capital, down in the seedy streets of Soho, another battle raged. Rival gangs with names such as the Italian Mob, the Hoxton Gang, the Elephant Mob and the St Pancras Boys all fought for control of the 'spielers' and lucrative gaming clubs.

The haunt of the Italian Mob was the Palm Beach Club, a small basement club in Wardour Street, and it was on the doorstep of this club on 20 April 1941 that a disturbance broke out between members of the Hoxton Gang and the doorman at the club, Pat Crowley. Hoxton's Teddy Fletcher was identified by club manager, Antonio Mancini, and promptly barred from the premises. As he walked away, he made threats to Mancini.

Gangster Antonio 'Babe' Mancini. The first man to be hanged by Albert Pierrepoint. (Author's collection)

Albert Pierrepoint made his debut as chief executioner at Pentonville on 31 October 1941. (Frank McKue)

Upstairs at the Palm Beach Club, Soho, where Harry Distleman was stabbed to death. (TNA:PRO)

Thirty-nine-year-old Antonio Mancini, an Italian immigrant known to his friends as 'Babe' or 'Baby-face', laughed off the threats. He was a well-known underworld tough, as much in demand for his skills with a razor and his fists as he was for his managerial skills, and being used to irate threats from the rival gangs, he often carried a knife, mainly for his own protection.

On the evening of Wednesday, 31 April, Fletcher and several of his friends returned to Wardour Street, but instead of heading to the basement, they took the stairs to a billiard club on the top floor. A fight soon broke out, which was quickly broken up, but in the early hours of the following morning, another disturbance erupted. Hearing that another fight was taking place, Mancini rushed upstairs, where he discovered several of the Hoxton Gang trading punches with some of Mancini's Italian friends. No sooner had he entered the room than he heard a shout from behind him: 'There's Babe – let's get him.'

Pulling out his knife, Mancini confronted Teddy Fletcher and 36-year-old Harry Distleman, known as 'Scarface'. In the fierce fight that ensued, snooker cues, billiard balls, chairs, knives and broken bottles were all used. Face-to-face with the knife-wielding Mancini, Fletcher was stabbed in the wrist, while Distleman received a 5in deep wound under his left armpit and slumped to the ground, fatally wounded. 'I'm stabbed – Babe's done it!' he cried with his final breath.

Following his arrest, Mancini claimed the killing was self-defence, but over forty witnesses testified to Mancini's rage during the fight, claiming he went berserk when attacked. At the Old Bailey on 4 July before Justice MacNaughton, two other men were convicted of attempted murder, while Mancini alone was convicted of murder and sentenced to death.

Mancini launched an appeal, claiming the judge had misdirected the jury with regards to a plea of manslaughter, but it was dismissed on the grounds that the extreme level of violence used prevented any chance of a manslaughter verdict. With the appeal dismissed, Mancini was given leave to appeal to the House of Lords. This second appeal was likewise dismissed, and he was returned to the death cell to await execution.

Mancini was the first person hanged by executioner Albert Pierrepoint. 'Cheerio,' he whispered, as the hangman placed the noose around his neck. Viewing the Italian's body in the prison mortuary following execution, Chief Inspector Arthur Thorp, who had been threatened by a number of Mancini's friends if he was hanged, observed that the killer had 'played too long and too hard with the fire of the underworld.'

70

BENEATH THE FLAGSTONES

❖ *Lionel Rupert Nathan Watson, 12 November 1941* ❖

Looking out of her upstairs window in the spring of 1941, Mrs Bound saw her neighbour digging away in his shirtsleeves in the garden below. 'I suppose you are digging for victory, Lionel,' she called out, jokingly. Having been unaware he had an audience up to that moment, the man put down his spade and wiped his brow. 'No, not this time,' he replied. 'I'm just burying some rubbish.'

Mrs Bound was fond of the family who had taken the downstairs flat at 9 Goring Way, Greenford, especially the little girl, Eileen, whom she often saw playing in the garden. It was odd, Mrs Bound had thought, that the child's mother, Phyllis, should have taken the child to Scotland without telling her, but people often did things on the spur of the moment during the Blitz. She had questioned the husband, 30-year-old Lionel Rupert Nathan Watson, about their sudden disappearance, but he assured her they were safe and well and would be returning soon.

Several weeks passed, and as the warmer weather arrived, a strange smell became obvious in the back garden. It seemed to be coming from beneath the flagstones near the coal shed, where Watson had been digging. A day or so later, Mrs Bound saw Watson enter the garden with a watering can, but instead of tending to the flowers, he glanced around before emptying the contents over the flagstones. Strangely, the liquid that came out of the can had a whitish colour and looked more like disinfectant than water.

On the morning of 30 June, Mrs Bound told a neighbour about the strange smell and what she had seen, and he decided to investigate. He entered the garden, raised the flagstones and poked around with a stick. Scraping away an inch of loose soil, he soon uncovered what looked like human flesh.

Police officers were called to Goring Way, and soon confirmed that two bodies were beneath the flagstones, covered in a white powder and smelling strongly of disinfectant. As the bodies were removed for examination by pathologist Sir Bernard Spilsbury, detectives learned that Watson worked as a bakelite moulder at Messrs Hoovers' factory in Perivale, and at 7 a.m. on the following morning, he was questioned at work.

Watson claimed responsibility for disposing of the bodies, but denied murder. He said he had met 28-year-old Phyllis Crocker when she had started working at the Perivale factory. Although he was married with four children of his own, Watson was at the time living apart from his wife, and he began an affair with Phyllis.

They took a flat in Greenford, where they lived with Phyllis's baby daughter, Eileen. Phyllis soon began to pester him to get married however, and he did so, bigamously, at the end of 1940. He claimed that on 19 May 1941, Phyllis had been complaining of headaches, and when he had arrived home from work on the following day, he found both her and the baby dead. He had panicked because if he went to the police, his bigamous marriage would be discovered and he would go to prison. Instead, he decided to bury the bodies in the garden and tell neighbours that Phyllis and her daughter had gone to Scotland. The post-mortem, however, told a very different tale. Both bodies contained cyanide, and Watson was known to have had access to sodium cyanide through his work in the bakelite factory.

At his Old Bailey trial, Watson claimed that Phyllis must have killed her child before committing suicide and that he had had no reason to commit murder. The prosecution provided the motive, maintaining that Watson had recently been making advances on a 17-year-old girl at the factory, showering her with gifts of money and jewellery, all belonging to Phyllis Crocker. They also revealed that the dead woman had been pregnant and suggested that Watson had killed her rather than face the extra responsibilities of fatherhood, now that he had found a new lover. This was enough for the jury to decide that Watson had killed his lover and her child simply to get them out of the way, and Mr Justice Cassels sentenced him to death.

71

'OLD MOULES'

❖ *Samuel Dashwood & George Silverosa, 10 September 1942* ❖

The two men loitered on the street corner and waited. Thursday was half-day closing in Shoreditch and other parts of the East End, and as the clock struck 1 p.m., the old man exited his shop and made to pull down the shutters.

Twenty-two-year-old George Silverosa, a machinist from Pitsea, spoke first: 'Are you game?' The other man, Sam Dashwood, looked across at the old man struggling with the shutter, 'Alright, but no violence.'

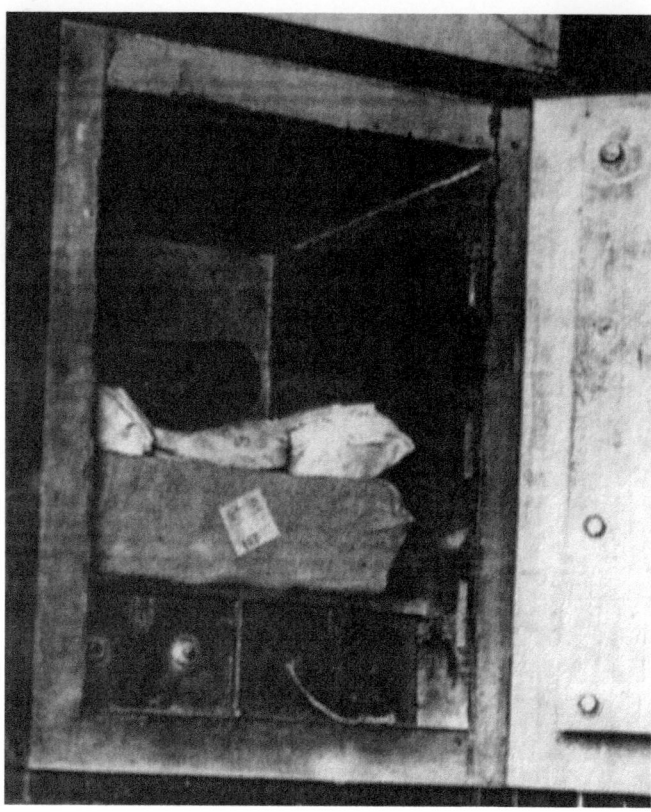

Left: *The safe where police found the tell-tale palm print.* (T.J. Leech Archive)

Below left: *Sam Dashwood.* (Author's collection)

Below right: *George Silverosa. Two days before his execution he made a failed attempt to murder his guards.* (Author's collection)

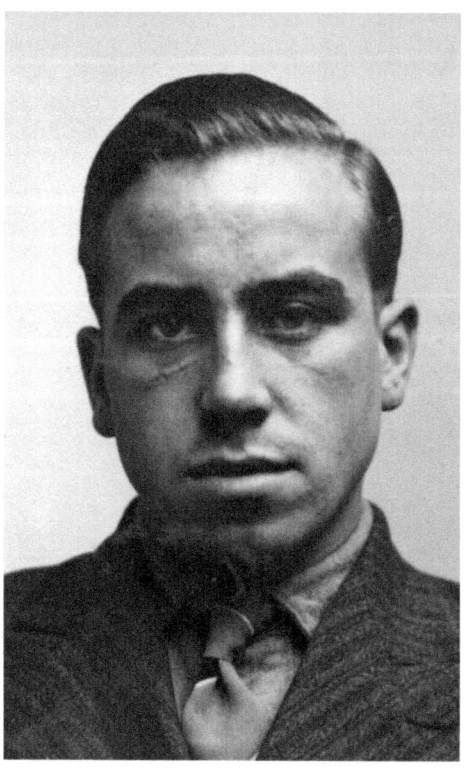

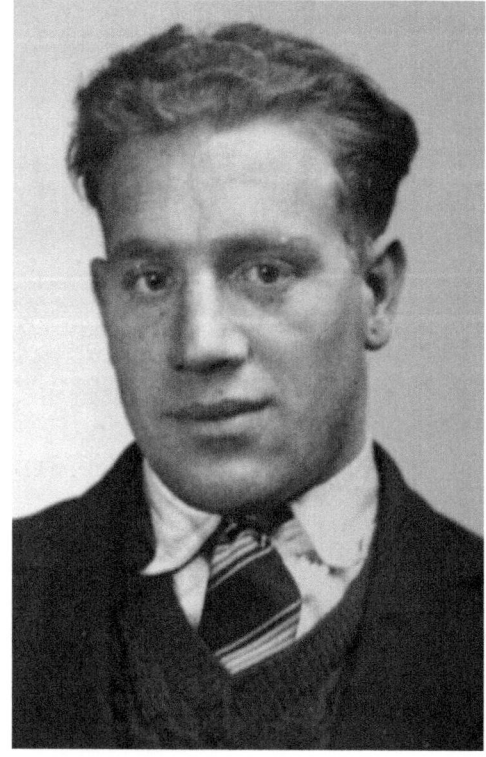

Leonard Moules had run the pawnbroker's shop in Shoreditch for as long as anyone could remember. Known locally as 'Old Moules', he was found unconscious in the basement of his shop on the afternoon of Thursday, 30 April 1942. He had severe injuries to his head and face, evidently inflicted by some blunt instrument, which was later revealed to be the handle of a gun. For eight days police sat by his bedside, awaiting any clue the old man might give them, but on Saturday, 9 May he died without regaining consciousness.

Detectives examining the scene of the attack had not found a single rogue fingerprint, but did find a palm print on the inside of the open safe. They reasoned that the killers were probably local men, and organised a detailed search of the maze of streets within a few miles of Hackney Road. After several false leads, they finally made a breakthrough when, on 15 May, a soldier told police he had overheard two men talking in a café around the time of the murder and that one had been carrying a gun. He gave their names as Sam and George. Further enquires led police to Silverosa, who made a statement:

'The man who was with me, whose name I now know as Sam Dashwood, or Glen, went in first and I followed. I closed the door and, as I turned round, I saw the old man falling down. I didn't see Sam strike him, but I surmised what he had done... I gave Sammy £20. Sammy kept the rings, which he sold, and I had my wages out of it – about £50 or £60.'

Dashwood was taken in for questioning and told police a slightly different tale. He said that Silverosa had gone in first and had struggled with the old man. The dog had started barking so Dashwood had battered it over the head. Seeing Old Moules about to blow a whistle, Silverosa had then struck him on the head with the butt of the gun.

They were tried side by side in July before Mr Justice Wrottersley. Neither chose to give evidence on his own behalf nor to go into the witness box, but on the third day of the trial, with evidence mounting against them, Dashwood shocked those assembled in the Old Bailey by dismissing his defence and asking for fresh counsel.

After a short recess, the request was refused, so Dashwood opted to defend himself. It was to no avail and, although it was shown that only Dashwood had used violence, on the following day both were jointly convicted and sentenced to death. 'Hard luck, George,' a friend shouted from the gallery. 'Don't worry,' he replied, as he was led from the dock.

Dashwood lodged an appeal on the grounds that his dismissal of his counsel during a murder trial proved that he must be insane. He asked for a retrial, but this was refused as it would have set a precedent.

Dashwood and Silverosa were two ex-borstal boys, both with a history of theft and violence. Two days before he was due to hang, Silverosa asked warders for permission to burn some private papers in the incinerator. This request was granted, but as he disposed of the last letter, Silverosa picked up the metal poker and turned on his guards, injuring both of them. He was overpowered and returned to his cell, where he stayed under maximum security until the following Thursday morning, when he made his last walk to the gallows alongside his partner in crime.

72

THE DESERTER

❖ *William Henry Turner, 24 March 1943* ❖

The stranger knocked on the door and asked for a room for the night. Rose Cook often took in lodgers at her rather grandly named home, Rookery House, at Abbeygate, Colchester, and so the request, late as it was, on the night of Tuesday, 29 December 1942, was not that unusual.

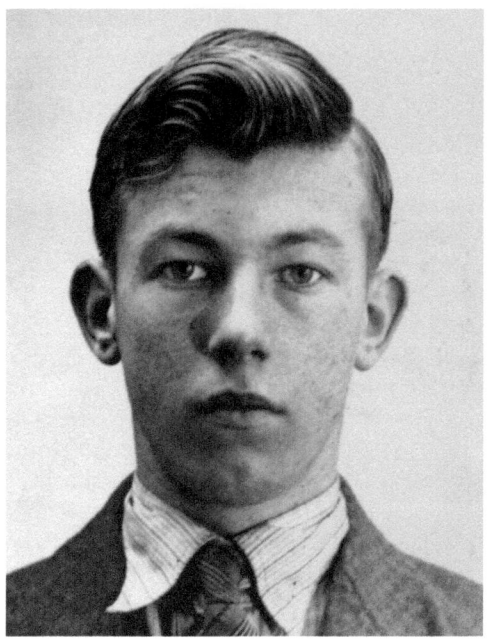 

Nineteen-year-old gang leader and deserter William Turner. (Author's collection)

Audley Road, Colchester, where Elizabeth Wade was strangled. (Author's collection)

The young soldier was wearing a corporal's uniform, and after agreeing on a price, he was shown to Rose's son's room on the upper floor. He was not asked, nor did he volunteer his name.

He left the next day in the early afternoon, and when Rose went to clean the room, she found that the young soldier had forced a lock on the wardrobe and stolen a number of her son's clothes. Rose Cook reported the theft to the local police and cursed herself for not finding out the identity of the thief.

Now sporting civilian clothes, the thief moved across town and booked a room at 48 North Hill, run by Ida Ruth Walford. He gave his name as Corporal Swann and he stayed until Saturday, 2 January 1943. Checking out, he again left with items that didn't belong to him, having forced open a suitcase in the room he had lodged. Mrs Walford called the police and they arrived sharply, while 'Corporal Swann' was still in the area.

Identified as Private William Turner, a 19-year-old Doncaster-born ex-borstal boy and army deserter from the Infantry Corps, he was charged with theft from both addresses in Colchester, and when searched, he was found to be carrying a large quantity of money.

Asked to explain the money, Turner immediately made a confession to a murder the police had as yet to discover. He told them he had strangled a woman at Audley Road, and when police went to investigate, they found the body of 82-year-old Elizabeth Wade, just as Turner had described.

His first trial at the Chelmsford Assizes was soon dissolved when one of the jury members made it clear that he opposed capital punishment. At his second trial, before Mr Justice Asquith, Turner offered a plea of guilty, which he later withdrew.

Turner sported a distinctive tattoo on his hand that marked him as the leader of the 'Five-Star Gang,' worn as a badge of his toughness and gangsterism. He had joined the army in November, but had absconded from the training unit on 28 December 1942, taking a revolver and ammunition.

According to Turner, he had been walking the streets looking for an easy target to rob. Arriving outside 19 Audley Road, he knocked, and when the old lady opened the door, he asked for a cup of tea. She kindly granted his request, and in return, he offered to do some gardening for her. After a short time she called him in, and, once in the kitchen, he grabbed her by the neck as she stood in front of the sink. She immediately went limp in his arms, whereupon he carried her into another room and laid her down on the floor. Before he had chance to search the house for valuables, a visitor had called asking for the old lady. Turner was able to bluff the caller into believing the lady was out, but when he returned to where he had left the old lady, he was shocked to find she was no longer breathing. He hid the body underneath a bed, before stealing some money and leaving.

Turner's counsel pressed for a verdict of manslaughter, as he had not intended to commit murder, and it was only because the old lady was so frail that his assault on her had proved fatal. Nevertheless, the old lady had died at his hands, and although the jury strongly recommended mercy on account of his youth, it did not save him from the gallows.

73

THE SUPREME FATALIST

❖ *Gerald Elphinstone Roe, 3 August 1943* ❖

Nigel Arnold was awakened by the screams. He glanced at his alarm clock and saw it was almost 6.50 a.m. on Monday, 17 May 1943. He got out of bed, looked through the window, and in the house across the road, he saw the figure of a woman in blue pyjamas being pulled about by a man whom he could not see clearly. Both figures disappeared, and with no further noise coming from the house, he assumed it had been a lovers' tiff and went back to bed.

Elizabeth Canfield was on her daily round delivering milk when she called at 9 Greenhill Park, Barnet. She was due to collect some money, and depositing the milk on the doorstep, she knocked on the door. Receiving no reply, she was about to walk back up the path when she was struck by the smell of gas. As Elizabeth opened the letterbox, the smell became much stronger, so she hurried up the street and sought out a policeman.

PC Warner accompanied the woman back to the house, and failing to rouse the occupants and being unable to force the front door, he went round the back and climbed through the kitchen window. On the kitchen floor was the body of a woman dressed in blue pyjamas. Warner climbed back out of the window, and looking down the street, he could see that the house across the way, no. 4, had a telephone line. From there he phoned for an ambulance and notified the station.

The owner of no. 4 was Nigel Arnold, the man who had heard the screams earlier that morning, and together they returned to the house, forced entry through the patio doors and switched off the gas stove. Arnold told the officer he recognised the woman as Elsie Roe and that a short time earlier, he had noticed her husband, Gerald, leaving the house, carrying two suitcases. He also told the policeman about the screams he had heard a few hours before.

Pathologist Keith Simpson carried out the post-mortem. He found that the woman had injuries to the head, several of which she had sustained as she lay on the floor. The cause of death, however, was carbon monoxide poisoning, and he estimated the time of death at 8 a.m.

Elsie's husband, a 43-year-old Indian-born engineer, was traced to Hampshire, where he was being billeted while engaged in war work with the Government Signals research department. Interviewed a few hours later, he was found to have bloodstains on his clothing. Unable to offer a satisfactory explanation for the bloodstains, he was placed under arrest and later charged with his wife's murder.

At his trial before Mr Justice Humphries at Hertfordshire Assizes in June – the first murder trial at Hertford in almost forty years – Roe denied any involvement in the death of his wife.

Following his arrest, he made a statement in which he said he had left the house at 8.45 a.m. on the morning of the murder, after taking Elsie a cup of tea. Prosecution evidence that a witness had heard screams and seen a struggle, supported by the pathologist's view that death had taken place approximately 45 minutes before Roe claimed he had left the house, destroyed his defence.

Roe refused to give any explanation or speak on his behalf in court, other than to offer a plea of insanity on the grounds of hereditary mental illness. Although it was shown that his mother had been an in-patient at an asylum, she had never been formally certified, and there was nothing to show it was hereditary.

Following conviction, Roe, described by one prison official as a supreme fatalist on account of his refusal to speak in court, appealed on the grounds that the gas stove may have been turned on accidentally, and as this was the actual cause of death, he should be found guilty only of manslaughter. Dismissing the appeal, the panel stated that while there was no proof that Roe had been the one to turn the stove on, the physical injuries to his wife, which Roe admitted inflicting, had been fundamental to her death and it was therefore immaterial who turned the gas on, and whether or not it had been deliberate.

74

THE OLD FLAME

❖ *Charles William Koopman, 15 December 1943* ❖

Dear Ernie. I am sorry to do this to you and please God forgive me, but your wife is very immoral. We are going the same way. We don't know you personally but we know your heart. When you get over the shock you will be better off.

The anonymous note on the armchair was short and to the point. Twenty-two-year-old Gladys Lavinia Brewer's neighbours suspected something was amiss when she had failed to draw her blackout curtains, and as morning turned into afternoon with still no stirring and no signs of Gladys and her 2-year-old daughter, Shirley, the police were called in. Forcing entry to the house on Grove Place, Ealing, officers found the bodies of Gladys and Shirley on the living room floor. They had been battered to death with a hammer, and lying beside the bodies was the note addressed to Gladys' husband, Ernie Brewer, who was serving overseas in the Navy.

Detectives soon figured out who they were looking for. One of the bodies was lying on an RAF tunic, which suggested the killer may have been an airman. This led police to Charles Koopman, a 22-year-old engineer of Hanwell.

Koopman had received his call-up papers on 23 August 1943, and when informed he would be posted to Bridlington in Yorkshire for his basic training, he deserted from his unit. Prior to his enlistment, Koopman and his wife, Patricia, had handed in their tenancy agreement and sold all their furniture, living off the proceeds. With their money spent and nowhere to hide, Koopman had contacted Gladys Brewer, an old flame whom he knew as 'Vini'. She allowed Koopman and his wife to share her apartment, but soon began to regret her offer.

On 8 September, after spending the night drinking with his wife, Koopman returned to the house, where he began teasing Gladys by turning the gas light up and down, and they began to quarrel. Koopman then picked up a hammer and battered her about the head, before killing the child in the same manner. He then fled the house with his wife, taking whatever jewellery and money they could find. The Koopmans were arrested in Slough, and, initially, both were charged with murder. Koopman maintained from the start that his wife had not been involved, and charges against her were dropped.

At his trial before Mr Justice Asquith at the Old Bailey on 27 October, Koopman admitted the attack, but claimed he was insane at the time. He admitted he had been teasing Gladys by turning down the gas when she was trying to read. She had remonstrated with him and he then picked up the hammer, intending to frighten her. He claimed that before he knew it, he had battered her to death, his wife finally stopping him from inflicting further injuries. It seems clear that Patricia Koopman did nothing, however, to stop her husband from going into the child's bedroom when he heard her crying. Koopman coldly told the court he had killed Shirley because he didn't think she should be without her mother.

Koopman's defence was insanity on three points: firstly, that he had had a reaction to an inoculation given when he received his RAF call up; secondly, that he was drunk at the time; and thirdly, that he was suffering from anxiety brought on by the fact that he was a deserter from the army.

Described as an ill-tempered and aggressive man, Koopman was sentenced to death, and this was despite the somewhat surprising protests of a group calling itself the 'Opponents of Compulsory Vaccinations,' which petitioned for a reprieve on his behalf, believing the effects of the vaccine had led him to commit the brutal double murder.

75

FOR THIRTY SHILLINGS

❖ *Christos Georghiou, 2 February 1944* ❖

Thirty-eight-year-old Christos Georghiou and 43-year-old Savvas Demetriades had been close friends and partners in a café near Cardiff docks. The business had been successful until an incident in early 1943, when Georghiou caught Demetriades slipping money into his pocket instead of putting it in the till. Although it was only 30s, it caused a fearsome argument, and despite the fact that the money was repaid, it was the end of the friendship, and the partnership dissolved.

The rift between the two increased following a quarrel over a woman, when Demetriades invited a lady Georghiou was enamoured with to a party. As Demetriades already had a girlfriend, he had done it primarily to antagonise Georghiou.

In April 1943, Georghiou left Cardiff and moved to London, and on 24 October, Demetriades travelled to London when a friend needed bail arranging. He contacted a friend, Nicola Costas, who owned a café, and Costas offered him the use of his spare room. Later that night, they called into a Soho café, where Demetriades and Georghiou met up for the first time. They did not speak to each other, and when Demetriades and his friend went to another café on Charlotte Street, Georghiou followed them there. Again they refused to speak to each other.

On the following afternoon, Demetriades called on Christos Costa, who owned a café on Dean Street, and after visiting the Old Bailey to arrange the bail for a friend, they returned to Soho. At 3 p.m., as they entered Old Compton Street, a hand appeared on Demetriades' shoulder and pushed him. He fell to the ground, and as he tried to get to his feet, the assailant stabbed him three times in the chest. Georghiou was arrested in Wealdstone and witnesses picked him out from an identity parade.

On 10 December, he appeared before Mr Justice Hilbery at the Old Bailey. Georghiou claimed to have no memory of the crime, declaring that he had been drinking in a number of public houses until 2.45 p.m. When he left the last pub, he was very drunk indeed, and the next thing he remembered was having an argument with someone and being pushed. He had no knowledge of what he did next, until he found himself vomiting in the toilets of the Dominion cinema. Nevertheless the jury believed he was guilty of a wicked murder and returned a guilty verdict.

THE HOLLOW KEYS

❖ *Oswald John Job, 16 March 1944* ❖

Educated at an English public school, Oswald Job had moved to Paris in his mid 20s. Born in Bromley in July 1885, the son of German parents, Job was a British passport holder, and when the Germans occupied France in 1940, he was interned in the St Denis Internment Camp along with other enemy passport holders.

Job soon became friendly with his German guards, and when approached by the German Intelligence services, he immediately offered his services, claiming he had always been sympathetic towards Germany. After three years' internment, the emaciated Job eventually arrived at the British Embassy in Madrid, carrying a Portuguese transit visa. His story seemed to check out, and as he didn't have enough money for passage back to England, he wired his brother, who agreed to act as guarantor for the air tickets.

The British Secret Service had noted Job's request to enter the country and, on arrival, he was interrogated and asked if he was working for the enemy. Three times he denied any involvement and he was allowed on his way. He found a room in Bayswater and soon Postal Censorship noticed the frequent exchange of letters between members of Job's family and former inmates at the St Denis Camp.

MI5 agents now faced a predicament. One of Job's contacts was a known double agent, and if Job was compromised, it could potentially blow their agent's cover, so they needed proof of his espionage activities. His apartment at Bayswater was visited, but a search of his property

INVISIBLE INK TRAITOR
HANGED AT PENTONVILLE
*Came Here in Disguise to Report
on Bomb Damage and Morale*

A German spy, who came to Britain to report on bomb damage and public morale, was hanged at Pentonville Prison to-day.

He was a British subject, Oswald (or Oscar) John Job, born in London of German parents. Secret writing material hidden in the hollows of keys was found on him. He is the 14th spy to be executed in Britain during this war.
The Home Office announce-

Newspaper headline announcing the execution of Oswald Job.
(T.J. Leech Archive)

Oswald John Job. (T.J. Leech Archive)

failed to unearth any evidence against him. Just as they were preparing to depart, a sharp-eyed officer spied a bunch of keys belonging to Job. For a 58-year-old man with no employment, and a small apartment with few doors requiring keys, the bunch had far more keys than necessary.

The keys were examined and a number were found to be hollow and to contain invisible ink crystals. Faced with this evidence, Job confessed under interrogation and claimed he had accepted the mission from the Germans as a way to escape internment.

Before Mr Justice Stable on 24 January 1944, Job reiterated that he had only promised to help the Germans in order to gain his freedom, but he could not adequately explain why he had failed to notify the authorities on arrival into the country, nor why he had then sent numerous letters back to his controllers at St Denis.

77

POUR DECOURAGER LES AUTRES

❖ *Pierre Richard Charles Neukermans, 23 June 1944* ❖

Pierre Richard Charles Neukermans was a 28-year-old former officer, invalided out of the Belgian Army in 1938. Following the German invasion of Belgium, Neukermans returned to Brussels and worked in his father-in-law's business, supplementing his income by selling food on the black market.

He was introduced to a German agent by a friend and readily agreed to work for the enemy. After receiving training, he landed in England on 16 July 1943, posing as a refugee. He said he had escaped from German occupied territory and wished to join the Free Belgian Army which was based in England. After questioning, Neukermans was allowed entry and in due course, contacted the Free Belgian authorities. Having been found to be medically unfit for military service, however, he gained employment in their government offices.

On 2 February 1944, British agents assigned the duty of monitoring immigrants, paid Neukermans a visit. Information had come into their possession that the people he had named as helping him escape from Belgium were known collaborators, and after interrogation, Neukermans admitted he had sent letters out of the country detailing convoy movements from England to the Belgian Congo.

Neukermans was tried before Mr Justice MacNaughten. The evidence against him was conclusive, and although he offered the defence that he was insane, he was convicted and hanged almost a year after landing in England. D-Day had now passed and the allies were in the ascendancy, so the authorities were quite free in releasing the details of Neukermans' arrest, trial and execution – as a warning to other agents. He was hanged '*pour decourager les autres*': to discourage others.

Pierre Neukermans. (Author's collection)

THE RELUCTANT SPY

❖ *Joseph Jan Van Hove, 12 July 1944* ❖

Joseph Jan van Hove was a 27-year-old Belgian waiter. Before the war, he had volunteered for the Belgian Army, but had been discharged when he developed a double hernia. In 1939 he moved to France, but returned to Belgium when France fell under German occupancy.

Van Hove had not been home long before he became involved in the black market. His activities brought him to the attention of the police in Antwerp, who issued a warrant for his arrest, but through a collaborator friend he obtained the help of the German invaders to avoid arrest. Soon he was recruited to work as an informer in northern France, reporting back the names of any of the Belgian workers on the new airfields who had sympathies with the Resistance.

He so impressed the Germans with his ruthless betrayal of fellow countrymen, that he was selected for training as an enemy agent and detailed to be sent to England. Following rudimentary training, in the middle of 1942 he was tasked with entering England by plane from Switzerland, only to be turned back at the Swiss border.

On his return to Belgium, the German intelligence services devised another plan. His new mission was to gain passage on a German merchant vessel to Sweden, where he would jump ship at Stockholm and present himself to the British authorities. Achieving the first stage of his mission, he explained to the authorities that he had deserted from the German ship and wished to travel to England to re-enlist in the Belgian Army.

Although suspecting he was a spy, the authorities allowed him to stay in Stockholm for several months, where he reported information on ship movements back to the Germans. In early February 1944, he secured a seat on a flight to Leuchars, in Scotland, where he was immediately detained.

Charged with treachery, Van Hove was taken to London for questioning. There he soon confessed that his mission was to spy for the Germans and he produced a matchstick and converted razor handle that contained ingredients for secret writing. Tried before Mr Justice Hallett at the Old Bailey on 23 May, his defence was that he had reluctantly travelled to Britain, with no intention of spying and fully intending to sign up with the Belgian Army.

Obviously, if this were true and he had not intended to spy, Van Hove could have surrendered himself on arrival rather than undergo several days of interrogation before finally confessing. This, together with the fact that he had been under surveillance in Sweden for some time, made it clear that he was guilty. He was convicted after a two-day trial and became the last foreigner in Britain to be executed for treachery.

79

IN SEARCH OF EXCITEMENT

❖ *Karl Gustav Hulten, 8 March 1945* ❖

Elizabeth Jones had moved to London in search of excitement. At 16-years-old, she married a soldier, but she walked out after he struck her during a quarrel on their wedding day. Two months later, in January 1943, she decided to leave her native South Wales and seek her

Elizabeth Jones. (Crime Picture Archive)

American soldier Karl Hulten. (Author's collection)

fortune in London. She soon found a room in Hammersmith and took a job in a seedy strip club in Soho, working as a dance hostess and striptease artiste under the name 'Georgina'.

In October 1944, she was introduced to Swedish-born American solder, Karl Hulten, a 22-year-old paratrooper, who, for the last six weeks, had been absent without leave from his unit. He told her his name was Ricky, and despite already having a steady girlfriend in London, Hulten was captivated by the vivacious Jones and asked her out. She agreed to meet that night, 3 October, outside a cinema, but thinking Hulten had stood her up, she set off back to her lodgings when a ten-wheel American truck pulled up and the driver told her to jump in.

Hulten told her the truck was stolen, and that back home in America he had been a 'Chicago Gangster'. It didn't take her long to realise that Hulten could give her the excitement she craved. They met up on the following evening and committed their first crime together when they robbed a girl near Reading. The next day, again at Reading, Hulten pulled out a gun during a robbery and they also robbed another young girl near Windsor.

In the early hours of 7 October, they flagged down a cab and asked the driver, George Heath, to take them to Chiswick. As Heath turned to collect his fare, Hulten drew his gun and fired once, wounding the driver in the chest. Hulten threatened Heath and told him to move across to the passenger seat. As the driver did so, Hulten took his place and they set out towards Staines. Heath died from his injuries as they drove, so they dumped his body in a ditch and returned to London in the stolen cab.

Heath's body was discovered later that morning. A description of his stolen cab was issued, and two days later, a police officer spotted it parked at Hammersmith. He called for backup and they watched and waited. At 9 p.m. that night, Hulten emerged from the house of his other girlfriend, and as soon as he climbed into the cab, he was placed under arrest.

He gave his name as Second Lieutenant Richard Allen of the US Army, and claimed he had been using the cab after finding it abandoned outside Newbury. Taken in for questioning, he soon confessed his name was Hulten, and that he was a deserter. Charged with murder, Hulten then told officers about his partner-in-crime, and Elizabeth Jones was picked up for questioning. She made a statement, denying any knowledge of the crime, and was allowed home, only for her to confide to an acquaintance that she had seen Hulten commit the murder. Jones was interviewed again and this time made a full confession, claiming, however, that she had only participated in the crimes because she lived in fear of Hulten. Faced with this information, Hulten responded by stating that if anything, Elizabeth had been the instigator, encouraging him to commit the crimes to give her the excitement she craved.

It was decided to charge both with murder, but first permission had to be sought from the American authorities to charge Hulten in a civil court. As Hulten was being charged along with a British subject, they decided to allow the Crown to prosecute, and on 16 January 1945, the two found themselves before Mr Justice Charles at the Old Bailey.

In what had become known as the 'cleft chin murder' due to the victim's facial features, both Hulten and Jones each tried to blame the other, with Hulten claiming the shooting was accidental and that he had only pulled out the gun at Jones's suggestion. The six-day trial ended when both were found guilty and sentenced to death. 'Lies! Lies! Why don't you tell them the truth?' Jones screamed at Hulten as she was led from the dock.

Much to the anger of Winston Churchill, Elizabeth Jones was reprieved just forty-eight hours before she was to go to the gallows. Her search for excitement cost her eight years of her young life. She was released from gaol in January 1954. For Hulten, there would be no reprieve and he became the last man hanged at Pentonville by veteran executioner Tom Pierrepoint.

80

THE COMRIE CAMP MURDER

❖ *Erich Koenig, Joachim Palme Goltz, Kurt Zuehlsdorf,*
Heinz Brueling & Josef Mertins, 6 October 1945 ❖

Thirty-five-year-old Sergeant Major Wolfgang Rosterg had been taken prisoner-of-war in September 1944. Unlike many he fought beside in the German Army, Rosterg was not a Nazi and had enlisted purely to fight for his country. Following his surrender, he was sent to a camp near Devizes, Wiltshire, where, due to his high standard of education, he soon became the camp interpreter. Rosterg was in the minority at the camp, as large numbers of prisoners were fanatical Nazis, desperate to escape and return to fight for the *Führer*.

In the winter of 1944, a mass breakout was planned, but word of the plan reached the British guards and the plan was thwarted. The ringleaders were removed to high security Comrie Camp in Perthshire, Scotland, and, for some reason never explained, Rosterg was also taken to Comrie. Although no word of the planned escape had come from him, the prisoners began to look for a scapegoat. Rosterg was immediately suspected, tried by kangaroo court and sentenced to death. In the early hours of 23 December 1944, Rosterg was dragged from his bed in Number 4 hut, mercilessly beaten and kicked before being hanged in the hut latrine.

When the body was discovered, a murder investigation was launched, and following information received, eight men were placed on trial for the murder. In addition to Koenig, Palme Goltz, Zuehlsdorf, Brueling and Mertins were Rolf Herzig, Herbart Wunderlich and Hans Klein.

They men were tried at a military court martial held in Kensington Palace Gardens, London, in July. None of the accused denied playing his part in the killing of Rosterg, and all seemed

Assistant hangman Harry Allen's diary recording the execution of the five Germans. (Author's collection)

perplexed as to why they were on trial for it. It was found that under the guidance of Koenig, Zuelsdorf had placed the rope around the man's neck, and the others had all beaten and kicked Rosterg as he was dragged to the latrine to his death. Several witnesses came forward and gave evidence on the proviso that their identities were kept secret for fear of reprisals, either against themselves or against their families back in Germany. On the third day, Hans Klein was acquitted due to a lack of sufficient evidence against him. The remaining seven endured a trial lasting ten days. It concluded with Wunderlich being acquitted, Herzig sentenced to life imprisonment, and the other five all being sentenced to death. They were just 20 years of age, with the exception of Brueling and Mertins, who were a year older.

Details of their executions are confusing, but it is almost certain they were hanged in five single executions. Koenig, the last to go to the gallows, shouted, 'Long live the Fatherland!' as the rope was placed around his neck.

81

THE INNOCENT VICTIM

❖ *Armin Kuehne & Emil Schmittendorf, 16 November 1945* ❖

The murder of 25-year-old Gerhardt Rettig in a PoW camp on the outskirts of Sheffield on 24 March 1945 was, in many ways, identical to the murder of Wolfgang Rosterg at Comrie Camp (see Chapter 80), just a few months earlier. Like Rosterg, Rettig was a regular German soldier, with little in common with the many 'Nazi' prisoners in the camp, and as in the previous case, it was the discovery of an escape tunnel that led to Rettig being killed by fellow inmates.

When a search made by guards unearthed the tunnel, inmates believed they had known exactly where to look and suspected that someone had tipped them off. Rettig had been seen on the previous afternoon passing a piece of paper through the barbed wire to one of the British guards, and he became the immediate suspect.

When word reached the German camp leader, who was convinced of Rettig's innocence, he advised Rettig and a friend that for their own safety, they should pack their kit and prepare to be transferred to another camp. Both hurried to gather their belongings, only to be interrupted by the 5.40 p.m. roll call. On return to their hut, they were seen packing their kit bags, and when some of the fanatical Nazis heard about this, they decided to confront them. A crowd of over twenty prisoners chased Rettig around the hut, caught up with him and beat him with their fists. Rettig's friend saw that the ringleaders appeared to be 21-year-old Kuehne and 31-year-old Schmittendorf, along with two other men, Heinz Ditzler and Juergen Kersting.

Rettig was pushed out of the hut, where a large crowd of up to a hundred men had gathered. They began chanting: 'Hang him, hang him!' The beatings began again with Schmittendorf kicking Rettig repeatedly in the head, until British guards were able to intervene and drag the stricken man to safety. Rettig was rushed to hospital where he died later that night. The four men identified as ringleaders were arrested and stood trial by military court martial at Kensington in August. All four men denied the attack. As in the previous trial of German prisoners, witnesses were not named for fear of reprisals, and after a trial lasting almost a week, Ditzler and Kersting were acquitted. Kuelne and Schmittendorf were hanged side by side.

82

SHOTS IN THE DARK

❖ *James McNicol, 21 December 1945* ❖

It was a time for celebration. The long war in Europe was over and on Thursday, 16 August 1945, the announcement that Japan had surrendered meant the war in the Far East was also at an end. This was the cue for further celebrations at the Heavy Anti-Aircraft Battery at Thorpe Bay, Essex. Earlier that evening, Royal Artillery Sergeant James McNicol had been out drinking with a colleague, Sergeant Leonard Cox. After consuming several pints at various pubs around the town, they returned to camp where a dance was taking place.

Trouble began when 30-year-old Sergeant McNicol saw his sometime ATS girlfriend, Jean Neale, dancing with an airman in civilian clothes. Worse still, the airman had been admitted to the dance as a guest of Sergeant Cox, and when McNicol confronted the couple and threw a glass of beer over them, it led to a quarrel with Sergeant Cox. Another Sergeant, Donald Kirkaldie, intervened, and the argument ended with both Cox and McNicol being dragged outside. McNicol, now very drunk, staggered off into the dark, while the others returned to the dance.

When festivities drew to a close, the servicemen made for their quarters. Kirkaldie, Cox and two other officers shared a hut on the camp, and at around 3 a.m. the following morning, Cox was awoken by the sound of someone forcing the door handle. He heard the sound of breaking glass and suddenly a hand reached through the broken windowpane and flicked on the light. Seconds later, a rifle barrel appeared through the broken pane, a shot rang out and Cox was wounded. The second shot hit Kirkaldie in the throat, killing him instantly.

McNicol was the immediate suspect and was arrested within the hour. He claimed that the killing was accidental and that he had fired the shots merely to frighten Cox and Kirkaldie.

Tried at Chelmsford Assizes in November, before Mr Justice Lewis, McNicol admitted under cross-examination that when he had fired the shots, he had intended to wound Cox in revenge for threats he had made against him. Jean Neale told the court that she had only been out with McNicol four times, and on the night before the murder, the prisoner had asked her to accompany him to an empty hut to have sex. When she refused, he had lost his temper, and realising that there was no future in the relationship, Jean had ended their brief courtship.

Sergeant Cox admitted that he had threatened McNicol, but denied saying he would kill him. He told the court that the two men had been friendly until the night of the quarrel, when Cox had told McNicol that if it hadn't been for the fact he would lose his stripes if caught fighting, he would have 'done for' the prisoner.

83

PRESSING DEBTS

❖ *John Riley Young, 21 December 1945* ❖

John Young's building business, Moore & Young, based at Ilford, was having financial problems, and the bank was pressing him to deal with his overdraft, which was now running at £1,500. Desperate to pay off his debt, Young hit on a scheme. In the latter months of the war, he had become friendly with 52-year-old Fred Lucas, a travelling jewellery dealer and salesman, who lived with his wife and daughter at their bungalow 'Cranham', at Undercliffe Gardens, Leigh-on-Sea.

Young approached Lucas, who also had a shop in London, and said he had a friend named Neal who was looking for a buyer for some gold sovereigns. He said his friend was looking for a quick sale and would accept £3,000. Lucas handed over the money. Young then used some of this to clear his overdraft and with the remainder he bought a new car.

On 6 June 1945, Young travelled to Leigh-on-Sea. Trying to find Lucas' bungalow, he asked a neighbour for directions, and arriving at the house, he told Lucas that there had been some problems and he no longer had the money or the sovereigns. Lucas called him a 'twister' and threatened to go to the police, at which Young picked up a heavy piece of furniture and battered him to death. Lucas's wife, Cissie, came into the room on hearing the disturbance and she too was also battered to death.

Eva Lucas returned home that evening and discovered the bodies of her parents. Detectives had several clues to go on. The neighbour told them of the stranger who had asked directions to the Lucas house on the morning of the murder. The killer had also left footprints and a trouser fly button beside the body.

Young had returned to London and called to see his sister at Barking, before later that afternoon attempting to commit suicide by slashing his wrists. When taken to hospital, it was found that the wounds were only superficial, and after being bandaged up, he was released. He returned to his sister's and stayed the night, but on the following day he was again rushed to hospital, having tried to gas himself.

Detectives had by now linked Young to the murders, and he was arrested in hospital. 'I have been expecting you. It was me and I want to get it off my chest,' he told detectives as they approached his bedside.

On 8 November, Young appeared before Mr Justice Lewis at the Chelmsford Assizes. His defence was insanity. The prosecution claimed that it was a brutal double murder: Young had pressing debts, and although he may not have intended to kill when he ventured out to meet Lucas, he had battered him to death when threatened with the police, and had then murdered Mrs Lucas to stop her identifying him as the killer of her husband.

THE LAST TRAITOR

❖ *Theodore John William Schurch, 4 January 1946* ❖

Born in London to Swiss parents, Theodore John William Schurch grew up in Wembley and became a supporter of Nazi ideology in his youth. In 1934, at the age of 15, he joined the British Union of Fascists (BUF) and two years later, he enlisted and became a private in the Royal Army Service Corp (RASC), stationed at Woolwich. Schurch claimed later that he had only joined the BUF to escape bullying at school, and it was here that he came into contact with an Italian agent named Bianchi.

He was attached to RASC Woolwich depot, and it was while serving in North Africa that he deserted his unit and was 'captured' by the Italians at Tobruk, to whom he readily offered his services as a spy, thus renewing his acquaintance with Bianchi. Schurch was placed with other PoWs in camps and would report back to his controllers any items of information that might be of use to them. In 1943, following the ousting of Mussolini, he was handed over to the Germans as a 'going concern' and continued to operate for the enemy until his arrest in Rome in 1945.

Tried by general court martial held at Chelsea on 10 September 1945, Schurch faced ten charges: nine of assisting the enemy, and one of deserting from his unit. He did not call any witnesses in his defence, but did give evidence under oath and was examined by his legal representative. Found guilty of all ten charges, Schurch became the last person to be executed for offences committed under the Treachery Act of 1940.

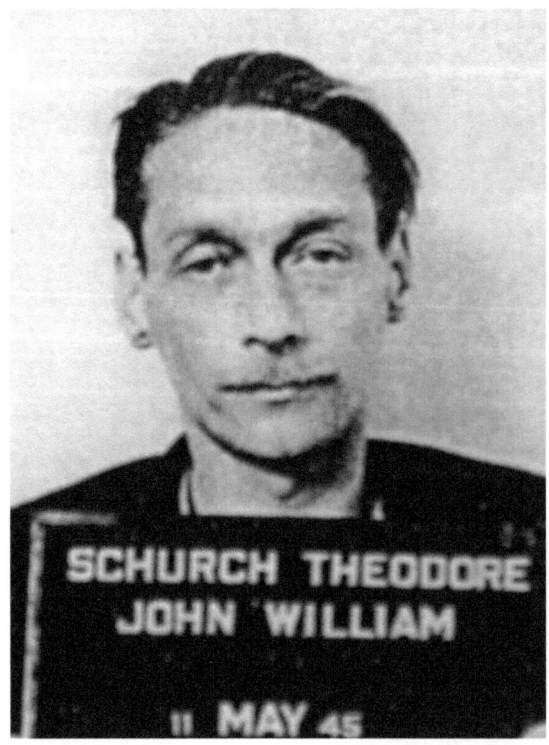

Theodore Schurch – the last traitor to be hanged.
(T.J. Leech Archive)

THE CHARMER

❖ *Neville George Clevely Heath, 16 October 1946* ❖

Dashing and smooth talking, 29-year-old Neville George Clevely Heath had built up an enviable reputation amongst his friends and colleagues. By the time the war had ended in Europe, he had racked up a number of fines for impersonating officers and for wearing medals and uniforms he was not entitled to, had been court-martialled several times and had even served a term in borstal for stealing. In June 1946 he became a murderer.

Margery Gardner was a pleasure-loving 32-year-old with a masochistic fondness for flagellation and bondage. She and Heath had booked into the Pembridge Court Hotel, Notting Hill Gate, once before for a night of mutual sexual gratification, only for her screams to alert security, who asked them to leave the hotel. The second time was to have fatal consequences.

On 15 June, Heath went to a dance in Chelsea where he met 19-year-old Yvonne Symonds. After spending the evening in a number of nightclubs, they agreed to meet again on the following day, and when Heath proposed marriage, she accepted. They spent the night at the Pembridge Court Hotel, and on the following morning, head over heels in love, Yvonne returned to her parents' home in Sussex.

On 20 June, Heath again met up with Margery Gardner. They spent the evening at the Panama Club in Cromwell Place before taking a taxi to the Pembridge Court Hotel, checking into room 4, signing the register as Lt-Col and Mrs N.G.C. Heath. On the following morning, the cleaner discovered the body of Margery Gardner in one of the beds. Covered with the bedclothes, she lay naked on her back, her ankles tied together with a handkerchief and marks on her wrists suggested her hands had also been tied. There were bruises to her face and chin and numerous diamond shaped marks on her body, which were found to have come from a leather whip. The list of injuries continued: both breasts had been bitten, the nipple of one was almost severed, and there were horrific sexual injuries.

Pathologist Professor Keith Simpson carried out a post-mortem and found that all the injuries had been carried out before death and that her cries must have been muffled either by a gag or a pillow held against her face. She had died of suffocation.

Later that day, Heath telephoned his fiancée in Worthing and arranged to travel down. There he discussed the murder with Yvonne, telling her it had happened in the same hotel room they had shared a few weeks before, and that he had actually seen the body. He told her he had met Margery on the day before she was murdered. She was with a male friend, and,

Neville Heath. (Author's collection)

having nowhere to go, Heath had loaned her the keys to his room so she could entertain her friend there.

When Heath's name was mentioned in the press in relation to the murder, Yvonne's horrified parents demanded an explanation. He reassured them it was just to clear up some further details and said he was returning to London that morning to deal with it. Instead, Heath wrote to Chief Inspector Barratt at Scotland Yard, repeating the story he had told his fiancée, but adding that he had found the body himself when he had returned to the room at 2 a.m. He claimed she had been in the company of a man named Jack, but that was all he could let them know.

Leaving Worthing that afternoon, Heath travelled along the coast to Bournemouth, booking into the Tollard Royal Hotel under the name Group Captain Rupert Brook. Here he attended a dance where he met a girl named Peggy. A week later, he bumped into Peggy again in the company of pretty 21-year-old Doreen Marshall. They began to chat and when Peggy said she had to go, Doreen stayed chatting with the handsome Group Captain, accepting his invitation for dinner later that evening. After a meal at the Norfolk Hotel, where Doreen was staying, they left for a walk. Doreen was not seen alive again.

Two days later, the manager of the Norfolk Hotel grew concerned over Miss Marshall's disappearance and contacted the manager of the Tollard Royal, knowing that it was one of their guests who had dined with Doreen. Heath denied that the woman he had dined with was Doreen Marshall, but agreed to talk to the police to help clear up the mystery.

Heath was invited to Bournemouth police station to look at a photograph of the missing girl, and when he arrived at the station, Doreen's father and sister were there. The sister's close resemblance to Doreen was so uncanny that Heath did a double take when he entered the station; a reaction spotted by Detective Constable Souter, who felt there was more to Group Captain Brook than he was letting on. He was also struck by the similarities he bore to the wanted picture of the Notting Hill murderer, Neville Heath.

Souter informed his superiors of his suspicions before asking the man if his name was Neville Heath. The man asked if he could return to his hotel and get his jacket and, suspicious now, Detective Inspector George Gates offered to collect it for him. The jacket was searched and it contained a cloakroom ticket for Bournemouth railway station, which, when redeemed, revealed a suitcase labelled 'Heath' containing items of clothing, a bloodstained scarf and a riding switch with a diamond-weave pattern.

Heath was returned to London where, on 8 July, he was charged with the murder of Margery Gardner. That evening, with Heath now in police custody, the body of Doreen Marshall was discovered at Bournemouth. Hidden by some bushes, the body was naked except for one shoe, with her clothes lying nearby. She had been struck several times on the head and her throat had been cut. Like the body found at Notting Hill, the injuries to Doreen's body were horrific. One nipple had been bitten off and she had been violated by what the pathologist thought was a tree branch.

Heath's three-day trial before Mr Justice Morris at the Old Bailey in September was the first major show trial in the post-war years. Crowds packed into the gallery to hear the defence argue that Heath was insane at the time of the murders. He was charged only with the first murder, that of Margery Gardner, and the prosecution offered medical evidence to show that although Heath was a sexual pervert and sadist, he was nevertheless sane, and was therefore fully responsible for his actions.

Neville Heath, whose charms had landed him almost any woman he set his eye on, paid for his crimes on 16 October. Asked if he would like a tot of whisky before the hangman entered, he nodded and added, 'In the circumstances you might make that a double!' He downed it in one, and as Pierrepoint entered, he smiled at his warders and spoke for the last time: 'Come on boys, let's be going!'

THE TELL-TALE CARTRIDGE

❖ *Arthur Robert Boyce, 1 November 1946* ❖

Arthur Boyce first met Elizabeth McLindon while working on Brighton's Palace Pier. Forty-five-year-old Boyce was a former regular soldier who, despite being above the age of conscription, had re-enlisted and fought throughout the war until victory had been assured. Following his demob, he had returned to Brighton, finding work as a painter and decorator. Boyce and 41-year-old Elizabeth soon became lovers and when, in May, 1946, she found work as housekeeper at 45 Chester Square, Belgravia, Boyce followed her to London.

The Chester Square house had been the wartime London home of King George of Greece, but following the sovereign's return to his own country, the day-to-day running of the house was undertaken by just a skeleton staff, and for the most part, Elizabeth lived in the house alone. Taking advantage of this situation, Boyce decided to move in with her, and on 1 June he was given a key to the staff quarters.

Elizabeth McLindon was last seen alive on 8 June, after watching the first post-war VE Day parade. A neighbour had seen her leave Chester Square, followed a short time later by Boyce, who seemed to be enraged. The following day, King George of Greece paid a fleeting visit to the house. Private secretary Sophocles Papanikoladu was dismayed to find milk bottles still on the doorstep and the housekeeper not on duty. He also noted that one of the basement rooms was locked. On 12 June, the king and some of his entourage returned to Chester Square and again, there was no sign of the housekeeper, although there was a letter for her on the doormat.

Arthur Boyce. (T.J. Leech Archive)

Elizabeth McLindon – shot dead by Boyce. (T.J. Leech Archive)

The writer of the letter signed himself 'Arthur', and asked Elizabeth to contact him urgently. Another letter in much the same vein followed on the following day, and, worried about the missing housekeeper and the locked room, the police were contacted. The door to the basement room was forced, and the mystery of missing Elizabeth McLindon was solved. She was sitting in a chair holding the mouthpiece of a telephone in her hand and had been shot through the back of the head. A .32 bullet and cartridge case were found at the scene.

Following investigations, Boyce was traced to Brighton where he made a statement to the effect that he had last seen Elizabeth on 8 June, when after watching the VE Day parade, they had returned to Chester Square. He said that they spent the afternoon in bed and their lovemaking had been interrupted by a call to the house to inform her of the king's impending visit later that evening. Elizabeth had told him to go back to Brighton where she would contact him when the king had returned to Greece. Boyce claimed that this was the last time he had seen her, and that he had written the notes to her as he was anxious about her disappearance.

Asked if he had a gun, Boyce admitted that he had possessed a Colt .45, but he had thrown it into the sea from the Palace Pier at Elizabeth's request. He also claimed that a man named John Rowland had offered him a gun for £9 but he didn't want to buy it and had handed it to Elizabeth, who said she was afraid of intruders at Chester Square.

Police located Rowland at an address in Wales. He gave a different version of events, saying that he had shared lodgings with Boyce in Fulham in the autumn of 1945, and when he moved back to Wales, he noticed that his gun was missing. He suspected that Boyce had taken it and had sent him a labelled box asking for its return. He then supplied detectives with a vital clue. Although he no longer had the gun, he did have a cartridge from it which he used as a spool for some sticking plaster. When it was examined alongside the one found at the murder scene, ballistics expert Robert Churchill claimed that both had been fired from the same gun.

Boyce was charged with murder, but the evidence against him was in the main circumstantial: he had lived with Elizabeth and had been seen with her on the day she died and was suspected of stealing the murder weapon. As regards to motive, detectives had found letters in Elizabeth's belongings suggesting that they had discussed marriage, which contradicted Boyce's claim that she was aware that he was already a married man. Boyce also had a string of convictions for larceny, and had been in court for deserting his wife and for bigamy many years before.

At his trial before Mr Justice Morris at the Old Bailey, Boyce protested his innocence, claiming the killer was one of Elizabeth's other lovers, and going as far as naming two men he claimed had done it. It was to no avail; the tell-tale cartridge provided the vital link and he was convicted after a short trial in September.

87

FOR CLOTHING COUPONS

❖ *John Fleming McCready Mathieson, 10 December 1946* ❖

In the early hours of Sunday, 21 July 1946, 23-year-old John Fleming McCready Mathieson, a sailor serving on HMS *Victory*, was taken into custody following an incident in a café in Holloway. Charged with being drunk and disorderly, he was held in the cells until the following morning when his case was heard by a local magistrate. Later that same morning, the body of a woman was discovered in the grounds of St Luke's Church at Holloway. Identified as 46-year-old Mrs Mona Vanderstay, a former weightlifter and variety artist 'strong-woman,' and mother of five children, she lived with her husband in nearby Camden Road, Holloway. Robert Vanderstay told police his wife had been out to the cinema on the Saturday night and he had been expecting her home before midnight.

Mrs Vanderstay had been strangled, her clothing torn at the front, and there were signs of a sexual assault. Her killer had seemingly also searched through her handbag, as a number of clothing coupons, a chequebook and her ID card were missing. The attacker had, however, failed to spot a small purse containing almost £12 in cash.

As detectives interviewed all those known to have been in the Holloway area around the time of the murder, Mathieson was re-interviewed in his cell. He was searched, and in his pockets were a chequebook in the name of Robert Vanderstay, as well as the clothing coupons and Mrs Vanderstay's ID card. He also had bloodstains on his uniform, which were later found to be of the same group B blood type as that of the murdered woman.

Tried before Mr Justice Stable at the Old Bailey on 21 October, Mathieson claimed to have no recollection of the actual attack. He said he had been drinking heavily on the Saturday night after a row with his girlfriend, which had blown up over her demands for clothing coupons. He admitted meeting Mona on a bus and said that they had gone into the churchyard together, where she had consented to have sex with him. He then claimed that she had told him to stop, but his memory was 'hazy' due to the drink, and he had no recollection of what happened next.

His defence claimed that Mathieson had carried out the attack while suffering from a form of sleepwalking, and therefore he was not responsible for his actions at the time, and was thereby not guilty of murder. The prosecution dismissed the line of his being too drunk or insane to form any intent by the fact that he had had the presence of mind to sort through the handbag, removing items which were of use to him, in particular the clothing coupons, and then discarding the remainder of the handbag's contents. The jury decided that Mathieson had been fully aware of what he was doing and found him guilty as charged.

'SLEEP-WALKING KILLER SMIRKS AT DEATH SENTENCE

FOUND guilty of murder and sentenced to death at the Old Bailey yesterday, a man smirked while sentence was pronounced.

He was in such a hurry to leave the court that he could hardly wait for the end of the death sentence

The sentenced man, John Fleming McCready Mathieson, 23, seaman, of H.M.S. Victory, Portsmouth, had been accused of murdering Mrs. Mona Victoria Vanderstay, 46, of Camden - road, Holloway, London, in St. Luke's Churchyard, near her home.

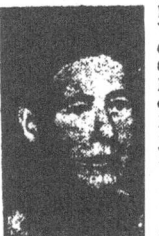

Mathieson

A doctor said for the defence that Mathieson, because of a war injury to his head and drinks he had taken that night, was in the same condition as a sleepwalker when he committed the crime.

Mr. Justice Stable said there was not a shred of evidence that Mathieson had ever been treated for any form of mental

Newspaper account of John Mathieson's trial. (Author's collection)

88

THE SECRET AFFAIR

❖ *Frederick William Reynolds, 26 March 1947* ❖

Frederick William Reynolds had served in the Fire Service during the early part of the war, but had been invalided out when he sustained a leg injury, and later that year he lost his wife in an air raid. Although he had been distraught at the death of his wife, Reynolds had been having an affair with a former workmate for several years before her death, one that had continued throughout the war and into peacetime.

In the winter of 1946, 37-year-old Reynolds was working as a bookmaker in Holloway while continuing his relationship with 40-year-old Beatrice Greenberg. Mrs Greenberg shared a house with her husband on Avenell Road, Highbury, and she hit on a routine with her lover that he would approach her house, whistling a popular Bing Crosby song. If her husband was out of the house she would sneak him in, but if he was in, she would put something in the window to warn Reynolds.

On the night of Tuesday, 17 December, after the pub had closed, Reynolds approached the house, whistling one of the usual tunes. There was no sign of Mrs Greenberg, so Reynolds walked up and down the street before returning. Approaching the window, he again whistled, and this time Mrs Greenberg appeared and let him in.

Reynolds was quite drunk, and what happened next was to be debated at his trial before Mr Justice Atkinson at the Old Bailey in February 1947. Reynolds claimed that she had told him he could not stay as her husband was due home any moment. They had quarrelled many times over her refusal to leave her husband to be with Reynolds, and it seems that he had asked her again that night. Minutes later, she let out a scream and pushed Reynolds against a wall. He claimed he didn't know what had happened, but it seems that he had pulled out a pistol and fired four shots into his mistress, killing her instantly. When the evidence was placed before him, Reynolds broke down and claimed: 'Now I know it was my hand that took her life, I am ready to die to be with her.'

His defence launched a failed appeal that the verdict should be reduced to manslaughter, as he had been too drunk to form any intent to kill.

89

SHOT DOWN IN THE STREET

❖ *Christopher James Geraghty & Charles Henry Jenkins, 19 September 1947* ❖

It is not every day, thank God, that innocent people are shot down in the streets of London, as occurred here. I describe this affair as an outrage – what else could it be called? (Mr Justice Hallett in summing up at the Old Bailey, 28 July 1947)

The planning was done, the Vauxhall 14 saloon positioned ready for a speedy getaway, and slipping knotted handkerchiefs over the lower part of their faces, the three men headed for the door. It was Monday, 28 April 1947, and staff at Jay's Jewellers, 73 Charlotte Street, in London's West End, were now back from lunch and ready for the afternoon trade when suddenly, at a few minutes after 2 p.m., the door burst open.

Proprietor Ernest Stock sized up the situation in an instant and decided he wasn't going to hand over his takings or his valuable goods meekly. As one of the young men pointed a gun and another rushed towards him, Stock slammed the safe shut, receiving a blow from the handle of the gun that knocked him bleeding to the ground. As mayhem erupted, the 70-year-old manager, Bertram Keates, reached down and pressed the alarm button.

Panic immediately spread amongst the thieves. This was not what they had imagined, and when Keates threw his wooden stool at them, one fired and narrowly missed hitting him, the bullet embedding itself in the wall above his head. Within seconds, they backed out into the street, empty-handed.

As robberies went, it had been a farce, but up to now, although Stock was battered and bruised, no one had been seriously hurt. Rushing into the crowded street, the thieves now faced another more serious problem. The stolen car they had carefully parked ready for a speedy getaway was now boxed in by a delivery lorry, and as the alarm bell rang and staff rushed out in the pursuit, the gang were forced to flee on foot.

Motorcyclist Alec de Antiquis, a 36-year-old father of six, saw what was happening and swung his powerful bike onto the pavement, blocking the path of the fleeing robbers. Ignoring their shouts to get out of the way, he paid for his courageous attempt to stop them with a bullet to the head. As he fell to the ground, fatally wounded, the gang reached the end of the road, turned the corner and disappeared into the crowds on Tottenham Court Road.

The brutal killing hit the headlines of newspapers across the country, and soon police received a vital lead. A taxi driver came forward to say he had seen two men run into an office block at 191 Tottenham Court Road on the afternoon of the murder. They appeared to have knotted handkerchiefs around their necks and were in a hurry.

Detectives searched the building, and in an empty office they discovered a knotted handkerchief and a raincoat, folded and stuffed inside a chimney. It seemed the owner had tried to conceal his identity by removing all the visible labels inside the coat, but unknown to him, inside the lining was a telltale manufacturer's label. This led to the coat being traced to a store in Deptford High Street. It was still a time of clothing coupons and shortages and, as a result, shopkeepers were obliged to record the name and address of every purchaser. The coat was logged in the book as being sold in December 1946, and led police to an address in Bermondsey. After a series of denials, the owner eventually told the police his wife had lent the coat to her brother, Charles Henry 'Harry' Jenkins.

Jenkins, a 23-year-old petty crook with a record of violence that included serious assault against a policeman, was placed under surveillance, and in due course, was picked up along with two associates, 20-year-old Christopher James 'Jim' Geraghty and 17-year-old Terry Rolt. Within days, two guns were found in the mud on the banks of the Thames, close to Jenkins's parents' house. Ballistic tests found that one gun had been the murder weapon, while the other had fired the bullet found inside the jewellers shop. All three men were questioned separately, and although Jenkins refused to testify against his close friend, Geraghty, he had no qualms about naming the youngster, Rolt, as having been involved in the robbery.

Charles Jenkins. (Author's collection)

Christopher Geraghty. (Author's collection)

Alec de Antiquis tended to by passers-by, having been shot down in the street. (TNA:PRO)

When Rolt was informed that he had been put in the frame, he in turn named Geraghty as the man who had shot dead Alec de Antiquis, and all three were charged with wilful murder.

Their trial before Mr Justice Hallett at the Old Bailey in July was to last six days. Neither Geraghty nor Rolt chose to give evidence, while Jenkins claimed he had an alibi for the time of the murder. After the judge's summing up, the jury took four hours to find all three guilty of murder. Rolt, at 17, being too young to face the death penalty, was to be detained at His Majesty's pleasure for a minimum of five years; Jenkins and Geraghty were sentenced to death.

As an interesting aside, on the afternoon of the murder, a passer-by on his way to nearby Fitzroy Street had had his journey interrupted by a police roadblock as the hue and cry went up following the shooting. Reaching his destination, he discovered he had witnessed the start of the investigation that was to lead to the arrest of the two men. Five months later, on a warm September morning, he was to play his part in the last act of the tragedy. The passer-by was hangman Albert Pierrepoint.

90

THE WATCHMAKER

❖ *Walter John Cross, 19 February 1948* ❖

A scream rang out, followed by a loud moan, then the slamming of a door. From the next-door window, neighbour Florence Wright hurriedly looked out and saw a man walk down the path, turn up his coat and disappear down the road. It was 9.30 p.m. on Friday, 14 November 1947, and hearing further moans coming from next door, Florence hurried to investigate.

Her neighbour was 55-year-old Percy Bushby, who lived alone with his cat at 11 King Edward Road, Barking. Florence knocked on the door and, receiving no reply, went inside and stumbled upon Percy's body. He had been strangled and the empty wallet on the table beside the body suggested that the motive was robbery.

Bushby had been disabled and earned a living as a watchmaker. His home also doubled as a shop and was often visited by customers at all hours. Police investigations soon led to Walter Cross, a Dagenham lorry driver, who was identified as the man seen leaving the house. Picked up the following day, Cross admitted that he and another man, Walter Bull, had been to the shop in early October in order to sell some items. They had returned on Wednesday, 12 November when Bull, who had recently repaired a lock at Bushby's house, had sold him a number of items. He ended his original statement by claiming he had not been to the house in Barking since that day and was not there on the night of the murder.

Under further questioning, Cross made a second statement admitting that he and Bull had planned to rob the old man. On a previous visit, Bull had spotted that the wallet Percy carried was full of notes. With the old man being disabled, they reasoned it would be easy to rob him.

On the night of the murder, Cross claimed that Bull had failed to make their rendezvous so he had gone to Barking alone. Cross had been given a key by Bull, who said it would open the new lock he had fitted to the old man's door. Cross claimed he had waited until darkness had fallen and then entered the premises using his key. To his horror, he saw Bushby coming towards him, but as the old man approached, he gave out a shout and then slumped to the floor in a faint. Cross said he had panicked, and after emptying the money from the man's wallet, had fled the house. He strenuously denied strangling the old man and claimed that someone else must have entered the house and committed the crime.

Bull was interviewed and claimed to have known Cross for only a month or so. He confirmed that along with Cross, he had visited the watchmaker but it was Cross who had spotted the wallet and Cross who had suggested the robbery. Bull was approached with the idea of committing the crime. Earlier on the day of the murder, Bull was asked again by Cross if he was prepared to assist in the robbery but had declined and had an alibi for the time of the murder.

Cross was convicted before Mr Justice Cassels at the Old Bailey in January 1948. His heavily pregnant wife, who was waiting outside the court as the jury returned, screamed and collapsed when she heard the verdict.

91

THE CARTOONIST

❖ *Harry Lewis, 21 April 1949* ❖

On the evening of Boxing Day 1948, commercial artist and lightening cartoonist Harry Saul Michaelson was attacked in his basement flat at Furzecroft, a block of flats on George Street, Marylebone. The 50-year-old shared the basement with his wife, who, at the time, was away on holiday with friends. Desperately trying with a towel to staunch the flow of blood from the head injuries he had sustained, Michaelson staggered into the lobby where he was able to attract the attention of the night porter, who called for medical assistance.

Michaelson was found to have a deep wound on his forehead and a fractured skull. He was taken to St Mary's Hospital, Paddington, where his condition soon deteriorated to the extent that he required emergency brain surgery later that same day. On the following morning

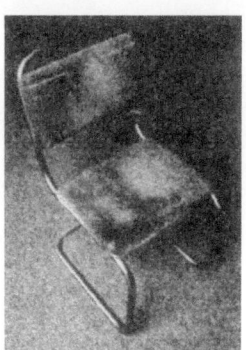

Left: *Lightening cartoonist Harry Saul Michaelson*. (Author's collection)

Below: *The murder weapon*. (TNA:PRO)

Michaelson died from his injuries. Detectives examined the flat, and while they could find no sign of forced entry, they did find the murder weapon: a tubular steel chair, stained with blood. Under examination, it also yielded several fingerprints, one of which led police to Harry Lewis, a well-known local thief of no recorded address.

Lewis was arrested on 18 January 1949. He was seen acting suspiciously outside a block of flats in St John's Wood, and was arrested, coincidentally, by one of the detectives working on the Michaelson case. Lewis claimed that, while wandering the streets with nowhere to go and with no money, he had spotted an open window in the basement flat on George Street. He had entered with a view to stealing and noticed that the occupant was asleep in bed. He removed the man's wallet, and as he made his way down the passage, he heard the man stir and call out. Lewis claimed Michaelson switched on the bedroom light, and in panic, he picked up the chair, and returning to the bedroom, struck Michaelson twice over the head before fleeing through the open window. He then flagged down a taxi and paid the fare with money he had stolen from the wallet.

Standing before the fearsome Lord Chief Justice Goddard at the Old Bailey on 7 March, Lewis' counsel offered a plea of guilty of manslaughter, claiming that the cause of death was the operation on Michaelson's fractured skull and not the actual assault. Pathologist Donald Teare gave evidence that, with the injuries Michaelson sustained, he would have died with or without the operation.

As he awaited execution, Lewis told his girlfriend that he rued the decision not to wear gloves when he committed the murder, which had yielded him just £5.

92

A SORDID TALE

❖ *Bernard Alfred Peter Cooper, 21 June 1949* ❖

At 8 p.m. on the evening of Friday, 1 April 1949, the body of 38-year-old Mary Cooper was found by her 14-year-old daughter, Sheila, at her home on Davisville Road, Shepherd's Bush. She had been strangled with one of her stockings, and her body was partly hidden beneath the mattress in her bedroom.

Her husband, Bernard, a 40-year-old painter, had been arrested that same afternoon in Islington, on a charge of being drunk and disorderly. Taken into the station, he was later released on bail on condition that he reported back the following morning. Aware that the police were now looking for him in connection with the murder, Cooper failed to report to the police station the next day and was at liberty for five days, before he was picked up on the evening of 6 April, when the caretaker at the Girl's County School on Maidstone Road, in Ashford, Kent, discovered an intruder on the premises. The caretaker contacted the police who arrived to discover it was their fugitive.

Cooper's statement to the police told a sordid tale. In the previous year, his teenage daughter had told the police she had been raped and had undergone a legally sanctioned abortion. Cooper now admitted that he had committed incest with the child and had been responsible for her condition. He had later confessed to his wife and she had forgiven him. He claimed that in the early hours of Friday morning, 1 April, during a quarrel, his wife had again brought up the subject, and told him he disgusted her. The row grew more heated, and Mary became hysterical. Cooper said he had first slapped her across the face and then, as she began to shout and attack him, he picked up one of her stockings and tied it around her throat.

After killing his wife, Cooper had gone into their daughter's room and woke Sheila, who had slept through the quarrel. He told her he had quarrelled with Mary and asked her if she would run away with him. She refused. Cooper then told her that Mary was very tired and wanted to stay in bed, and that afternoon he had gone out and got drunk.

Sheila's version was slightly different. She said that when she and the other two children got up on 1 April, her father told them that Mary had had a bad night, but was now asleep and should not be disturbed. He had left the house, as if to go to work, and it was not until the evening that Sheila had checked on her mother and was horrified to find her dead.

Following a short Old Bailey trial on 18 May, before Mr Justice Hallett, the jury took just eleven minutes to find Cooper guilty of murder.

93

DESPERATE MEASURES

❖ *William Claude Hodson Jones, 28 September 1949* ❖

While I was stationed in Rotenburg in Germany I shot a girl in the woods. I want to get it off my chest. Now perhaps you will do something about my transfer! (Confession written by William Jones at Dartmoor Gaol, May 1949)

The murder of the pretty young girl had long been filed as unsolved. In July 1945, the body of 19-year-old Waltraut Lehman was discovered in woodland near Rotenburg, in West Germany. She had been shot dead while picking flowers. Troops from the British Liberation Army (BLA) stationed nearby were questioned, but there was little in the way of clues left at the scene, and with post-war Germany still in turmoil, the murder hunt was soon wound down and resources deployed elsewhere. It was to be four years before a remarkable confession reopened the case and led to a former soldier making the short walk to the gallows.

William Claude Hodson Jones grew tired of counting the minutes. In his cell in the dank, dark corridors of Dartmoor Gaol, the six years that stretched ahead of him became unbearable. Maybe if he was closer to his home in Yorkshire it would be marginally more tolerable, but plea after plea for a transfer had fallen on deaf ears, and so he was forced to take desperate measures.

Waltraut Lehman. (TNA:PRO)

Jones asked to see the governor and made another request for a transfer. Again he was turned down. He then asked for a sheet of paper and began to write a confession to the murder of Waltraut Lehman. Jones claimed that he had met the pretty teenager in the woods, and after chatting for a few minutes, they reached an agreement. In exchange for some chocolate, she consented to have sex with the soldier. He quickly got his side of the bargain, but as she dressed and asked for the chocolate, Jones apologised and said he didn't have any.

She flew into a rage and began to insult him, calling him a filthy English pig. They exchanged insults and she again called him a pig. Jones said if she called him that again, he would shoot her.

'Shoot then, pig!' she mocked, as she walked away. He then callously picked up his rifle and shot her in the back.

Chief Inspector Fred Narborough of Scotland Yard's murder squad was detailed to check out the remarkable story and travelled to West Germany, where he was able to trace witnesses who had seen the soldier and the girl in the area around the time of the murder. Jones had also claimed to have stolen the girl's ring and sold it to a soldier. Narborough traced the ring to a soldier's wife in Hackney, and relatives of the dead girl positively identified it.

A little over a week after his confession, Jones stood before Mr Justice Streatfeild at the Old Bailey, accused of murder. His defence offered a plea of insanity and Jones' mother travelled down from Doncaster to testify that as a child, he had received a kick to the head from a horse, from which time he had been short tempered and irritable during a new moon.

Instead of getting the transfer to a northern prison, Jones found himself in the condemned cell at Pentonville, where, three weeks later, the man who preferred death to Dartmoor was hanged.

94

THE SON-IN-LAW

❖ *Daniel Raven, 6 January 1950* ❖

It was supposed to be a happy occasion. Dapper 23-year-old Jew, Daniel Raven, an advertising executive, and his young wife Marie were celebrating the birth of their first child. On Monday, 10 October, he went to visit his wife and son at a Muswell Hill nursing home. Also there, doting on their new grandson, were Marie's parents, 49-year-old Leopold and 47-year-old Esther Goodman. Marie's parents, both Russian Jews, left just after 9 p.m., and shortly afterwards, her husband bade her goodnight and left.

At 10.30 p.m., a police officer telephoned Raven to inform him there had been a terrible incident at his in-laws' home and to ask him to attend. Forty minutes earlier, another relative had called at the Goodman's house in Ashcombe Gardens, Edgeware, and found the battered bodies of Leopold and Esther.

Detectives looking for clues to the brutal double murder were puzzled as to the motive. The Goodmans were a wealthy couple, and even a cursory search found large quantities of money in a drawer and in the safe. The motive would not, therefore, have been robbery. Perhaps then, the killer had had a grudge against the couple, which meant the list of suspects would include those closest to the couple, including their immediate relatives. When Daniel Raven arrived at the house, he seemed shocked and upset, but detective's suspicions were aroused when they noticed that his clothes appeared to be freshly laundered. Raven explained that he had just had a bath and changed into the clean clothes when he received the telephone call.

Having obtained Raven's keys, police entered his home in nearby Edgwarebury Lane shortly before midnight, and immediately noticed a strong smell of burning. They entered the kitchen where, in the coke-burning boiler, they found the charred remains of a suit and shirt. Able to retrieve parts of the suit, it was sent for examination, and traces of blood were found. Tests showed that they were the same rare 'AB' blood group as Leopold Goodman.

At Raven's trial before Mr Justice Cassells at the Old Bailey, the prosecution outlined their case. They suggested that, after leaving the nursing home, Raven had driven to his in-laws', battered them both to death with the heavy, aluminium base of a television aerial, and then returned home, where he had tried to clean the blood off his clothes. He had expected to have had more time to remove all traces of blood from his clothing and from the car seat, but the surprise visit to the Goodman's house by his brother-in-law had started the murder enquiry, and Raven had been questioned before he could hide the evidence.

Raven admitted that he had called on the Goodmans after leaving the nursing home, but had left them alive and well. He said that he had then called on a cousin, but finding no one there, returned to Ashcombe Gardens, where he learned that the murder had been committed. He had then panicked, believing he would be blamed for the crimes, as he had recently fallen out with Leopold, and it was well known in the family that he did not get on with Mrs Goodman. No real motive was ever discovered, but it was thought that Raven had taken offence at some comment made by his wife's parents at the nursing home.

Raven was duly found guilty of murder and at his appeal, his counsel forlornly tried a different approach, suggesting that a plane crash (which had led to him being discharged from the RAF) had rendered Raven insane and prone to blackouts.

Daniel Raven. (Author's collection)

HANGED AND INNOCENT?

❖ *Timothy John Evans, 9 March 1950* ❖

Timothy Evans' conscience was troubling him. His pretty young wife had died a week or so before, and the kindly neighbour who rented the ground floor flat in the same house had offered to dispose of her body and save him from a possible murder charge. There was also his baby daughter, who was being cared for by a couple his neighbour knew, and there were the endless questions his relatives had been asking since his return to his native South Wales in early November.

Deciding it was time to set the record straight and get it off his chest, 25-year-old Evans walked into Merthyr Tydfil police station on 20 November 1949, and asked to speak to a detective. Evans then told a remarkable tale that had officers in London hurrying to check out his story.

Evans said he had moved to London with his 19-year-old wife, Beryl, and shortly after the birth of their daughter, Geraldine, he took lodgings at 10 Rillington Place, Notting Hill. Beryl had recently fallen pregnant again, and as his wages as a van-driver could barely support a family of three, let alone four, Beryl had suggested an abortion. They had quarrelled, but she was adamant she would not have another child, and he eventually agreed to help. Evans said he met a man in a transport café who gave him a bottle of liquid which would terminate the pregnancy.

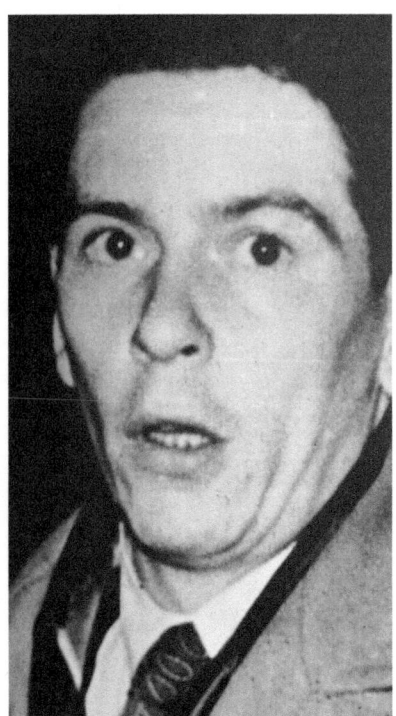

Timothy John Evans. (Crime Picture Archive)

On the following day, 8 November, Evans returned home to find the abortion had obviously gone wrong and his wife was dead. He decided to dispose of the body, and on the following morning he deposited it down a drain in the street outside his home.

Officers in London rushed to Rillington Place. The manhole cover was outside, as Evans had described, but there was no sign of any body, and it had taken four burly officers to prise open the cover, which appeared not to have been lifted for several years. They spoke to neighbours at 10 Rillington Place, who confirmed that Beryl and Geraldine Evans were both missing.

Back in Wales, Evans was questioned again and told of the findings of the London police. Shocked and confused, he made a second statement, this time with a few changes. Beryl had been pregnant and had wanted an abortion. There had been no bottle of liquid bought from a man in a café; instead he had been offered help from John Christie, who lived in the ground floor flat at Rillington Place.

Christie had offered to help arrange an abortion, and when Evans had returned home from work, he found his wife dead, lying on their bed, covered by an eiderdown. She was bleeding from her mouth, nose and from between her legs. Christie told him the operation had gone wrong, and that they had to hide the body or both would go to prison. Christie said he would put the body down the drain outside, where it would be washed out to sea. Evans believed this had been done and also that Christie knew a couple in Acton who would look after baby Geraldine.

Evans was removed to London for further questioning as officers returned to Rillington Place, where a search of the wash-house unearthed the bodies of his wife and child. Both had been strangled. He now made a third statement, this time admitting that he was responsible for the two deaths, claiming that he and Beryl had argued over money after she had run up too many debts. He had then strangled her with a piece of rope, and on the following day, strangled Geraldine with his tie, hiding them both in the wash-house.

It had long been the custom in British courts when the accused was charged with multiple killings to proceed with a charge against one victim. Evans was charged with the murder of Geraldine Evans, as the prosecution felt this allowed for the best chance of a conviction, since there could be no defence of manslaughter through provocation in the case of the child.

Tried before Mr Justice Lewis at the Old Bailey in January 1950, Evans retracted the confession in which he had admitted responsibility for the deaths of his wife and child, and instead blamed Christie for the murders. Christie, a former wartime reserve policeman, made a plausible witness and denied all knowledge of the crime. Evans, whose low intelligence meant he was easily confused by the prosecution's questioning, made a poor showing in the dock and could not explain why he had made two false statements before telling the truth. Why should the jury believe this third statement if Evans had already admitting lying before?

Evans was hanged on 9 March 1950. Weighing just 137lb, he was given a drop of 8ft. Assistant hangman Syd Dernley recorded later that he clearly heard Evans' neck break as he plunged to his death at the end of the hangman's rope.

With Evans lying in a felon's grave at Pentonville, that seemed to be the end of the matter. Three years later, the case hit the headlines again when the crimes of Rillington Place resident, John Reginald Halliday Christie, horrified the world.

Christie was convicted of murdering at least seven women, one of whom was Beryl Evans. He denied murdering baby Geraldine, however, and although it was for this crime that Evans had been executed, it did throw doubt on Evans' conviction.

The Brabin inquiry was set up to look into the case, and although it did not find that Evans was innocent, it did determine that while it was Evans who had probably killed his wife, it was likely that it was Christie who had murdered Geraldine. Since Evans had been convicted of the murder of his daughter, the inquiry found he had been convicted of the wrong murder, and he was granted a posthumous pardon.

96

THE URGE TO DESTROY

❖ *John O'Connor, 24 October 1951* ❖

Eugenie le Maire liked nothing more that to share a cup of tea and a bit of gossip with the tenants who rented out the bed-sitting room at her home. The 84-year-old French grandmother ran a small boarding house on Perham Road, West Kensington, and one of those who joined her for regular chats in the kitchen was 29-year-old Londonderry-born labourer, John O'Connor.

In the early hours of Saturday, 11 August 1951, Eugenie le Maire was found dead in a basement at the house. She had been raped, strangled and then stabbed twice. Police issued a wanted notice for O'Connor, and on the following afternoon he surrendered to police in Barnet and made a detailed confession.

O'Connor said that on the Friday night he had visited several West End pubs, arriving home by taxi shortly after midnight. Eugenie was still awake and pottering about in the kitchen when he entered the house, and as he started to climb the stairs, she called out and offered to make him a cup of tea. Entering the kitchen, O'Connor suddenly seized the old lady by the throat and attempted to strangle her. As she lost consciousness and slumped to the floor, O'Connor then savagely raped her before going up to his room. A short time later, he ventured back down to the kitchen and, finding the old lady still lying on the floor, he picked up a bread knife and plunged it twice into her chest. He then went to bed and slept through until 10.30 a.m. the following day, when he fled the house.

When he appeared before Mr Justice Barry at the Old Bailey on 2 October, O'Connor faced three possible verdicts: not guilty, guilty of murder or guilty but insane. His confession had effectively ruled out the first option, and it was left to his counsel to plead for his life by showing his client was insane.

A prisoner was always presumed sane unless evidence was produced to show otherwise, and O'Connor as good as put the noose around his own neck when he refused to give his counsel permission to fight his corner and offer evidence that he was insane. Only the prosecution's evidence was heard, which included a statement the prisoner had made following his arrest in which he claimed he felt the 'urge to destroy her'.

With O'Connor refusing to go into the witness box, and with no evidence called for the defence, the jury took just ten minutes to return the only possible verdict: guilty of murder. There was no appeal against the sentence and the execution date was set for the first Tuesday after three Sundays had passed following sentence. O'Connor was hanged twenty-two days later.

97

THE DRUG DEALER

❖ Backary Manneh, 27 May 1952 ❖

Joseph Aaku's injuries were so severe it looked as if he had been attacked by a madman. He had been battered in the face, his nose was broken and he had been stabbed several times in the back of the neck, one wound being so severe it had cut through his spinal cord.

It was late Friday night, 4 January 1952, when residents of Oakley Square, Camden, heard screaming and shouting coming from one of the houses. Several people looked out onto the street and saw a coloured man hastily leave no. 10 and set off briskly down the street. A neighbour hurried into the house and found the stricken Aaku. He was rushed to the National Temperance Hospital where he died later that night. Detectives discovered that the killer had been wounded in the attack, as two different blood types were found at the scene. The dead man had type 'A' blood, while traces of blood group 'O' were also found at the crime scene.

They had also found a probable motive. Apart from the fact that Aaku's rolled gold watch was missing, his room also contained a large quantity of marijuana, too much for individual use, which led detectives to believe there may have been some fall out over a drug deal.

They began questioning scores of coloured men who congregated in the local cafés, milk bars and lodging houses, and five days later, they spoke to Backary Manneh. Like Aaku, he worked as a cleaner at nearby Euston station, and as Manneh described his movements on the previous Friday, they noticed that his right hand was badly bruised and cut. Manneh claimed he had been mugged by three white men while walking down Tottenham Court Road on the Saturday night.

Manneh's hand injury was bad enough to require hospital treatment, and on 10 January he attended St George's Hospital. Two days later he was again questioned, and he repeated his

DRUG TRAFFIC MURDER

Death Sentence Protest At Old Bailey

AFTER A TRIAL LASTING THREE DAYS, BACKARY MANNEH (26), A WEST AFRICAN, DESCRIBED AS A DRIVER, OF LIVERPOOL ROAD N.1, WAS SENTENCED TO DEATH AT THE OLD BAILEY FOR THE MURDER OF JOSEPH AAKU, ANOTHER NEGRO, WHO WAS FOUND STABBED IN THE BACK AT HIS LODGINGS IN OAKLEY SQUARE N.W.1, ON THE NIGHT OF JANUARY 6

early testimony. Unknown to Manneh, detectives knew he wasn't telling the truth. A friend had told police he had seen Manneh sporting a bandage on his injured hand on Saturday afternoon, several hours before he claimed to have been mugged, and another friend told police he had bought a rolled gold watch from Manneh. The watch had been taken to a local watchmaker for repair, and when the back was removed, traces of blood were discovered. The watch was identified as having belonged to Aaku.

On 14 January, Manneh was arrested and charged with the murder of Joseph Aaku. He had damaged his hand punching the victim in the face. His three-day trial at the Old Bailey was notable, firstly for the fact that Manneh swore that every one of the forty prosecution witnesses was lying, and secondly, when trial judge Mr Justice Gorman donned the black cap in order to pass sentence of death, a spectator in the public gallery leapt to his feet and shouted: 'Take the black cap off and abide by the law of God. Thou shalt not kill!'

Joseph Aaku had been a big-time drug dealer. Besides the large amount of marijuana found stashed in his room, detectives also unearthed his diary, which listed the names and addresses of scores of contacts and suppliers, and as a result of his brutal murder, dozens of arrests were made and large quantities of narcotics seized, both in London and many other parts of the country.

98

THOSE FATAL SECONDS

❖ *John Howard Godar, 5 September 1952* ❖

At a few minutes before midnight on Friday, 6 June 1952, taxi driver Hughie Gillespie picked up a couple from Uxbridge railway station. Told to drive to an address in Maple Cross, the driver's assumption that it would be just another routine journey was rudely shattered when, as they approached the destination, the female passenger suddenly let out a fearful scream.

Gillespie slammed on the brakes, and turning to look over his shoulder, he heard a thump on the window, and then silence. He climbed out, rushed to the rear of the cab, and opening the door, saw the body of attractive 20-year-old brunette Maureen Cox slumped on the floor and covered in blood. Sitting beside her, 31-year-old film cameraman John Godar spoke solemnly. 'I think I've hurt her. Take me to the police station.'

Above left: *Maureen Cox, stabbed to death by John Godar.* (T.J. Leech Archive)

Above right: *Godar under arrest.* (T.J. Leech Archive)

Left: *Letter confirming the execution of John Godar.* (Author's collection)

Tel. No. : WHItehall 8100

Ext. ....

Any communication on the subject of this letter should be addressed to :—

THE UNDER SECRETARY OF STATE,

Home Office, London, S.W.I.

and the following number quoted :

.....CCS. 124/1 ...

Your Ref. ....

W P.84346

HOME OFFICE,

WHITEHALL.

2nd September, 1952.

Sir,

I am directed by the Secretary of State to inform you that, having had under his consideration the case of John Howard Godar, now lying under sentence of death in Pentonville Prison, he has failed to discover any sufficient ground to justify him in advising Her Majesty to interfere with the due course of law.

I am, Sir,

Your obedient Servant,

FaN Ewsay

The Secretary,
    Prison Commission,
        Horseferry House,
            Dean Ryle Street,
                S.W.1.

Gillespie climbed back into his cab and hurried towards Uxbridge police station, where police found that Maureen Cox had been stabbed almost fifty times: there were twenty wounds to her face, twenty to her chest, and eight to her throat. Lying on the floor was a stiletto knife.

Interviewed by Chief Inspector Richardson, Godar simply claimed; 'I would sooner let it go. I just want to go where she is, and as quickly as possible.' Asked why he had done it, he simply stated that it was through jealousy.

Looking into the background of the case, detectives found that Godar and Maureen Cox had been dating for almost a year, but recently certain revelations had caused her to reassess their relationship. Maureen had discovered that Godar was divorced with a young child, and as a result, she began to look around at other suitors. Godar suspected there was a cooling in their relationship and had decided to take drastic measures if she was to end their affair.

It was while they were returning to her home in the cab that she had confirmed his worst fears, and when she told him she intended to go on a date with another man on the following Sunday, he went berserk. Godar drew out a knife and attacked Maureen in a savage frenzy.

Godar's sanity was the main issue when he appeared before Mr Justice Barry at the Old Bailey on 7 July. The defence called Dr Rossiter Lewis to testify that Godar was suffering from a mental condition that caused a period of temporary insanity, lasting less than a minute, and it was during those fatal seconds that he had committed the murder.

This was countered by Dr Matheson, Chief Medical Officer at Brixton Prison, who said he had observed Godar at length while the prisoner was on remand awaiting trial, and he could find no evidence of insanity.

The defence failed to convince the court of Godar's insanity and he was duly convicted. A campaign for a reprieve on the grounds of insanity was rejected, which angered his supporters, as it came just a few weeks after child killer John Straffen had been reprieved, having been found insane and sent to Broadmoor.

Following Godar's execution, his mother wrote an angry letter to the Home Secretary condemning the decision. 'Why do you reprieve Straffen, who killed three little children, and execute my son? I am feeling very bitter because my son did not get a fair chance.'

99

THE FANTASIST

❖ *Dennis George Muldowney, 30 September 1952* ❖

I killer her. Let's get away from here and get it over quickly. (Statement made by Dennis Muldowney following his arrest, 15 June 1952)

Dennis George Muldowney lived in a fantasy world. The 41-year-old Wigan-born porter resided at the Reform Club, on Pall Mall, where it appears he built up an imaginary relationship with a lady who had served the British government so bravely during the war that she was awarded a number of honours in recognition of her courage.

Krystyna Skarbek was born in Poland in 1915, but was living in East Africa when the Second World War broke out. She offered to assist the British government and was sent to Hungary to help establish a resistance force; she was later dropped into France and worked with the resistance. She had been arrested twice by the Gestapo and managed on both occasions to escape. After fleeing Hungary, she later served in Turkey, before ending the war working in Italy. At the conclusion of hostilities, she moved to England, taking up British citizenship and changing her name to Christine Granville. She was rewarded for her valour

War heroine Christine Glanville.
(T.J. Leech Archive)

Dennis Muldowney. (T.J. Leech Archive)

with the George Medal and an OBE, while the French government awarded her the Croix de Guerre.

On 15 June 1952, Christine was stabbed to death in the foyer of the Shelbourne Hotel, Kensington. A knife was plunged into her chest with such force it penetrated her heart. Muldowney was arrested immediately and claimed that it was jealousy which had made him commit the crime. His story was then picked up by the media of the day.

According to Muldowney, he and Christine had been lovers, and he had killed her when he found out that she had been unfaithful. He said that he had seen her and a Polish man together in April and had decided that he would kill Christine and then take his own life. He claimed that they had quarrelled and that he had not seen her again until the day of the murder.

Seeing her enter the hotel, Muldowney had followed her inside and asked her to return a number of letters he had written to her. He said she told him she had burned them, that she wanted nothing more to do with him, and that she was leaving for the Continent on the following day. In a rage, he pulled out a knife and plunged it into her heart.

At his trial before Mr Justice Donovan at the Old Bailey on 11 September, Muldowney insisted on pleading guilty and refused all offers of legal representation. It was then merely a matter of reciting the prosecution's evidence, which was based in the main on Muldowney's own testimony.

Following the inevitable death sentence, relatives of the dead woman claimed there was no truth whatsoever in what Muldowney had claimed. They were adamant that Muldowney lived in a fantasy world and the relationship between himself and Christine Granville was all a figment of his imagination.

'I JUST DON'T WANT TO SEE YOU ANYMORE'

❖ *Raymond John Cull, 30 September 1952* ❖

She had been a very young bride. At barely 17-years-old, Jeannie Cull was almost eight years younger than her husband, Raymond. Cull worked as a labourer and they shared a house together on Thorne Close, Northolt. Soon the age difference, and perhaps doubts at getting married so young, began to show. The couple began arguing over the slightest things, but mainly it was his jealousy whenever she talked to her friends, in particular male friends. After weeks of tiresome quarrels and accusations of her seeing other men, Jeannie packed her bags and moved back with her parents at nearby Shadwell Drive.

Cull was devastated and wrote long letters, begging her to return home. They were all in vain. The break served only to strengthen her belief that she had made the wrong decision in getting married so young, and so, on Saturday, 28 June 1952, she pushed a short note through his letterbox to explain her decision. It began, 'Please understand I just don't want to see you anymore...'

Later that night, at a few minutes before midnight, Jeannie's father heard a terrible scream coming from her bedroom. He scrambled out of bed, ran across the corridor and, pushing the door open, was horrified to find the body of his daughter lying on the floor. Cull was standing over her holding a 14in long, bloodstained bayonet in his hand. He brandished the bayonet in the direction of his father-in-law before chasing the older man down the stairs so he could make good his escape.

Cull then called at his sister's house where, ashen faced, he told her, 'I think I have stabbed Jeannie.' She poured him a drink and then telephoned for the police, who had already been alerted and were on the lookout for Raymond.

When the police arrived, Cull handed over the bayonet saying; 'I did it with this, Guv. She has been two-timing me.'

Cull said he been out drinking that evening and had consumed about seventeen pints of beer. He had decided he wanted to speak to Jeannie and had taken the bayonet with him to frighten her father should he have tried to stop him from entering the house. Cull said he had walked to Shadwell Drive, and when he had found that all the doors were locked, he gained entry by climbing through a window, taking off his shoes so no one would hear him creep up the stairs. He said he had entered the room where his wife was sleeping and woke her. Seeing the knife in his hand, she made a grab for it and during the struggle in the darkness, she fell onto the blade.

Cull was tried before Mr Justice Donovan at the Old Bailey. Pathologist Dr Donald Teare dismissed the claims of a fall onto the blade, stating that the only way such injuries could have been inflicted was if the blade had been swung with great force. This ruled out an accident, and with a motive – his jealousy at her leaving him – the jury found him guilty of murder, but with a recommendation for mercy.

Teenage bride Jeannie Cull – killed by her estranged husband. (T.J. Leech Archive)

WHEN FRIENDS FALL OUT

❖ *Peter Cyril Johnson, 9 October 1952* ❖

The public in the gallery of Number One Court at the Old Bailey had taken their seats, Mr Justice Donovan was presiding over events, and the defendant, Peter Johnson, was about to take the stand. It was Wednesday, 17 September 1952, and Johnson, a 24-year-old Jamaican barrow boy from Brixton, was standing trial for the brutal murder of his former friend, Charles Mead, at Bethnal Green.

Johnson and Mead, both street traders, had been close friends for several years and had spent most days in each other's company. On the night of Saturday, 28 June, they had been in a Bethnal Green public house when a quarrel broke out following a game of cards. The argument became so heated that the two men went outside to fight, ending with Johnson victorious.

They retired to a friend's house where both men cleaned themselves up, before heading back towards Mead's house on Minerva Street. As they made their way back, they resumed their fight, and this time Mead received horrific head injuries which were to cost him his life.

When Johnson was cross-examined in court about events that night, he jumped to his feet and cried out, 'Leave me alone!' He then began to struggle with his guards in the dock, and as extra warders rushed to give assistance, a violent struggle took place. As Johnson was bundled out of the dock and down to the cells below, one of Johnson's relatives in the public gallery began screaming and had to be ushered out of the court. There was an attempt to continue proceedings, but Johnson was unwilling to cooperate, so it was decided to postpone the trial until the following day.

The prosecution counsel claimed that, as the two men had made their way down the street, Johnson had picked up a jagged lump of concrete, weighing over 16lb, and had used it to batter his friend to death.

While Johnson did not deny the killing, he maintained that it was in self-defence, after Mead had first wielded the piece of concrete against him. Having managed to disarm Mead, Johnson claimed he had then held the concrete in his hand while he removed his jacket during the struggle. Asked to demonstrate this to the jury, Johnson was unable to do so satisfactorily. He became even more agitated when prosecution counsel, Christmas Humphreys, further pressed him on an earlier statement that he was alleged to have made to detectives, in which he claimed he had deliberately struck Mead as he lay on the ground. Trapped by his own words, Johnson then announced that he wished to change his plea.

The jury took just thirty minutes to decide Johnson was guilty of murder. Passing sentence, Mr Justice Donovan told the court of the prisoner's long record of violence. Johnson merely shrugged his shoulders and smiled as he was escorted to the cells below.

THE HOUSE OF DEATH

❖ *John Reginald Halliday Christie, 15 July 1953* ❖

It remains one of the most notorious addresses in criminal history, and although any trace of it has long since vanished and its name has been erased from the map, the memory of the horrors that took place at 10 Rillington Place, Notting Hill , will never be forgotten.

By the time the Second World War had broken out, John Christie had served prison sentences for assault and petty theft, but with the Blitz at its height, his past misdemeanours were ignored, and he found a position as a special constable in the War Reserve Police. With great zeal, Christie would patrol at night, enforcing the blackout regulations and clamping down on petty crime and any other offences that came under his jurisdiction.

In August 1943, he met Ruth Fuerst, a munitions factory worker whom he managed to lure back to his ground floor flat. They met up several times and she eventually consented to have sex, only for Christie to strangle her as they made love. After concealing her body temporarily under the floorboards in his front room, he later dug a grave in the back garden, and on the following night, during the blackout, he buried his first victim.

Muriel Eady had known Christie for several months, and when she complained of bronchitis, which was not helped by the thick London smog, he told her he had a cure for her ailment. Disguising the smell of household gas by means of a solution of Friar's Balsam, Christie rendered Muriel unconscious before he raped and strangled her, finally burying her in the back garden.

John Reginald Halliday Christie. (TNA:PRO)

Christie did not kill again until 1949 when Timothy Evans, along with his wife Beryl and baby daughter Geraldine took occupancy of the top floor flat at 10 Rillington Place (see Chapter 95). Evans was hanged in March 1950 for the murder of his daughter, and Christie's name drifted out of the spotlight.

It was not to last long. At the end of 1952, Christie's long-suffering wife disappeared. She had been strangled and concealed beneath the floorboards in the front room. In January 1953, with the freedom of an empty house, Christie picked up prostitute, Hectorina Maclennan, took her home and strangled her in a deckchair after persuading her to try his cure for bronchitis. He then concealed her body in an alcove in the kitchen, papering over a false wall he had created with a sheet of hardboard. Later that month, Kathleen Maloney and Rita Nelson were both strangled, either during or immediately after intercourse had taken place. They too were concealed in the same alcove.

On 13 March, with four bodies hidden inside the house and two others buried in the garden, Christie walked out of Rillington Place and never returned. On 24 March, tenant Beresford Brown entered the kitchen in Christie's recently vacated flat and, knocking on the kitchen wall, noticed that it sounded hollow. Tearing back the wallpaper and flimsy hardboard, he peered into the recess and reeled back at what he discovered.

The house of death now filled the newspapers as the body count grew on a daily basis. A search of the premises unearthed the body of Mrs Christie and the remains of Christie's other victims in the garden. In total, six women were found at Rillington Place.

Christie was now the most wanted man in the country, and on 31 March, PC Thomas Ledger, walking along the embankment near Putney Bridge, noticed a shabby, unshaven man leaning against the wall and staring absent-mindedly down at the river. Asked his name, he said he was called Waddington, his wife's maiden name, but it was when he gave an address in Notting Hill that Ledger became suspicious. He asked him to take off his hat, and the hunt for Christie ended.

Taken to Putney police station, Christie readily confessed and stated: 'The more the merrier' when admitting he had killed Mrs Evans and her child.

The trial of John Reginald Halliday Christie, perhaps the most notorious in an era of sensational murder trials, began at the Old Bailey on 22 June 1953. It was to last four days, and in an attempt to cheat the hangman, Christie pleaded guilty but insane. The bulk of the evidence was concerned with Christie's mental state, as there was no disputing that Christie had committed multiple murders. It took the jury just eighty-five minutes to dismiss the insanity plea and to return a verdict of guilty of murder.

Hangman Albert Pierrepoint later claimed that Christie had a look of sheer hatred on his face as he was led, stumbling and faltering, blinking and half blind without his trademark horn-rimmed spectacles, the few short steps to the gallows, where he took with him the secret of the true number of his victims.

In the light of events in 1953, the case against Timothy Evans was reopened, and in 1965 he became the first man in the twentieth century to have his conviction overturned. He would not be the last.

103

LIKE A MADMAN

❖ *George James Newland, 23 December 1953* ❖

It was while doing national service at a military camp on the outskirts of Orsett, near Grays, Essex, that 21-year-old George Newland had first met 65-year-old Henry Tandy and his wife Honor. The Tandys rented a bungalow on the Southfield's Estate, which bordered onto the camp, and they supplemented their pension by selling cigarettes and cups of tea to soldiers at the camp. Known affectionately to the couple as 'Ginger', Newland was a frequent caller at the bungalow, and the Tandys came to regard the young Londoner as a friend.

Newland finished his national service early in 1953 and found a job as a caster at a company which made toy metal cars. He returned to his home at Cogan Avenue, Walthamstow, and it was from there, on the morning of Saturday, 30 May 1953, that he travelled to Orsett. Instead of paying a friendly visit, he was on a murderous mission: concealed in his pocket was a hammer he had taken from his father's toolbox.

Shortly after 9 a.m., a paperboy recognised Newland approaching the Tandys' bungalow. Newland was greeted warmly by the Tandys and ushered inside. A lodger who rented a building next to the bungalow heard the greeting: 'Come in, Ginger...'

Later that morning, the old couple were found badly battered on the kitchen floor. Henry had died from his wounds, but Honor was to make a full recovery and appear as the main prosecution witness when Newland stood trial for murder at the Chelmsford Assizes in November. Honor Tandy told the court that no sooner had Newland entered the house than he pulled out the hammer and began to attack both her and her husband. 'He looked like a madman,' she sobbed.

Detectives had picked up Newland within hours of the attack. His haul was a measly £8 and 5s, and when a cheque belonging to the murdered man was found hidden in Newland's bedroom, he was arrested. He immediately admitted responsibility, claiming he was sorry for what he had done.

The court heard that the motive for the crime was his need of money to buy a new suit. Thinking of a way to get money, he was influenced by a 'cosh-boy' film he had watched at the local cinema which gave him the idea for the robbery. It was then he hatched his cruel and terrible plan.

'*Ginger' Newland following his arrest.* (T.J. Leech Archive)

Sentenced to death by Mr Justice Streatfeild after his plea of insanity failed, as did his subsequent appeal, Newland was hanged by Albert Pierrepoint two days before Christmas.

104

PARTNERS IN CRIME

❖ *Ian Arthur Grant & Kenneth Gilbert, 17 June 1954* ❖

It appeared to be a carefully planned robbery, but apart from the paltry sum of £2 in cash, only a large quantity of cigarettes was missing. On the morning of Tuesday, 9 March 1954, George Smart, the 53-year-old night porter at the Aban Court Hotel, Harrington Gardens, Kensington, was found beaten and gagged in the servants' quarters. Police soon worked out that those responsible had gained access via the coal cellar, but then, presumably having been disturbed by Smart, they had battered him about the head before tying him up and sticking a towel into his mouth. The pathologist later found it was the gag which had caused his death, as he had died of asphyxiation.

Shortly after the discovery of the body at his workplace in Olympia, Ian Grant read that the porter had died and told a fellow employee named Chapman that he and Kenny Gilbert had 'done a man in'. Grant told Chapman he had stashed the cigarettes in the left luggage office at Victoria station and asked him if he would pick them up for him. Chapman immediately contacted the police. Grant and Gilbert shared lodgings together on Harwood Road in Fulham, and were arrested and charged with murder later that same day. Police investigations found that Gilbert had worked at the Aban Court during the summer of 1953 and was familiar with the layout of the hotel.

Tried before Mr Justice Glynn-Jones at the Old Bailey in May, both pleaded not guilty to murder, but accepted they were responsible for the death of George Smart. Grant said he had

Newspaper account of the Gilbert and Grant case. (Author's collection)

punched the porter in the stomach when Smart came at him holding a heavy torch, as he feared he was about to be hit, but it was Gilbert who then struck Smart several times in the face and had tied him up. For his part, Gilbert admitted hitting Smart but claimed that he had only struck him twice before gagging him, and that he did not strike him after he had been tied up.

It was a clear-cut case and the jury, finding both men equally responsible, soon returned a guilty verdict. At their appeal hearing, defence counsel tried to suggest that since neither man had set out with the intention of killing Smart, the crime should be reduced to that of manslaughter. The appeal was dismissed on the grounds that since they had ventured out on a robbery and were prepared to use violence to overcome any resistance, then the charge must be one of murder.

Kenny Gilbert and Ian Grant were the last men hanged side by side. Following a report by the Royal Commission in 1953, it was decided that henceforth in cases of two people being jointly convicted of the same charge, in order to give the less experienced second executioner the chance to practise his skills, the condemned men would be hanged at different prisons on the same morning.

105

THE ACCOMPLICE

❖ *Joseph Chrimes, 28 April 1959* ❖

On Friday, 2 January 1959, the body of 60-year-old widow Nora Summerfield was found at her bungalow in Harlington Road, Hillingdon, Middlesex. Known locally as the 'Cider Queen' or the 'Merry Widow' due to her fondness for drink, she had last been seen alive as she celebrated New Year's Eve in a local pub. Pathologist Donald Teare put the time of death at around the early hours of the New Year, and found that death was due to head injuries inflicted by a heavy tyre lever.

Police soon had two men in custody. Joseph Chrimes, a 30-year-old wood stainer, and 18-year-old unemployed Ronald Pritchard were picked up following a tip-off. Chrimes had discussed his plans to break into Norah Summerfield's bungalow with a man named Michael Ulrich, and these two met up with Pritchard near the bungalow on New Year's Eve. Ulrich decided he wanted no part in the robbery and went home. On the following day, before the crime had been discovered, Chrimes confessed to Ulrich's brother that he had 'done the old lady in.'

Both Chrimes and Pritchard admitted that they were responsible for stealing items from the bungalow, including a clock, a cigarette case, some spoons and other items, but each put the blame for the murder on the other. Chrimes claimed that it was Pritchard who had battered Norah to death, but Pritchard's version was very different.

He said that after they had broken into the bungalow, the old lady appeared and Chrimes began to strike her with the tyre lever. Pritchard claimed he had tried to stop his friend but Chrimes pushed him out of the way and continued beating her until she died.

Both were charged with capital murder but when the case came before Mr Justice Donovan at the Old Bailey, although both men pleaded guilty to breaking and entering, the prosecution now stated that Pritchard had turned King's Evidence and they would be offering no evidence against him on the charge of murder. On the contrary, he would now supply the main prosecution evidence against his partner in crime.

The all male jury had retired for just seventy minutes before returning to court to ask the judge to explain why no evidence had been offered against Pritchard on the charge of murder. Mr Justice Donovan explained that this had not been the prosecution's case, which had offered evidence that it was Chrimes alone who had struck the fatal blow. Pritchard could only have been guilty if he had been actively urging Chrimes to commit the murder and this had not been suggested. Pritchard was subsequently convicted of breaking and entering, and larceny, and was sent to borstal; Chrimes was convicted of capital murder and sentenced to death.

Awaiting execution, Chrimes sent a short message to Pritchard: 'Tell him to be a good lad and keep out of the cafés. That's where I went wrong.'

On the day before his execution, Chrimes promised to write a letter explaining that Pritchard had taken no part in the actual killing, but when the letter arrived at Pritchard's house, after the execution had been carried out, it simply said: 'I have nothing against him'.

The new Homicide Act of 1957 had spared Pritchard's life. Prior to its passing, the prosecution would not have needed to show who dealt the fatal blow or even if violence was contemplated. If the accomplice had remained with the killer and the crime had continued, the accomplice would have been equally guilty.

Hangman Harry Allen. He hanged three of the four men executed at Pentonville following the passing of the Homicide Act in 1957. (Author's collection)

MANHUNT

When Rosalie Marwood told her husband that she didn't feel well enough to go out to celebrate their first wedding anniversary and would instead stay home and watch television, her husband Ronald decided that he would still go out and celebrate with friends. It was Sunday, 14 December 1958 and by the time the 25-year-old burly scaffolder and several friends left the Spanish Patriots public house near Waterloo station, they had each consumed about ten bottles of brown ale. They moved on to a club in Bow Road where a similar amount was downed, and as the night drew to a close, they then piled into three cars and arrived outside Gray's Dance Hall on Seven Sisters Road in Holloway.

Trouble had been brewing between rival gangs for several weeks and threats had been made that it would be resolved this evening. As the hall emptied, trouble broke out. Scuffles erupted and someone pulled out a small axe, swinging it at Marwood's head and knocking him to the ground. As the fight spilled out into the road, a policeman arrived on the scene, and when Marwood got to his feet and stumbled down the street, he saw a friend being quizzed by police constable Ray Summers.

Marwood believed his friend was being unduly hassled and went to remonstrate. Summers pushed Marwood and told him to go away. Marwood said later he had no idea what he did next, but seconds later, PC Summers fell to the ground with a knife wound in the back. Marwood ran down the street, discarding a bloodstained 10in underwater diver's knife as he fled.

On the following morning, police interviewed anyone connected with the gangs involved, and Marwood was one of the first men spoken to. With nothing yet linking him to the murder, Marwood told detectives he had been in Finsbury Park all evening and he was released. When further evidence put Marwood at the scene of the crime, detectives went back to interview him, only to find that he had fled.

A manhunt was launched, and as Marwood went to ground, charges were pressed against some of those involved in the fight outside the dance hall. Eight of the youths received varying terms of imprisonment. In early January 1959, detectives issued a photograph of Marwood who they believed was being shielded by friends. Aware that he faced a capital murder charge, Marwood was a man living in fear of his life, but eventually, after over six weeks on the run, he gave himself up.

Scaffolder Ronald Marwood. (Crime Picture Archive)

Throughout his Old Bailey trial, Marwood maintained that he had not even been aware of the knife in his hand and he claimed that he had had no intention of even hurting the policeman, let alone killing him. Nevertheless, it was never in dispute that when he went out that evening he was carrying a lethal weapon, an act which had resulted in the death of a policeman.

Sentenced to death by Mr Justice Gorman, Marwood was the first man convicted of the murder of a policeman under the newly formed Homicide Act. Yet despite the brutal nature of the fight, and the murder of an unarmed officer struck down in the line of duty, a campaign for Marwood's life to be spared drew great support. One hundred and fifty, mostly Labour Members of Parliament signed an appeal, and a petition by members of the public attracted over 10,000 signatures.

As the hour of execution neared, demonstrations took place inside Pentonville. While the hangmen waited in their quarters and the light in Marwood's cell burned through the night for the last time, trouble flared inside the gaol. The noise reached such a level that it was alleged that Marwood asked the gaolers if they would ask the demonstrators to stop and allow him some peace on his final night on earth. On the following morning, a crowd of over a thousand people assembled outside the prison gates as inside, Ronald Marwood, whose anniversary celebrations had gone horribly wrong, walked bravely to the gallows.

There is a sad footnote to this case. Within a year of the murder there was further tragedy. PC Summers' heartbroken fiancée, Sheila 'Peggy' McKenzie, was at a dance hall in north London when she collapsed and died. She was just 21 years old.

107

COMMON DESIGN

❖ *Norman James Harris, 10 November 1960* ❖

It was Saturday evening, 25 June 1960, and 21-year-old engineer Alan Jee and his new fiancée, Jacqueline Herbert, had just spent the evening at the cinema. They had announced their engagement on the previous day, and, after seeing her safely home, Jee caught a bus to Hounslow, alighting close to Inwood Park. He then set off on foot to his home on Hall Road, Isleworth. The last part of the journey involved walking down a footpath at the bottom of James Street, which would take him to a bridge over the railway line near Chatsworth Crescent and then on to Hall Road.

As he approached the footpath, he noticed four youths dressed in the 'teddy boy' fashion of the day, waiting in the dark at the far end. Jee had reached the end of the path when one of the gang stepped in front of him, and without any provocation, punched him in the face.

'What do you want me for?' Jee cried, falling to the ground. Two of the youths held him down, while another rummaged through his pockets, but with just a handful of coppers and some silver, Jee was not the lucrative target they had hoped for. As the others left the young engineer lying on the ground, one of the gang walked back and repeatedly kicked him in the head. With his anger sated, he rejoined his friends.

Jee was found lying on the ground and rushed to hospital, where he died from his injuries two days later, the pathologist having found that the kicks to the head had proved fatal.

A witness on James Street saw the fleeing youths and was able to give descriptions to the police. Several young men were interviewed in the days following the murder, but it was a tip off which led to police re-interviewing one of them.

TWO YOUTHS EXECUTED FOR FOOTPATH MURDER

PRISON DISTURBANCE DENIED

Francis Forsyth, aged 18, and Norman Harris, aged 23, were executed in London yesterday for their part in the capital murder of Allan Edward Jee, aged 23, on a footpath at Hounslow, Middlesex, in June. Forsyth was executed at Wandsworth prison and Harris at Pentonville.

Groups of people stood outside both prisons until shortly after 9 a.m., the time fixed for the executions.

The Home Office later described as untrue a rumour that prisoners in Wandsworth had demonstrated during Wednesday night. They said the prison governor had officially denied talk of a disturbance.

The Oxford Union Society, before its weekly debate last night, adjourned for a token period in protest against the executions.

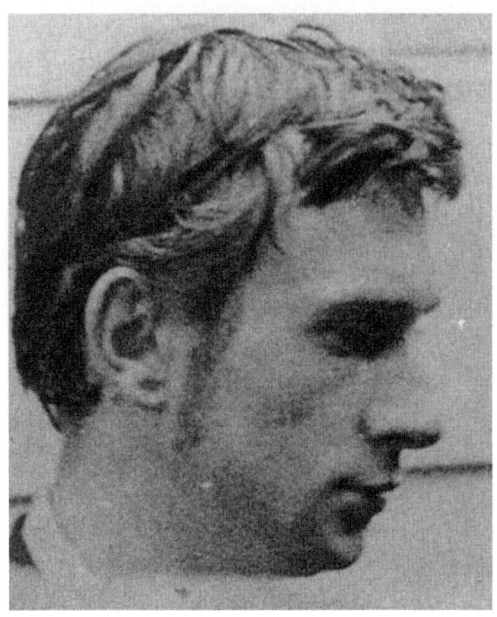

Newspaper account of the Hounslow Footpath Murder. (Author's collection)

Norman Harris. (T.J. Leech Archive)

THE OFFICE OF THE UNDER SHERIFF OF MIDDLESEX.

14, Norfolk Street,
Strand,
London W.C.2.

TEMple Bar 0188   25th October, 1960.

R.L. Stewart, Esq.,
2, Birchenlea Street,
CHADDERTON,
Lancs.

Dear Sir,

                    Norman James Harris

        The Sheriff of Middlesex has appointed Thursday the 10th November 1960 at 9 a.m. for the execution of the above named who is now lying under sentence of death at Pentonville Prison.

        I shall be obliged if you will let me know if you will be available on that day for the purpose of carrying into effect the sentence of the Court. Upon the assumption that you will be available, I am sending you herewith Memorandum of Conditions in duplicate which I shall be grateful if you will sign and return to me as soon as possible.

        Will you also please confirm that you and your assistant will be at the Prison at 4.30 p.m. on Wednesday the 9th November for the purpose of examining the apparatus.

                    Yours faithfully,

                    UNDER SHERIFF.

Letter to hangman Jock Stewart. (Author's collection)

On 17 July, a witness came forward say that a friend of his had been boasting about the attack, and this led police to 18-year-old Francis Forsyth, known to his friends as 'Flossie'. The same witness also gave police the names of three other youths whom he had seen with Forsyth in a coffee bar on the night of the attack. Norman Harris, a 23-year-old unemployed driver, had first been spoken to two days after Jee had died, but had given a satisfactory account of his movements at the time of the attack and was allowed to go. Within forty-eight hours, detectives had four youths in custody, and after intense questioning, Forsyth, Harris, 23-year-old Christopher Darby and 17-year-old Terence Lutt were all charged with murder.

Before Mr Justice Winn at the Old Bailey in September, evidence was heard that it was Lutt who had struck the first blow, knocking Jee to the ground, while Harris had gone through his pockets as Lutt and Forsyth held him down. Forsyth, who had been wearing pointed 'winkle-picker' shoes, was found to have delivered the fatal kicks to the head. Only Darby claimed to have used no violence. He said it had been his and Harris' intention to commit a robbery, but at Lutt's suggestion, they had decided to 'jump' someone.

The prosecution sought to prove that they had acted with 'common design' and that all were equally culpable in the murder. On 26 September, after a deliberation by the jury of just forty minutes, all four were found guilty. Harris and Forsyth were convicted of capital murder and sentenced to death, Darby was convicted of non-capital murder and sentenced to life imprisonment, while Lutt, deemed the main protagonist, was also convicted of capital murder, but at 17, was too young to be hanged, and was sentenced to be detained at Her Majesty's pleasure.

On 10 November, Flossie Forsyth was hanged at Wandsworth, a national newspaper reporting that he had spent a fitful night repeatedly crying out that he did not want to die. At exactly the same time, Harris was hanged at Pentonville. Hangman Jock Stewart recalled later that Harris had attempted to put his own head in the noose and it delayed things by a few seconds as the eyelet was facing the wrong way, but the execution went 'very well'.

108

PORTRAIT OF A KILLER

❖ *Edwin Albert Arthur Bush, 6 July 1961* ❖

On Wednesday, 1 March 1961, over thirty police officers from across the country attended a three-day course at Scotland Yard. The class had been set up to familiarise detectives and instruct them in the use of a new Identikit system, which used various parts of the face to construct a likeness. Invented by an American two years earlier, the system was to have immediate success on its introduction to these shores.

On 2 March 1961, a half-caste man walked into Louis Meier's antique shop on Cecil Court, off Charing Cross Road, and enquired about the cost of a dress sword. Told the price, he left, and walking across the passageway, entered another shop where he asked the owner what he would pay for an antique sword. The owner told him to bring the sword in to be valued and they would work out a fair price.

On the following day, the man returned to the first shop where, during a struggle, Mrs Elsie Batten, Meier's 65-year-old assistant, was battered and stabbed to death. Missing from the shop was an antique dress sword.

One of those who had completed the Identikit course was Detective Sergeant Dagg, who was stationed in the district where the murder took place. Under the command of Superintendent Powell, officers spoke to other shopkeepers in the area and heard about the young half-caste

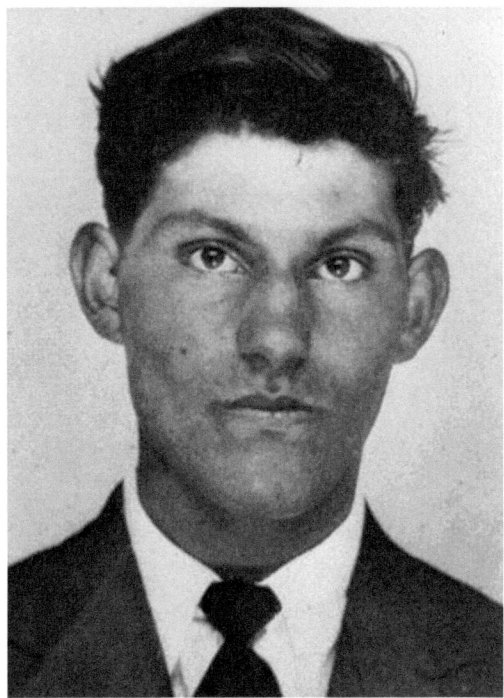

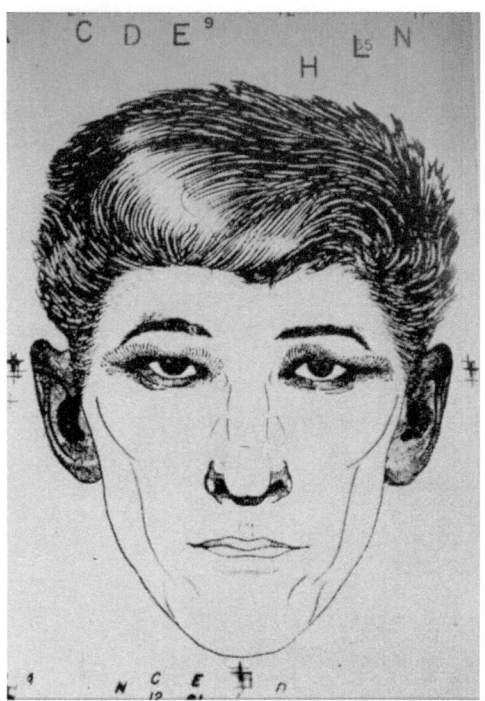

Edwin Bush. (Crime Picture Archive)

Identikit picture used to convict Edwin Bush. (TNA: PRO)

who had enquired the previous day about selling a similar sword. They then found that the same man had left a sword at another shop for valuation a few hours earlier. It appeared that, after stealing the sword and carrying out the brutal attack, the killer had immediately tried to offload it.

With three people having seen the suspect, Dagg interviewed them separately, building up a portrait of the killer that all agreed was a good likeness. It was so accurate that four days later a constable on duty in Soho saw a man who resembled the wanted man and took him into custody.

He gave his name as Edwin Albert Arthur Bush and said he was half English, half Indian. Under questioning, Bush, who was celebrating his 21st birthday on the day of his arrest, denied any involvement in the murder and offered an alibi for the time of the attack. When this was found to be false, he admitted the assault, claiming that he had lost his temper when Mrs Batten had made a racist remark when he tried to haggle over the price of the sword.

When the case came before Mr Justice Stephenson at the Old Bailey in May, Bush was indicted on a charge of capital murder, the prosecution claiming that he had committed murder during the theft of the sword. Bush claimed that robbery had not been the motive and that he had stabbed Mrs Batten when he had lost his temper after she had referred to him as a 'nigger'. The judge directed the jury that if they believed that the racist comment was the only reason for the murder, then Bush would be guilty of non-capital murder and face life imprisonment, but if they believed that theft was also the motive, then it was capital murder.

With the jury believing him guilty of the latter, Edwin Bush became the last man to be hanged at Pentonville.

APPENDIX

List of persons hanged at Pentonville 1902–1961

Date of Execution	Convict	Executioner	Assistant(s)
30 September 1902	John Macdonald	William Billington	Henry Pierrcpoint
11 November, 1902	Henry Williams	William Billington	Henry Pierrepoint
9 December, 1902	Thomas Fairclough Barrow	William Billington	John Billington
10 November, 1903	Charles Jeremiah Slowe	William Billington	John Billington
12 July, 1904	John Sullivan	William Billington	Henry Pierrepoint
13 December, 1904	Joseph Potter	William Billington	Henry Pierrepoint
	Charles Wade		
26 April, 1905	Alfred Bridgeman	John Billington	Henry Pierrepoint
15 August, 1905	Arthur Devereux	Henry Pierrepoint	John Ellis
7 November, 1905	George William Butler	Henry Pierrepoint	John Ellis
6 January, 1909	John Esmond Murphy	Henry Pierrepoint	William Willis
20 May, 1909	Morris Reuben	Henry Pierrepoint	William Willis
	Marks Reuben		Thomas Pierrepoint
17 August, 1909	Madar Dal Dhingra	Henry Pierrepoint	Thomas Pierrepoint
1 March, 1910	George Henry Perry	Henry Pierrepoint	William Willis
23 November, 1910	Hawley Harvey Crippen	John Ellis	William Willis
21 December, 1910	Noah Woolf	John Ellis	Thomas Pierrepoint
24 May, 1911	Michael Collins	John Ellis	Thomas Pierrepoint
17 October, 1911[+]	Francisco Carlos Godhino	John Ellis	William Cunduit
	Edward Hill		Albert Lumb
6 March, 1912	Myer Abramovitch	John Ellis	Albert Lumb
18 April, 1912	Frederick Henry Seddon	John Ellis	Thomas Pierrepoint
29 January, 1913	Edward Hopwood	Thomas Pierrepoint	Albert Lumb
8 July, 1913	Henry Longden	John Ellis	William Willis
27 November, 1913	Frederick Albert Robertson	John Ellis	William Willis
1 January, 1916	Lee Kun	John Ellis	George Brown
3 August, 1916	Roger Casement	John Ellis	Robert Baxter
17 April, 1917	William James Robinson	John Ellis	Robert Baxter
2 March, 1918	Louis Marie Joseph Voisin	John Ellis	Edward Taylor
10 July, 1919	Henry Perry (Beckett)	John Ellis	William Willis
31 July, 1919	Thomas Foster	John Ellis	Edward Taylor
7 October, 1919	Frank George Warren	John Ellis	George Brown
27 July, 1920	Arthur A.C. Goslett	John Ellis	Edward Taylor
30 December, 1920	Mark Goodmacher	William Willis	Robert Baxter
11 April, 1922	Frederick Alex Keeling	John Ellis	Seth Mills
18 April, 1922	Edmund Hugh Tonbridge	John Ellis	Robert Baxter
7 June, 1922	Henry Julius Jacoby	John Ellis	Thomas Phillips
5 September, 1922	William James Yeldham	John Ellis	William Willis
9 January, 1923	Frederick Edward Bywaters	William Willis	Seth Mills
5 April, 1923	Bernard Pomroy	John Ellis	Edward Taylor
4 July, 1923	Rowland Duck	John Ellis	Robert Wilson
2 April, 1925	George William Barton	Robert Baxter	Robert Wilson

14 August, 1925[+]	William John Cronin	Robert Baxter	Henry Pollard
	[+]Arthur Henry Bishop		Edward Taylor
			Robert Wilson
24 March, 1926	Eugene De Vere	Robert Baxter	Thomas Phillips
27 July, 1926	Johannes J.C. Mommers	Robert Baxter	William Willis
2 November, 1926	Hashan Khan Samander	Robert Baxter	Thomas Phillips
29 March, 1927	James Frederick Stratton	Robert Baxter	Lionel Mann
12 August, 1927	John Robinson	Robert Baxter	Robert Wilson
31 May, 1928	Frederick Guy Browne	Robert Baxter	Henry Pollard
6 June, 1928	Frederick Stewart	Robert Baxter	Thomas Phillips
20 February, 1929	Frank Hollington	Robert Baxter	Robert Wilson
27 February, 1929	William John Holmyard	Robert Baxter	Lionel Mann
3 June, 1931	Alexander Anastassiou	Robert Baxter	Henry Pollard
5 August, 1931	William Shelley	Robert Baxter	Lionel Mann
	Oliver Newman		Robert Wilson
			Thomas Phillips
23 February, 1932	William Harold Goddard	Robert Baxter	Thomas Phillips
4 May, 1932	Maurice Freedman	Robert Baxter	Robert Wilson
8 June, 1933	Jack Samuel Puttnam	Robert Baxter	Stanley Cross
10 August, 1933	Varnavas Loizi Antorka	Robert Baxter	Henry Pollard
11 October, 1933	Robert James Kirby	Robert Baxter	Robert Wilson
9 October, 1934	Harry Tuffney	Robert Baxter	Alfred Allen
14 November, 1934	John Frederick Stockwell	Robert Baxter	Robert Wilson
13 March, 1935	Charles Malcolm Lake	Robert Baxter	Henry Pollard
30 October, 1935	Allan James Grierson	Robert Baxter	Henry Pollard
13 August, 1937	Leslie George Stone	Thomas Pierrepoint	Alfred Allen
17 August, 1937	Frederick George Murphy	Alfred Allen	Thomas Phillips
18 November, 1937	John Thomas Rodgers	Thomas Pierrepoint	Henry Pollard
31 July, 1940	Udham Singh	Stanley Cross	Albert Pierrepoint
10 December, 1940	Jose Waldburg	Stanley Cross	Albert Pierrepoint
	Carl Meier		Henry Critchell
			Harry Kirk
17 December, 1940	Charles.Van Den Kieboom	Stanley Cross	Herbert Morris
31 October, 1941	Antonio Mancini	Albert Pierrepoint	Stephen Wade
12 November, 1941	Lionel Rupert N. Watson	Thomas Pierrepoint	Henry Critchell
10 September, 1942	Samuel Dashwood	Albert Pierrepoint	Stephen Wade
	George Silverosa		Herbert Morris
			Harry Kirk
24 March, 1943	William Henry Turner	Thomas Pierrepoint	Henry Critchell
3 August, 1943	Gerald Elphinstone Roe	Albert Pierrepoint	Stephen Wade
15 December, 1943	Charles William Koopman	Thomas Pierrepoint	Stephen Wade
2 February, 1944	Christos Georghiou	Albert Pierrepoint	Herbert Morris
16 March, 1944	Oswald John Job	Albert Pierrepoint	Harry Kirk
23 June, 1944	Pierre R. C. Neukermans	Albert Pierrepoint	Alex Riley
12 July, 1944	Joseph Jan Van Hove	Albert Pierrepoint	Stephen Wade
8 March, 1945	Karl Gustav Hulten	Thomas Pierrepoint	Henry Critchell
6 October, 1945	Erich Koenig	Albert Pierrepoint	Stephen Wade
	Joachim Palme Goltz		Harry B. Allen
	Kurt Zeuhlsdorf		
	Heintz Brueling		
	Josef Mertins	*(five single executions)*	
16 November, 1945	Armin Kuelne	Albert Pierrepoint	Alex Riley
	Emil Schmittendorf		
21 December, 1945[*]	James McNicol	Albert Pierrepoint	Herbert Morris

21 December, 1945*	John Riley Young	Albert Pierrepoint	Stephen Wade
4 January, 1946	Theodore William Schurch	Albert Pierrepoint	Alex Riley
16 October, 1946	Neville George C. Heath	Albert Pierrepoint	Harry Kirk
1 November, 1946	Arthur Robert Boyce	Albert Pierrepoint	Henry Critchell
10 Dcember, 1946	John Mathieson	Albert Pierrepoint	Harry B. Allen
26 March, 1947	Frederick William Reynolds	Albert Pierrepoint	Harry Kirk
19 September, 1947	Christopher J. Geraghty	Albert Pierrepoint	Henry Critchell
	Charles Henry Jenkins		Harry B. Allen
19 February, 1948	Walter John Cross	Albert Pierrepoint	Harry B. Allen
21 April, 1949	Harry Lewis	Albert Pierrepoint	Harry B. Allen
21 June, 1949	Bernard Alfred P. Cooper	Albert Pierrepoint	Harry Kirk
28 September, 1949	William Claude H. Jones	Albert Pierrepoint	Harry B. Allen
6 January, 1950	Daniel Raven	Albert Pierrepoint	Harry Kirk
9 March, 1950	Timothy John Evans	Albert Pierrepoint	Sydney Dernley
24 October, 1951	John O'Connor	Albert Pierrepoint	Herbert Allen
27 May, 1952	Backary Manneh	Albert Pierrepoint	Harry Smith
7 September, 1952	John Howard Godar	Albert Pierrepoint	Robert L. Stewart
30 September, 1952+	Dennis G. Muldowney	Albert Pierrepoint	Harry Smith
	Raymond John Cull		Robert L. Stewart
9 October, 1952	Peter Cyril Johnson	Albert Pierrepoint	Harry B. Allen
15 July, 1953	John Reginald H. Christie	Albert Pierrepoint	Harry Smith
23 December, 1953	George James Newland	Albert Pierrepoint	Harry B. Allen
17 June, 1954	Ian Arthur Grant	Albert Pierrepoint	Joseph Broadbent
	Kenneth Gilbert		Harry Smith
			Royston Rickard
28 April, 1959	Joseph Chrimes	Harry B. Allen	Royston Rickard
8 May, 1959	Ronald Henry Marwood	Harry B. Allen	Harry Robinson
10 November, 1960	Norman James Harris	Robert L. Stewart	Royston Rickard
6 July, 1961	Edwin Albert Arthur Bush	Harry B. Allen	John Underhill

+ Signifies double executions where the killers were not connected and were hanged for separate crimes.
* Signifies two hangings on the same day but at different times.

INDEX